SPSS®
Statistical Algorithms

2nd Edition

$$ln\left(\frac{\mu}{1-\mu}\right) = \eta = \beta_0 + \beta_1 X_1 + \ldots + \beta_k X_k.$$

$$L = -w\left(y ln p + (1-y) ln (1-p)\right)$$

$$h(t|x) = h_0(t)\, e^{x'\beta}$$

$$L(\beta) = \prod_{j=1}^{m}\prod_{i=1}^{k_j} \frac{e^{S_{ji}'\beta}}{\left(\sum_{l \in R_{ji}} w_l e^{x_l'\beta}\right)^{d_{ji}}}$$

$$P = \frac{e^{A+BT}}{1+e^{A+BT}}$$

$$Y = W\beta + E$$

SPSS

SPSS Inc.

SPSS Inc.
444 N. Michigan Avenue
Chicago, Illinois 60611
Tel: (312) 329-2400
Fax: (312) 329-3668

For more information about SPSS® software products, please write or call

Marketing Department
SPSS Inc.
444 North Michigan Avenue
Chicago, IL 60611
Tel: (312) 329-3500
Fax: (312) 329-3668

SPSS® Statistical Algorithms, 2nd Edition

Printed in the United States of America.

3 4 5 6 7 8 9 0   93 92

ISBN 0-918469-89-9

Library of Congress Catalog Card Number: 89-069858

Contacting SPSS Inc.

If you would like to be on our mailing list, write to us at one of the addresses below. We will send you a copy of our newsletter and let you know about SPSS Inc. activities in your area.

SPSS Inc.
444 North Michigan Ave.
Chicago, IL 60611
Tel: (312) 329-2400
Fax: (312) 329-3668

SPSS Federal Systems
12030 Sunrise Valley Dr.
Suite 300
Reston, VA 22091
Tel: (703) 391-6020
Fax (703) 391-6002

SPSS Latin America
444 North Michigan Ave.
Chicago, IL 60611
Tel: (312) 329-3556
Fax: (312) 329-3668

SPSS Benelux BV
P.O. Box 115
4200 AC Gorinchem
The Netherlands
Tel: +31.1830.36711
Fax: +31.1830.35839

SPSS UK Ltd.
SPSS House
5 London Street
Chertsey
Surrey KT16 8AP
United Kingdom
Tel: +44.932.566262
Fax: +44.932.567020

SPSS UK Ltd., New Delhi
No. 3 Business Centre
Ashok Hotel
Chanakyapuri
New Delhi 110 021
India
Tel: +91.11.600121 x1029
Fax: +91.11.6873216

SPSS GmbH Software
Steinsdorfstrasse 19
D-8000 Munich 22
Germany
Tel:+49.89.2283008
Fax: +49.89.2285413

SPSS Scandinavia AB
Sjöängsvägen 21
S-191 72 Sollentuna
Sweden
Tel: +46.8.7549450
Fax: +46.8.7548816

SPSS Asia Pacific Pte. Ltd.
10 Anson Road, #34-07
International Plaza
Singapore 0207
Singapore
Tel: +65.221.2577
Fax: +65.221.9920

SPSS Japan Inc.
Gyoen Sky Bldg.
2-1-11, Shinjuku
Shinjuku-ku
Tokyo 160
Japan
Tel: +81.3.33505261
Fax: +81.3.33505245

SPSS Australasia Pty. Ltd.
121 Walker Street
North Sydney, NSW 2060
Australia
Tel: +61.2.954.5660
Toll-free: +008.024.836
Fax: +61.2.954.5616

Contents

Introduction

Starting with the first statistics course, students learn that there are often several equivalent ways to compute the same quantity. For example, the variance can be obtained using either of the following formula:

$$s^2 = \sum_{i=1}^{N} (x_i - \bar{x})^2 / (N-1)$$

$$s^2 = \left(\sum_{i=1}^{N} x_i^2 - \left(\sum_{i=1}^{N} x_i \right)^2 / N \right) / (N-1)$$

Since the formulas are algebraically equal, the one preferred is often the one easier to use (or remember). For small data sets consisting of "nice" numbers, the arbitrary choice of several computational methods is usually of little consequence. However, for handling large data sets or "troublesome" numbers, the choice of computational algorithms can become very important, even when those algorithms are to be executed by a computer. Care must be taken to choose an algorithm which produces accurate results under a wide variety of conditions without requiring extensive computer time. Often these two considerations must be balanced against each other.

It will be noted that the same statistic is often computed differently in the various routines. The precision of the calculations and the desirability of computing many statistics in the same procedure are among the reasons for this. For example, in the paired T-TEST procedure, the need to compute both the correlation coefficient and the standard error of the difference led to selection of a different algorithm than would have been chosen for computation of only the standard error. Of course, personal preferences of many designers and programmers throughout the years have also influenced the choice of algorithms. As new routines are added and old ones are updated, any unnecessary diversity is being replaced by a consistent core of algorithms.

This text represents the algorithms present in releases 4 and 5 of SPSS and SPSS/PC+, in the base system, Statistics or Professional Statistics option (where separate from the base), Advanced Statistics, Trends and Categories. Except where required for clarity, algorithms for facilities new to Release 5 are not differentiated within the text; this book is designed as a resource for those interested in the specific calculations of procedures within their software rather than as a catalog of available features.

Missing Values

Since similar options for treatment of missing values are available in many procedures, treatment of missing values has often not been specified in each chapter. Instead, the following rules should be used:

- If listwise deletion has been specified and a missing value is encountered, the case is not included in the analysis. This is equivalent, for purposes of following the algorithms, to setting the case weight to zero.

- If variable-wise deletion is in effect, a case has zero weight when the variable with missing values is involved in computations.

- If pairwise deletion has been specified, a case has zero weight when one or both of a pair of variables included in a computation is zero.

- If missing-value declarations are to be ignored, all cases are always included in the computations.

  It should be noted again that the computer routines do not alter case weights for cases with missing data, but instead actually exclude them from the computations. Missing-value specifications do not apply when a variable is used for weighting. All values are treated as weights.

Autocorrelation and Partial Autocorrelation Functions (ACF / PACF)

General

Procedures ACF and PACF print and plot the sample autocorrelation and partial autocorrelation functions of a series of data.

Notation

x_i ith observation of input series, $i = 1, \ldots, n$

r_k kth lag sample autocorrelation

$\hat{\phi}_{kk}$ kth lag sample partial autocorrelation

Basic Statistics

The following formulas are used if no missing values are encountered. If missing values are present, see the section on Missing Values for modification of some formulas.

Sample Autocorrelation r_k

$$r_k = \frac{\sum_{i=1}^{n-k} (x_i - \bar{x})(x_{i+k} - \bar{x})}{\sum_{i=1}^{n} (x_i - \bar{x})^2}$$

where $\bar{x}$ is the average of the n observations.

Standard Error of r_k

There are two formulas for the standard error of r_k based on different assumptions about the autocorrelation.

Under the assumption that the true MA order of the process is k-1, the approximate variance of r_k given by Bartlett (1946) is

$$Var(r_k) \cong \frac{1}{n}\left(1 + 2\sum_{l=1}^{k-1} r_l^2\right)$$

The standard error is the square root (see Box & Jenkins (1976), p. 35).

Under the assumption that the process is white noise,

$$Var(r_k) \cong \frac{1}{n}\left(\frac{n-k}{n+2}\right)$$

Box-Ljung Statistic

At lag k, the Box-Ljung statistic is defined by

$$Q_k = n(n+2)\sum_{l=1}^{k}\frac{r_l^2}{n-l}$$

When n is large, Q_k has a chi-square distribution with degrees of freedom k-p-q, where p and q are autoregressive and moving average orders respectively. The significance level of Q_k is calculated from the chi-square distribution with k-p-q degrees of freedom.

Sample Partial Autocorrelation

$$\hat{\phi}_{11} = r_1$$

$$\hat{\phi}_{22} = (r_2 - r_1^2)/(1 - r_1^2)$$

$$\hat{\phi}_{kj} = \hat{\phi}_{k-1,j} - \phi_{kk}\phi_{k-1,k-j} \quad k = 2, \ldots, \quad j = 1, 2, \ldots, k-1$$

$$\hat{\phi}_{kk} = \left(r_k - \sum_{j=1}^{k-1}\phi_{k-1,j}r_{k-j}\right) \Big/ \left(1 - \sum_{j=1}^{k-1}\phi_{k-1,j}r_j\right), k = 3, \ldots$$

Standard Error of $\hat{\phi}_{kk}$

Quenouville (1949) has shown that, under the assumption that the AR (p) model is correct and $p \le k-1$,

$$\hat{\phi}_{kk} \cong N(0, \frac{1}{n}).$$

Thus

$$Var(\hat{\phi}_{kk}) \cong \frac{1}{n}$$

Series with Missing Values

If there are missing values in x, the following statistics are computed differently. The approach for handling missing values in ACF/PACF can be found in Cryer (1986). First, let us define

$\bar{x}$ = average of nonmissing $x_1, \ldots, x_n$,

$$a_i = \begin{cases} x_i - \bar{x}, & \text{if } x_i \text{ is not missing} \\ \text{SYSMIS} & \text{if } x_i \text{ is missing} \end{cases}$$

for $k = 0,1,2,\ldots$, and $j = 1,\ldots,n$

$$b_j^{(k)} = \begin{cases} a_j a_{j+k} & \text{if both are not missing} \\ \text{SYSMIS} & \text{otherwise} \end{cases}$$

m_k = the number of nonmissing values in $b_1^{(k)},\ldots,b_{n-k}^{(k)}$.

m_o = the number of nonmissing values in x.

Sample Autocorrelation

$$r_k = \frac{\text{sum of nonmissing } b_1^{(k)},\ldots,b_{n-k}^{(k)}}{\text{sum of nonmissing } b_1^{(o)},\ldots,b_n^{(o)}}$$

Standard Error of r_k

$$\text{Standard Error } (r_k) = \sqrt{\frac{1}{m_o}\left(1+\sum_{l=1}^{k-1} r_l^2\right)} \qquad \text{(MA assumption)}$$

$$\text{Standard Error } (r_k) = \sqrt{\frac{m_k}{(m_o+2)\,m_o}} \qquad \text{(white noise)}$$

Box-Ljung Statistic

$$Q = m_o(m_o+2)\sum_{l=1}^{k}\frac{r_l^2}{m_l}$$

Standard Error of $\hat{\phi}_{kk}$

$$\text{Standard Error } (\hat{\phi}_{kk}) \cong \sqrt{\frac{1}{m_o}}$$

References

Bartlett (1946)

Box & Jenkins (1976)

Cryer (1986)

Quenouville (1949)

ALSCAL

Initial Configuration

The first step is to estimate an additive constant c_k , which is added to the observed proximity measures, e.g., o_{ijk}. Thus,

$$o^*_{ijk} = o_{ijk} + c_k$$

such that for all triples the triangular inequality holds:

$$o^*_{ijk} + o^*_{jlk} \geq o^*_{ilk}$$

and positivity holds $o^*_{ijk} \geq 0$,

where

o^*_{ijk} is the adjusted proximity between stimulus *i* and stimulus *j* for subject *k*

o^*_{jlk} is the adjusted proximity between stimulus *j* and stimulus *l* for subject *k*

o^*_{ilk} is the adjusted proximity between stimulus *i* and stimulus *l* for subject *k*

The constant c_k, which is added, is as small as possible to estimate a zero point for the dissimilarity data, thus bringing the data more nearly in line with the ratio level of measurement. This step is necessary to make the B^*_k matrix, described below, positive semidefinite, i.e., with no imaginary roots.

The next step is to compute a scalar products matrix B^{**}_k for each subject *k* by double centering O^*_k , the adjusted proximity matrix for each subject. An element of the B^{**}_k matrix b^{**}_{ijk} is computed as follows:

$$b^{**}_{ijk} = -\frac{1}{2}\left(o^{*2}_{ijk} - o^{*2}_{i.k} - o^{*2}_{.jk} + o^{*2}_{..k}\right)$$

where

$o^*_{i.k}$ are the row means for the adjusted proximities for subject *k*

$o^*_{.jk}$ are the column means for the adjusted proximities for subject *k*

$o^*_{..k}$ is the grand mean for subject *k*

Double centering to convert distances to scalar products is necessary because a scalar products matrix is required to compute an initial configuration using the Young-Householder-Torgerson procedure.

Next the individual subject matrices are normalized so that they have the same variance. The normalized matrix B^*_k is found for each subject. The elements of the matrix are

$$b^*_{ijk} = \frac{b^{**}_{ijk}}{\left[\sum_i \sum_j \left(b^{**}_{ijk}\right)^2 / \left(n\left(n-1\right)\right)\right]^{1/2}}$$

where n is the number of stimuli, and $(n)(n\text{-}1)$ is the number of elements in the B_k^{**} matrix off the diagonal. The denominator is both the root mean square and the standard deviation of the unnormalized scalar products matrix B^{**}. (It is both because $b_{..k}^{**} = 0$, due to double centering.) B_k^* is thus a matrix with elements b_{ijk}^*, which are scalar products for individual subject k. Normalization of individual subjects' matrices equates the contribution of each individual to the formation of a mean scalar products matrix and thus the resulting initial configuration.

Next an average scalar products matrix B^* over the subjects is computed. The elements of this matrix are

$$b_{ij.}^* = \frac{\sum_k b_{ijk}^*}{m},$$

where m is the number of subjects.

The average B^* matrix used in the previous step is used to compute an initial stimulus configuration using the classical Young-Householder multidimensional scaling procedure

$$B^* = XX',$$

where X is an $(n \times r)$ matrix of n stimulus points on r dimensions, and X' is the transpose of the X matrix, i.e., the rows and columns are interchanged. The X matrix is the initial configuration.

For the weighted ALSCAL matrix model, initial weight configuration matrices W_k for each of the m subjects are computed. The initial weight matrices W_k are $r \times r$ matrices, where r is the number of dimensions. Later the diagonals of W_k will form rows of the W matrix, which is an n x r matrix. The matrices W_k are determined such that $B_k^* = YW_kY'$, where $Y{=}XT$ and $TT' = I$, and where T is an orthogonal rotation of the configuration X to a new orientation Y. T is computed by the Schönemann-de Leeuw procedure discussed by Young, Takane, and Lewyckyj (1978). T rotates X so that W_k is as diagonal as possible (i.e., off-diagonal elements are as close to "0" as possible on the average over subjects). Off-diagonal elements represent a departure from the model (which assumes that subjects weight only the dimensions of the stimulus space).

Optimization Algorithm

The optimization algorithm is a series of steps which are repeated (iterated) until the final solution is achieved. The steps for the optimization algorithm are performed successively because disparities, weights, and coordinates cannot be solved for simultaneously.

Distances

Distances are computed according to the weighted Euclidean model

$$d_{ijk}^2 = \sum_{a=1}^{r} w_{ka} (x_{ia} - x_{ja})^2$$

where:

w_{ka} is the weight for subject k on a dimension a,

x_{ia} is the coordinate of stimulus i on dimension a,

x_{ja} is the coordinate of stimulus j on dimension a.

The first set of distances is computed from the coordinates and weights found in the previous steps. Subsequently, new distances are computed from new coordinates found in the iteration process (described below).

Optimal Scaling

Optimal scaling for ordinal data uses Kruskal's least-squares monotonic transformation. This yields disparities that are a monotonic transformation of the data *and* that are as much like the distances (in a least squares sense) as possible. Ideally, we want the distances to be in exactly the same rank order as the data, but usually they are not. So we locate a new set of numbers, called disparities, which are in the same rank order as the data and which fit the distances as well as possible. When we see an order violation we replace the numbers that are out of order with a block of values that are the mean of the out-of-order numbers.

When there are ties in the data, the optimal scaling process is changed somewhat. Kruskal's primary and secondary procedures are used in ALSCAL.

Normalization

The disparities computed previously are now normalized for technical reasons related to the alternating least squares algorithm (see Young, de Leeuw, and Takane, 1979). During the course of the optimization process, we want to minimize a measure of error called SSTRESS. But the monotone regression procedure described above only minimizes the numerator of the SSTRESS formula. Thus, the formula below is applied to readjust the length of the disparities vector so that SSTRESS is minimized:

$$D_k^{*N} = D_k^{*} (D'_k D_k) (D'_k D_k^{*})^{-1}$$

where:

D_k^{*} is a column vector with $\frac{n(n-1)}{2}$ elements containing all the disparities for subject k,

D_k is a column vector with $\frac{n(n-1)}{2}$ elements containing all the distances for subject k,

$D'_k D_k$ is the sum of the squared distances,

$D'_k D_k^{*}$ is the sum of the cross products.

The normalized disparities vector D_k^{*N} is a conditional least squares estimate for the distances, i.e., it is the least squares estimate for a given iteration. The previous D^* values are replaced by D^{*N} values, and subsequent steps utilize the normalized disparities.

SSTRESS

The Takane-Young-de Leeuw formula is used:

$$\text{SSTRESS (1)} = S = \left[\frac{1}{m} \sum_{k=1}^{m} \left[\frac{\sum_i \sum_j (d_{ijk}^2 - d_{ijk}^{*2})^2}{\sum_i \sum_j d_{ijk}^{*4}} \right] \right]^{1/2}$$

where d_{ijk}^{*} values are the normalized disparity measures computed previously, and d_{ijk} are computed as shown above. Thus SSTRESS is computed from the normalized disparities and the previous set of coordinates and weights.

Termination

The current value of SSTRESS is compared to the value of SSTRESS from the previous iteration. If the improvement is less than a specified value (default equals .001), iteration stops and the output stage has been reached. If not, the program proceeds to the next step. (This step is skipped on the first iteration.)

Model Estimation

In ALSCAL the weights and coordinates cannot be solved for simultaneously, so we do it successively. Thus, the model estimation phase consists of two steps: (i) estimation of subject weights and (ii) estimation of stimulus coordinates.

- (i) Estimation of subject weights. (This step is skipped for the simple, i.e., unweighted, Euclidean model.)

A conditional least-squares estimate of the weights is computed at each iteration:

$$W \cong D^* P (P'P)^{-1}$$

This derivation of the computation formula is as follows:

We have found disparities such that

$$d^*_{ijk} \cong d^2_{ijk},$$

where

$$d^2_{ijk} = \sum_{a=1}^{r} w_{ka} (x_{ia} - x_{ja})^2 .$$

Let p_{ija} be the unweighted distance between stimuli i and j as projected onto dimension a, i.e.,

$$p_{ija} = (x_{ia} - x_{ja})^2.$$

Then

$$d^{*2}_{ijk} \cong d^2_{ijk} = \sum_{a=1}^{r} w_{ka} p_{ija} .$$

In matrix notation this is expressed as $D^* = WP'$, where D^* is now an $(m \times \frac{n(n-1)}{2})$ matrix having one row for every subject and one column for each stimulus pair; W is an $(m \times r)$ matrix having one row for every subject and one column for each dimension; and P' has one row for every dimension and one column for every stimulus pair.

We wish to solve for W, $WP' \cong D^*$, which we do by noting that

$$WP'P(P'P)^{-1} = D^* P (P'P)^{-1}.$$

Therefore,

$$W = D^* P (P'P)^{-1}$$

and we have the conditional least squares estimate for W. We have in fact minimized SSTRESS at this point relative to the previously computed values for stimulus coordinates and optimal scaling. We replace the old subject weights with the newly estimated values.

- (ii) Estimation of Stimulus Coordinates.

The next step is to estimate coordinates, one at a time, using the previously computed values for D^* (disparities) and weights. Coordinates are determined one at a time by minimizing SSTRESS with regard to a given coordinate. Equation 2 (below) allows us to solve for a given coordinate x_{le}:

$$\frac{\partial S}{\partial x_{le}} = \frac{1}{m}\sum c_k \frac{\partial S_k}{\partial x_{le}} \tag{1}$$

$$\frac{\partial S_k}{\partial x_{le}} = 4w_{ke}^2 \sum_j (x_{le}^3 - 3x_{le}^2 x_{je} + 2x_{le}x_{je}^2 - b_{ljke}^2 x_{le} + b_{ljke}^2 x_{je}) \tag{2}$$

Equation 2 can be substituted back into equation 1. This equation with one unknown, x_{le}, is then set equal to zero and solved by standard techniques. All the other coordinates except x_{le} are assumed to be constant while we solve for x_{le}.

Immediately upon solving for x_{le}, we replace the value for x_{le} used on the previous iteration with the newly obtained value, and then proceed to estimate the value for another coordinate. We successively obtain values for each coordinate of point l, one at a time, replacing old values with new ones. This continues for point l until the estimates stabilize. We then move to a new point and proceed until new coordinates for all stimuli are estimated. We then return to the beginning of the optimization algorithm (the previous step above) and start another iteration.

References

Bloxom (1978)

Carroll & Chang (1970)

Carroll & Chang (1972)

Carroll, Pruzansky, & Kruskal (1980)

Harshman (1970)

Jones & Young (1972)

MacCallum (1977)

Mardia (1972)

Mardia, Kent, & Bibby (1979)

Null & Sarle (1982)

Schiffman, Reynolds, & Young (1981)

Takane, de Leeuw, & Young (1977)

Tucker (1972)

Young, Easterling, & Forsyth (1984)

Young & Lewyckyj (1979)

Young, Takane, & Lewyckyi (1978)

ANACOR

General

The ANACOR algorithm consists of three major parts: (1) a singular value decomposition (SVD), (2) centering and rescaling of the data and various rescalings of the results, and (3) variance estimation by the delta method. Other names for SVD are "Eckart-Young decomposition," after Eckart and Young (1936), who introduced the technique in psychometrics, and "basic structure" (Horst, 1963). The rescalings and centering, including their rationale, are well explained in Benzécri (1969), Nishisato (1980), Gifi (1981), and Greenacre (1984). Those who are interested in the general framework of matrix approximation and reduction of dimensionality with positive definite row and column metrics are referred to Rao (1980). The delta method is a method that can be used for the derivation of asymptotic distributions and is particularly useful for the approximation of the variance of complex statistics. There are many versions of the delta method, differing in the assumptions made and in the strength of the approximation (Rao, 1973, ch. 6; Bishop et al., 1975, ch. 14; Wolter, 1985, ch. 6).

Notation

k_1	number of rows (row objects)
k_2	number of columns (column objects)
p	number of dimensions

Data-Related Quantities

f_{ij}	nonnegative data value for row i and column j: collected in table F
f_{i+}	marginal total of row i, $i = 1, \ldots, k_1$
f_{+j}	marginal total of column j, $j = 1, \ldots, k_2$
N	grand total of F

Scores and Statistics

r_{is}	score of row object i on dimension s
c_{js}	score of column object j on dimension s
I	total inertia

Basic Calculations

One way to phrase the ANACOR objective (cf. Heiser, 1981) is to say that we wish to find row scores $\{r_{is}\}$ and column scores $\{c_{js}\}$ so that the function

$$\sigma(\{r_{is}\};\{c_{js}\}) = \sum_i \sum_j f_{ij} \sum_s (r_{is} - c_{js})^2$$

is minimal, under the standardization restriction either that

$$\sum_i f_{i+} r_{is} r_{it} = \delta^{st}$$

or

$$\sum_j f_{+j}\, c_{js} c_{jt} = \delta^{st},$$

where δ^{st} is Kronecker's delta and t is an alternative index for dimensions. The trivial set of scores $(\{1\},\{1\})$ is excluded.

The ANACOR algorithm can be subdivided into five steps, as explained below.

1. Data scaling and centering

The first step is to form the auxiliary matrix Z with general element

$$z_{ij} = \frac{f_{ij}}{\sqrt{f_{i+} f_{+j}}} - \frac{\sqrt{f_{i+} f_{+j}}}{N}.$$

2. Singular value decomposition

Let the singular value decomposition of Z be denoted by

$$Z = K \Lambda L',$$

with $K'K = I$, $L'L = I$, and Λ diagonal. This decomposition is calculated by a routine based on Golub and Reinsch (1971). It involves Householder reduction to bidiagonal form and diagonalization by a QR procedure with shifts. The routine requires an array with more rows than columns, so when $k_1 < k_2$ the original table is transposed and the parameter transfer is permuted accordingly.

3. Adjustment to the row and column metric

The arrays of both the left-hand singular vectors and the right-hand singular vectors are adjusted row-wise to form scores that are standardized in the row and in the column marginal proportions, respectively:

$$r_{is} = k_{is} / \sqrt{f_{i+}/N},$$

$$c_{js} = l_{js} / \sqrt{f_{+j}/N}.$$

This way, both sets of scores satisfy the standardization restrictions simultaneously.

4. Determination of variances and covariances

For the application of the delta method to the results of generalized eigenvalue methods under multinomial sampling, the reader is referred to Gifi (1981, ch. 12) and Israëls (1987, Appendix B). It is shown there that N times the variance-covariance matrix of a function ϕ of the observed cell proportions $p = \{p_{ij} = f_{ij}/N\}$ asymptotically reaches the form

$$N \times COV(\phi(p)) \cong \sum_i \sum_j \pi_{ij} \left(\frac{\partial \phi}{\partial p_{ij}}\right) \left(\frac{\partial \phi}{\partial p_{ij}}\right)' - \left(\sum_i \sum_j \pi_{ij} \frac{\partial \phi}{\partial p_{ij}}\right) \left(\sum_i \sum_j \pi_{ij} \frac{\partial \phi}{\partial p_{ij}}\right)'$$

Here the quantities π_{ij} are the cell probabilities of the multinomial distribution, and $\partial \phi / \partial p_{ij}$ are the partial derivatives of ϕ (which is either a generalized eigenvalue or a generalized eigenvector) with respect to the observed cell proportion. Expressions for these partial derivatives can also be found in the above-mentioned references.

5. Normalization of row and column scores

Depending on the normalization option chosen, the scores are normalized, which implies a compensatory rescaling of the coordinate axes of the row scores and the column scores. The general formula for the weighted sum of squares that results from this rescaling is

$$\text{row scores: } \sum_i f_{i+} r_{is}^2 = N\lambda_s (1 + q)$$

$$\text{column scores: } \sum_j f_{+j} c_{js}^2 = N\lambda_s (1 - q).$$

The parameter q can be chosen freely or it can be specified according to the following designations:

canonical: $q = 0$
row principal: $q = 1$
column principal: $q = -1$

There is a fifth possibility, choosing the designation "principal," that does not fit into this scheme. It implies that the weighted sum of squares of both sets of scores becomes equal to $N\lambda_s^2$. The estimated variances and covariances are adjusted according to the type of normalization chosen.

Diagnostics

After printing the data, ANACOR optionally also prints a table of row profiles and column profiles, which are $\{f_{ij}/f_{i+}\}$ and $\{f_{ij}/f_{+j}\}$, respectively.

Singular values, maximum rank, and inertia

All singular values λ_s defined in step 2 are printed up to a maximum of $\min\{(k_1 - 1), (k_2 - 1)\}$. Small singular values and corresponding dimensions are suppressed when they don't exceed the quantity $(k_1 k_2)^{1/2} 10^{-7}$; in this case a warning message is issued. Dimensionwise inertia and total inertia are given by the relationships

$$I = \sum_s \lambda_s^2 = \sum_s \sum_i \frac{f_{i+} r_{is}^2}{N}$$

where the right-hand part of this equality is true only if the normalization is row principal (but for the other normalizations similar relationships are easily derived from step 5). The quantities "proportion explained" are equal to inertia divided by total inertia: λ_s^2/I.

Scores and contributions

This output is given first for rows, then for columns, and always preceded by a column of marginal proportions (f_{i+}/N and f_{+j}/N , respectively). The table of scores is printed in p dimensions. The contribution to the inertia of each dimension is given by

$$\tau_{is} = \frac{f_{i+}}{N} \frac{r_{is}^2}{\lambda_s^2}$$

$$\tau_{js} = \frac{f_{+j}}{N} c_{js}^2$$

The above formula is true only under the row principal normalization option. For the other normalizations, similar relationships are again easily derived from step 5. The contribution of dimensions to the inertia of each point is given by, for $s,t = 1,...p$,

$$\sigma_{is} = r_{is}^2 / \sum_t r_{it}^2$$

$$\sigma_{js} = c_{js}^2 / \sum_t c_{jt}^2$$

Variances and correlation matrix of singular values and scores

The computation of variances and covariances is explained in step 4. Since the row and column scores are linear functions of the singular vectors, an adjustment is necessary depending on the normalization option chosen. From these adjusted variances and covariances the correlations are derived in the standard way.

Permutations of the input table

For each dimension s, let $\rho(i|s)$ be the permutation of the first k_1 integers that would sort the sth column of $\{r_{is}\}$ in ascending order. Similarly, let $\rho(j|s)$ be the permutation of the first k_2 integers that would sort the sth column of $\{c_{js}\}$ in ascending order. Then the permuted data matrix is given by $\{f_{\rho(i|s),\rho(j|s)}\}$.

References

Benzécri (1969)

Bishop, Fienberg, & Holland (1975)

Eckart & Young (1936)

Gifi (1981)

Golub & Reinsch (1971)

Greenacre (1984)

Heiser (1981)

Horst (1963)

Israëls (1987)

Nishisato (1980)

Rao (1973)

Rao (1980)

Wolter (1985)

ANOVA

Model and Matrix Computations

Notation

N	number of cases
F	number of factors
CN	number of covariates
k_i	number of levels of factor i
Y_k	value of the dependent variable for case k
Z_{jk}	value of the jth covariate for case k
w_k	weight for case k
W	sum of weights of all cases

The Model

A linear model with covariates can be written in matrix notation as

$$Y = X\underset{\sim}{\beta} + Z\underset{\sim}{C} + \underset{\sim}{e} \qquad (1)$$

where

Y	$N\times1$ vector of values of the dependent variable
X	design matrix ($N\times p$) of rank $q < p$
$\underset{\sim}{\beta}$	vector of parameters ($p\times1$)
Z	matrix of covariates ($N\times CN$)
$\underset{\sim}{C}$	vector of covariate coefficients ($CN\times1$)
$\underset{\sim}{e}$	vector of error terms ($N\times1$)

Constraints

To reparameterize Equation 1 to a full rank model, a set of non-estimable conditions is needed. The constraint imposed on non-regression models is that all parameters involving level 1 of any factor are set to zero.

For the regression model, the constraints are that the analysis of variance parameter estimates for each main effect and each order of interactions sum to zero. The interactions must also sum to zero over each level of subscripts.

For a standard two way ANOVA model with the main effects α_i and β_j, and interaction parameter γ_{ij}, the constraints can be expressed as

$$\alpha_1 = \beta_1 = \gamma_{1j} = \gamma_{i1} = 0 \text{ non-regression}$$

$$\alpha_{\cdot} = \beta_{\cdot} = \gamma_{i.} = \gamma_{.j} = 0 \quad \text{regression}$$

where . indicates summation.

Computation of Matrices

- $X'X$

Non-regression Model

The $X'X$ matrix contains the sum of weights of the cases which contain a particular combination of parameters. All parameters which involve level 1 of any of the factors are excluded from the matrix. For a two-way design with $k_1 = 2$ and $k_2 = 3$, the symmetric matrix would look like the following:

	α_2	β_2	β_3	γ_{22}	γ_{23}
α_2	$N_{2.}$	N_{22}	N_{23}	N_{22}	N_{23}
β_2		$N_{.2}$	0	N_{22}	0
β_3			$N_{.3}$	0	N_{23}
γ_{22}				N_{22}	0
γ_{23}					N_{23}

The elements $N_{i.}$ or $N_{.j}$ on the diagonal are the sums of weights of cases which have level i of α or level j of β. Off-diagonal elements are sums of weights of cases cross-classified by parameter combinations. Thus, $N_{.3}$ is the sum of weights of cases in level 3 of main effect β, while N_{22} is the sum of weights of cases with α_2 and β_2.

Regression Model

A row of the design matrix X is formed for each case. The row is generated as follows:

If a case belongs to one of the 2 to k_i levels of factor i, a code of 1 is placed in the column corresponding to the level and 0 in all other $k_i - 1$ columns associated with factor i. If the case belongs in the first level of factor i, -1 is placed in *all* the $k_i - 1$ columns associated with factor i. This is repeated for each factor. The entries for the interaction terms are obtained as products of the entries in the corresponding main effect columns. This vector of dummy variables for a case will be denoted as $d(i)$, $i = 1,..., NC$, where NC is the number of columns in the reparameterized design matrix. After the vector $\underset{\sim}{d}$ is generated for case k, the ij^{th} cell of $X'X$ is incremented by $d(i)\,d(j)\,w_k$, where $i = 1,..., NC$ and $j \geq i$.

Checking and Adjustment for the Mean

After all cases have been processed, the diagonal entries of $X'X$ are examined. Rows and columns corresponding to zero diagonals are deleted and the number of levels of a factor is reduced accordingly. If a factor has only one level, the analysis will be terminated with a message. If the first specified level of a factor is missing, the first non-empty level will be deleted from the matrix for non-regression models. For regression designs, the first level cannot be missing. All entries of $X'X$ are subsequently adjusted for means.

The highest order of interactions in the model can be selected. This will affect the generation of $X'X$. If none of these options is chosen, the program will generate the highest order of interactions allowed by the number of factors. If sub-matrices corresponding to main effects or interactions in the reparameterized model are not of full rank, a message is printed and the order of the model is reduced accordingly.

- Cross-Product Matrices for Continuous Variables

Provisional means algorithms are used to compute the adjusted-for-the-means cross-product matrices.

- Matrix of covariates $Z'Z$

The covariance of covariates m and l after case k has been processed is:

$$Z_{ml}(k) = Z_{ml}(k-1) + \frac{w_k\left(W_k Z_{lk} - \sum_{j=1}^{k} w_j Z_{lj}\right)\left(W_k Z_{mk} - \sum_{j=1}^{k} w_j Z_{mj}\right)}{W_k W_{k-1}}$$

where W_k is the sum of weights of the first k cases.

- The vector $Z'Y$

The covariance between the mth covariate and the dependent variable after case k has been processed is:

$$Y_m(k) = Y_m(k-1) + \frac{w_k\left(W_k Y_k - \sum_{j=1}^{k} w_j Y_j\right)\left(W_k Z_{mk} - \sum_{j=1}^{k} w_j Z_{mj}\right)}{W_k W_{k-1}}$$

- The scalar $Y'Y$

The corrected sum of squares for the dependent variable after case k has been processed is:

$$Y'Y(k) = Y'Y(k-1) + \frac{w_k\left(W_k Y_k - \sum_{j=1}^{k} w_j Y_j\right)^2}{W_k W_{k-1}}$$

- The vector $X'Y$

$X'Y$ is a vector with NC rows. The ith element is:

$$X'Y_i = \sum_{k=1}^{N} Y_k w_k \delta_k,$$

where, for non-regression models, $\delta_k = 1$ if case k has the factor combination in column i of $X'X$; $\delta_k = 0$ otherwise. For regression models, $\delta_k = d(i)$, where $d(i)$ is the dummy variable for column i of case k. The final entries are adjusted for the mean.

- Matrix $X'Z$

The (i, m) th entry is:

$$X'Z_{im} = \sum_{k=1}^{N} Z_{mk} w_k \delta_k$$

where δ_k has been defined previously. The final entries are adjusted for the mean.

Computation of ANOVA Sum of Squares

The full rank model with covariates

$$Y = X\beta + ZC + e$$

can also be expressed as

$$Y = X_k b_k + X_m b_m + ZC + e$$

where X and b are partitioned as

$$X = [X_k | X_m] \text{ and } \beta = \begin{bmatrix} b_k \\ \hline b_m \end{bmatrix}$$

The normal equations are then

$$\begin{bmatrix} Z'Z & Z'X_k & Z'X_m \\ X'_k Z & X'_k X_k & X'_k X_m \\ X'_m Z & X'_m X_k & X'_m X_m \end{bmatrix} \begin{bmatrix} \hat{C} \\ \hat{b}_k \\ \hat{b}_m \end{bmatrix} = \begin{bmatrix} Z'Y \\ X'_k Y \\ X'_m Y \end{bmatrix} \qquad (2)$$

The normal equations for any reduced model can be obtained by excluding those entries from Equation 2 corresponding to terms which do not appear in the reduced model.

Thus, for the model excluding b_m,

$$Y = X_k b_k + ZC$$

the solution to the normal equation is:

$$\begin{bmatrix} \tilde{C} \\ \tilde{b}_k \end{bmatrix} = \begin{bmatrix} Z'Z & Z'X_k \\ X'_k Z & X'_k X_k \end{bmatrix}^{-1} \begin{bmatrix} Z'Y \\ X'_k Y \end{bmatrix} \qquad (3)$$

The sum of squares due to fitting the complete model (explained SS) is

$$R(C, b_k, b_m) = [\hat{C}' \; \hat{b}'_k \; \hat{b}'_m] \begin{bmatrix} Z'Y \\ X'_k Y \\ X'_m Y \end{bmatrix} = \hat{C}'Z'Y + \hat{b}'_k X'_k Y + \hat{b}'_m X_m Y$$

For the reduced model it is

$$R(C, b_k) = [\tilde{C}' \; \tilde{b}'_k] \begin{bmatrix} Z'Y \\ X'_k Y \end{bmatrix} = \tilde{C}'Z'Y + \tilde{b}'_k X'_k Y$$

The residual (unexplained) sum of squares for the complete model is $RSS = Y'Y - R(C, b_k, b_m)$ and similarly for the reduced model. The total sum of squares is $Y'Y$. The reduction in the sum of squares due to including b_m in a model which already includes b_k and C will be denoted as $R(b_m | C, b_k)$. This can also be expressed as

$$R(b_m | C, b_k) = R(C, b_m, b_k) - R(C, b_k) .$$

There are several ways to compute $R(b_m | C, b_k)$. The sum of squares due to the full model, as well as the sum of squares due to the reduced model, can each be calculated, and the difference obtained. (Method 1.)

$$R(b_m | C, b_k) = \hat{C}'Z'Y + \hat{b}_k' X_k' Y + \hat{b}_m' X_m Y - \tilde{C}'Z'Y - \tilde{b}_k' X_k' Y$$

A sometimes computationally more efficient procedure is to calculate

$$R(b_m | C, b_k) = \hat{b}_m' T_m^{-1} \hat{b}_m$$

where $\hat{b}_m$ are the estimates obtained from fitting the full model and T_m is the partition of the inverse matrix corresponding to b_m. (Method 2.)

$$\begin{bmatrix} Z'Z & Z'X_k & Z'X_m \\ X_k'Z & X_k'X_k & X_k'X_m \\ X_m'Z & X_m'X_k & X_m'X_m \end{bmatrix}^{-1} = \begin{bmatrix} T_c & T_{ck} & T_{cm} \\ T_{kc} & T_k & T_{km} \\ T_{mc} & T_{mk} & T_m \end{bmatrix}$$

Models and Options

Notation

Let b be partitioned as

$$b = \begin{pmatrix} M \\ D \end{pmatrix} = \begin{bmatrix} m_1 \\ \cdot \\ \cdot \\ \cdot \\ m_F \\ \text{---------} \\ d_1 \\ \cdot \\ \cdot \\ \cdot \\ d_{F-1} \end{bmatrix}$$

where:

M	vector of main effect coefficients
m_i	vector of coefficients for main effect i

$m^{(i)}$	M excluding m_i
M^{i*}	M including only m_1 through m_{i-1}
D	vector of interaction coefficients
d_k	vector of kth order interaction coefficients
d_{k_i}	vector of coefficients for the ith of the kth order interactions
$D^{(k)}$	D excluding d_k
D^{k*}	D including only d_1 through d_{k-1}
$d_k^{(i)}$	d_k excluding d_{k_i}
C	vector of covariate coefficients
$C^{(i)}$	C excluding c_i
C^{i*}	C including only c_1 through c_{i-1}

Models

Different types of sums of squares can be calculated in ANOVA.

Sum of Squares for Type of Effects

	Covariates	**Main Effects**	**Interactions**
Experimental and Hierarchical	$R(C)$	$R(M\|C)$	$R(d_k \mid C, M, D^{k*})$
Covariates with Main Effects	$R(C, M)$	$R(C, M)$	$R(d_k \mid C, M, D^{k*})$
Covariates after Main Effects	$R(C\|M)$	$R(M)$	$R(d_k \mid C, M, D^{k*})$
Regression	$R(C\|M, D)$	$R(M\|C, D)$	$R(d_k \mid C, M, D^{(k)})$

All sums of squares are calculated as described in the introduction. Reductions in sums of squares $(R(A|B))$ are computed using Method 1. Since all cross-product matrices have been corrected for the mean, all sums of squares are adjusted for the mean.

Sums of Squares Within Effects

	Covariates	Main Effects	Interactions
Default Experimental	$R(c_i \mid C^{(i)})$	$R(m_i \mid C, M^{(i)})$	$R(d_{k_i} \mid C, M, D^{k^*} d_k^{(i)})$
Covariates with Main Effects	$R(c_i \mid M, C^{(i)})$	$R(m_i \mid C, M^{(i)})$	same as default
Covariates after Main Effects	$R(c_i \mid M, C^{(i)})$	$R(m_i \mid M^{(i)})$	same as default
Regression	$R(c_i \mid M, C^{(i)}, D)$	$R(m_i \mid M^{(i)}, C, D)$	$R(d_{k_i} \mid C, M, D^{(k_i)})$
Hierarchical	$R(c_i \mid C^{i^*})$	$R(m_i \mid C, M^{i^*})$	same as default
Hierarchical and Covariates with Main Effects or Hierarchical and Covariates after Main Effects	$R(c_i \mid C^{i^*}, M)$	$R(m_i \mid M^{i^*})$	same as default

Reductions in sums of squares are calculated using Method 2, except for specifications involving the Hierarchical approach. For these, Method 1 is used. All sums of squares are adjusted for the mean.

Degrees of Freedom

- Main effects

$$df_M = \sum_{i=1}^{F} (k_i - 1)$$

- Main effect i

  $(k_i - 1)$

- Covariates

  $df_c = CN$

- Covariate i

  1

- Interactions d_r

  df_r = number of linearly independent columns corresponding to interaction d_r in $X'X$

- Interaction d_{r_i}

  df = number of independent columns corresponding to interaction d_{r_i} in $X'X$

- Model

$$df_{Model} = df_M + df_c + \sum_{r=1}^{F-1} df_r$$

- Residual

  $W - 1 - df_{Model}$

- Total

  $W - 1$

Multiple Classification Analysis

Notation

Y_{ijk}	value of the dependent variable for the kth case in level j of main effect i
n_{ij}	sum of weights of observations in level j of main effect i
k_i	number of nonempty levels in the ith main effect
W	sum of weights of all observations

Basic Computations

- Mean of dependent variable in level j of main effect i

$$\bar{Y}_{ij} = \sum_{k=1}^{n_{ij}} Y_{ijk} / n_{ij}$$

- Grand mean

$$\bar{Y} = \sum\sum\sum Y_{ijk} / W$$

- Coefficient estimates

  The computation of the coefficient for the main effects only model (b_{ij}) and coefficients for the main effects and covariates only model $(\tilde{b}_{ij})$ are obtained as previously described.

Calculation of the MCA Statistics (Andrews et al. (1973))

Deviations

For each level of each main effect the following are computed:

- Unadjusted deviations

The unadjusted deviation from the grand mean for the jth level of the ith factor:

$$m_{ij} = \bar{Y}_{ij.} - \bar{Y}$$

- Deviations adjusted for the main effects

$$m_{ij}^{1} = b_{ij} - \sum_{j=2}^{k_i} b_{ij} n_{ij} / W, \quad \text{where} \quad b_{i1} = 0.$$

- Deviations adjusted for main effects and covariates (only for models with covariates)

$$m_{ij}^{2} = \tilde{b}_{ij} - \sum_{j=2}^{k_i} \tilde{b}_{ij} n_{ij} / W, \quad \text{where} \quad \tilde{b}_{i1} = 0.$$

- ETA and beta coefficients

For each main effect i the following are computed:

$$\text{ETA}_i = \sqrt{\sum_{j=2}^{k_i} n_{ij} (\bar{Y}_{ij.} - \bar{Y})^2 / Y'Y}$$

- Beta adjusted for main effects

$$\text{Beta}_i = \sqrt{\sum_{j=2}^{k_i} n_{ij} (m_{ij}^{1})^2 / Y'Y}$$

- Beta adjusted for main effects and covariates

$$\text{Beta}_i = \sqrt{\sum_{j=2}^{k_i} n_{ij} (m^2{}_{ij})^2 / Y'Y}$$

- Squared multiple correlation coefficients

Main effects model

$$R_m^2 = \frac{R(M)}{Y'Y}$$

Main effects and covariates model

$$R_{mc}^2 = \frac{R(M, C)}{Y'Y}$$

The computations of $R(M)$, $R(M,C)$, and $Y'Y$ are outlined previously.

Unstandardized Regression Coefficients for Covariates

Estimates for the C vector, obtained the first time covariates are entered into the model, are printed.

Cell Means and Sample Sizes

Cell means and sample sizes for each combination of factor levels are obtained from the $X'Y$ and $X'X$ matrices prior to correction for the mean.

$$\bar{Y}_i = \frac{(X'Y)_i}{(X'X)_{ii}} \qquad i = 1,\ldots, CN$$

Means for combinations involving the first level of a factor are obtained by subtraction from marginal totals.

Matrix Inversion

The Cholesky decomposition (Stewart 1973) is used to triangularize the matrix. If the tolerance is less than 10^{-5}, the matrix is considered singular.

References

Andrews, Morgan, Sonquist, & Klem (1973)

Searle (1966)

Searle (1971)

Stewart (1973)

AREG

General

In the ordinary regression model the errors are assumed to be uncorrelated. The model considered here has the form

$$y_t = a + \sum_{i=1}^{p} b_i x_{ti} + u_t \qquad t=1,\ldots,n$$
$$u_t = \rho u_{t-1} + \varepsilon_t \tag{1}$$

where ε_t is an uncorrelated random error with variance σ^2 and zero mean. The error terms u_t follow a first-order autoregressive process. The constant term a can be included or excluded as specified. In the discussion below, if a is not included, it is set to be zero and not involved in the subsequent computation.

Two computational methods—Prais-Winsten and Cochrane-Orcutt—are described here.

Cochrane-Orcutt Method

Note that model (1) can be rewritten in two equivalent forms as:

$$y_t - \rho y_{t-1} = a(1-\rho) + \sum_{i=1}^{p} b_i (x_{ti} - \rho x_{(t-1)i}) + \varepsilon_t \tag{2}$$

$$y_t - a - \sum_{i-1}^{p} b_i x_{ti} = \rho\left(y_{t-1} - a - \sum_{i=1}^{p} b_i x_{(t-1)i}\right) + \varepsilon_t \tag{3}$$

Defining $y_t^* = y_t - \rho y_{t-1}$ and $x_{ti}^* = x_{ti} - \rho x_{(t-1)i}$ for $t=2,\ldots,n$, equation (2) can be rewritten as

$$y_t^* = a(1-\rho) + \sum_{i=1}^{p} b_i x_{ti}^* + \varepsilon_t \tag{2*}$$

Starting with an initial value for ρ, the differences y_t^* and x_{ti}^* in (2*) are computed and OLS then applied to (2*) to estimate a and b_i. These estimates in turn can be used in (3) to update $\hat{\rho}$ and the standard error of the estimate $\hat{\rho}$.

Initial Results

An initial value for ρ can be pre-set by the user or set to be 0 by default. The OLS method is used to obtain an initial estimate for a (if constant term is included) and b_i.

- ANOVA

Based on the OLS results, an analysis of variance table is constructed in which the degrees of freedom for regression are p, the number of X variables in (1), while the degrees of freedom for the residual are n-p*-1 if initial $\rho \neq 0$ and are $n - p^*$ otherwise. p* is the number of coefficients in (1). The sums of squares, mean squares, and other statistics are computed as in the REGRESSION procedure.

Intermediate Results

At each iteration, the following statistics are calculated:

- Rho

  An updated value for ρ is computed as

$$\hat{\rho} = \frac{\sum_{t=2}^{n} \tilde{u}_t \tilde{u}_{t-1}}{\sum_{t=1}^{n} \tilde{u}_t^2}$$

  where the residuals $\tilde{u}_t$ are obtained from (1).

- Standard Error of rho

  An estimate of the standard error of $\hat{\rho}$

$$SE(\hat{\rho}) = \sqrt{\frac{1 - \hat{\rho}^2}{n - 1 - p^*}}$$

  where $p^* = p+1$ if there is a constant term; p otherwise.

- Durbin-Watson Statistic

$$DW = \frac{\sum_{i=1}^{n-1} (\tilde{\varepsilon}_{i+1} - \tilde{\varepsilon}_i)^2}{\sum_{i=1}^{n} \tilde{\varepsilon}_i^2}$$

  where

$$\tilde{\varepsilon}_1 = \sqrt{1 - \hat{\rho}^2}\tilde{u}_1$$

$$\tilde{\varepsilon}_i = \tilde{u}_i - \hat{\rho}\tilde{u}_{i-1} \qquad i = 2,\ldots,n$$

- Mean Square Error

  An estimate of the variance of ε_t

$$MSE = \frac{\sum_{t=2}^{n} (\tilde{u}_t - \hat{\rho}\tilde{u}_{t-1})^2}{n - 2 - p^*}$$

Final Results

Iteration terminates if either all the parameters change by less than a specified value (default 0.001) or the number of iterations exceeds the cutoff value (default 10).

The following variables are computed for each case:

- FIT

Fitted responses are computed as

$$\tilde{y}_1 = \hat{y}_1$$

and

$$\tilde{y}_t = \hat{y}_t + \hat{\rho}\hat{u}_{t-1} \quad t = 2,\ldots,n$$

in which $\hat{\rho}$ is the final estimate of ρ, and

$$\hat{y}_t = \hat{a} + \sum_{i=1}^{p} \hat{b}_i x_{ti}$$

$$\hat{u}_t = y_t - \hat{y}_t \qquad t = 1,\ldots,n$$

- ERR

Residuals are computed as

$$\tilde{\varepsilon}_t = y_t - \tilde{y}_t \quad t = 2,\ldots,n$$

$$\tilde{\varepsilon}_1 = \sqrt{1-\hat{\rho}^2}\,(y_1 - \tilde{y}_1)$$

- SEP

Standard error of predicted value at time t

$$SEP_1 = \sqrt{MSE}\sqrt{\left(\frac{1}{1-\hat{\rho}^2} + \tilde{h}_1\right)}$$

and

$$SEP_t = \sqrt{MSE}\sqrt{(1 + \tilde{h}_t)} \qquad t=2,\ldots,n$$

where

$$\tilde{h}_i = X_i (X^{*\prime} X^*)^{-1} X_i'$$

in which X_i is the predictor vector at time i with the first component 1 if a constant term is included in (2*). X^* is a $(n-1) \times p^*$ design matrix for (2*). The first column has value of $1 - \hat{\rho}$ if a constant term is included in (2*).

- LCL and UCL

95% prediction interval for the future y_k is

$$\tilde{y}_k \pm t_{n-1-p^*\,;\,0.025} SEP_k$$

- Other Statistics

Other statistics such as Multiple R, R-Squared, Adjusted R-Squared, etc., are computed. Consult the REGRESSION procedure for details.

Prais-Winsten Method

This method is a modification of the Cochrane-Orcutt method in that the first case gets explicit treatment. By adding an extra equation to (2*), the model has the form of

$$(1-\rho)y_1 = a(1-\rho) + \sum_{i=1}^{p} b_i(1-\rho)x_{1i} + (1-\rho)u_1$$

$$y_t^* = a(1-\rho) + \sum_{i=1}^{p} b_i x_{ti}^* + \varepsilon_t \qquad \text{for } t = 2,\ldots,n \tag{4}$$

Like the Cochrane-Orcutt method, an initial value of ρ can be set by the user or a default value of 0 can be used. The iterative process of estimating the parameters is performed via weighted least squares (WLS). The weights used in WLS computation are $w_1 = (1-\hat{\rho}^2)/(1-\hat{\rho})^2$ and $w_i = 1$ for i=2,..., n. The computation of the variance of ε_t and the variance of $\hat{\rho}$ is the same as that of the WLS in the REGRESSION procedure.

Initial Results

The WLS method is used to obtain initial parameter estimates.

- ANOVA

The degrees of freedom are p for regression and n-p* for residuals.

Intermediate Results

The formulas for RHO, SE Rho, DW, and MSE are exactly the same as those in the Cochrane-Orcutt method. The degrees of freedom for residuals, however, are n-1-p*.

Final Results

- SEP

Standard error of predicted value at time t is computed as

$$SEP_1 = \sqrt{MSE}\sqrt{\left(\frac{1}{1-\hat{\rho}^2} + \tilde{h}_1\right)}$$

$$SEP_t = \sqrt{MSE}\sqrt{(1+\tilde{h}_t)} \qquad \text{for } t = 2,\ldots,n$$

where $\tilde{h}$ is computed as

$$\tilde{h}_i = X_i(X^{*\prime}X^*)^{-1}X_i'$$

in which X_i is the predictor vector at time i and X^* is a $n \times p^*$ design matrix for (4). If a constant term is included in the model, the first column of X^* has a constant value of $1-\hat{\rho}$, the first row of X^* is $\sqrt{w_1}(x_{11},\ldots,x_{1p})$, and $p^* = p+1$.

- LCL and UCL

95% prediction interval for y_k at time k is

$$\tilde{y}_k \pm t_{n-p^*;\,0.025}\mathrm{SEP}_k$$

ARIMA

Algorithms for the ARIMA procedure are not available at this printing.

Cross Correlation Function (CCF)

Notation

X, Y	any two series of length n
$r_{xy}(k)$	sample cross correlation coefficient at lag k
S_x	standard deviation of series X
S_y	standard deviation of series Y
$C_{xy}(k)$	sample cross covariance at lag k

Cross Correlation

The cross correlation coefficient at lag k is estimated by

$$r_{xy}(k) = \frac{C_{xy}(k)}{S_x S_y}$$

where

$$C_{xy}(k) = \begin{cases} \frac{1}{n}\sum_{t=1}^{n-k}(x_t - \bar{x})(y_{t+k} - \bar{y}) & k = 0, 1, 2, \ldots \\ \frac{1}{n}\sum_{t=1}^{n+k}(y_t - \bar{y})(x_{t-k} - \bar{x}) & k = -1, -2, \ldots \end{cases}$$

$$S_x = \sqrt{\frac{1}{n}\sum_{t=1}^{n}(x_t - \bar{x})^2}$$

$$S_y = \sqrt{\frac{1}{n}\sum_{t=1}^{n}(y_t - \bar{y})^2}$$

The cross correlation function is not symmetric about $k = 0$.

Approximate standard error of $r_{xy}(k)$ is

$$SE(r_{xy}(k)) \cong \sqrt{\frac{1}{n - |k|}} \quad k = 0, \pm 1, \pm 2, \ldots$$

The standard error is based on the assumption that the series are not cross correlated and one of the series is white noise. (The general formula for the standard error can be found in Box and Jenkins (1976), p. 376, 11.1.7).

CLUSTER

Cluster Measures

Six measures are available:

Squared Euclidean Distance

This measure is the default. You should use this measure whenever you use centroid, median, or Ward's method of clustering. With this measure, the distance between two cases (*x* and *y*) is the sum of the squared differences between the values of the clustering variables.

$$s_{xy} = \Sigma_i (x_i - y_i)^2$$

Euclidean Distance

The distance between two cases is the square root of the sum of the squared differences between the values of the clustering variables.

$$s_{xy} = \sqrt{\Sigma_i (x_i - y_i)^2}$$

Cosine of Vectors of Variables

This is a pattern similarity measure.

$$s_{xy} = \frac{\Sigma_i (x_i y_i)}{\sqrt{(\Sigma_i x_i^2)(\Sigma_i y_i^2)}}$$

Distance in Absolute Power—Power (*p*, *r*)

The distance between two cases is the *r*th root of the sum of the absolute differences to the *p*th power between the values of the clustering variables. Appropriate selection of the integer parameters *p* and *r* yields Euclidean, squared Euclidean, Minkowski, city-block, minimum, maximum, and many other distance metrics.

$$s_{xy} = (\Sigma_i |x_i - y_i|^p)^{1/r}$$

City-Block or Manhattan Distance

The distance between two cases is the sum of the absolute differences between the values of the clustering variables.

$$s_{xy} = \Sigma_i |x_i - y_i|$$

Chebychev Distance

The distance between two cases is the maximum absolute difference between the values of the clustering variables.

$$s_{xy} = max_i |x_i - y_i|$$

Clustering Methods

Notation

S	matrix of similarity or dissimilarity measures
s_{ij}	similarity or dissimilarity measure between cluster i and cluster j
N_i	number of cases in cluster i

General Procedure

Begin with N clusters each containing one case. Denote the clusters *1* through N.

- Find the most similar pair of clusters p and q $(p > q)$. Denote this similarity s_{pq}. If a dissimilarity measure is used, large values indicate dissimilarity. If a similarity measure is used, small values indicate dissimilarity.

- Reduce the number of clusters by one through merger of clusters p and q. Label the new cluster $t\,(=q)$ and update similarity matrix (by the method specified) to reflect revised similarities or dissimilarities between cluster t and all other clusters. Delete the row and column of S corresponding to cluster p.

- Perform the previous two steps until all entities are in one cluster.

- For each of the following methods, the similarity or dissimilarity matrix S is updated to reflect revised similarities or dissimilarities (s_{tr}) between the new cluster t and all other clusters r as given below.

Average Linkage between Groups

Before the first merge, let $N_i = 1$ for $i = 1$ to N. Update s_{tr} by

$$s_{tr} = s_{pr} + s_{qr}$$

Update N_t by

$$N_t = N_p + N_q$$

and then choose the most similar pair based on the value

$$s_{ij} / (N_i N_j)$$

Average Linkage within Groups

Before the first merge, let $SUM_i = 0$ and $N_i = 1$ for $i = 1$ to N. Update s_{tr} by

$$s_{tr} = s_{pr} + s_{qr}$$

Update SUM_t and N_t by

$$SUM_t = SUM_p + SUM_q + s_{pq}$$

$$N_t = N_p + N_q$$

and choose the most similar pair based on

$$\frac{SUM_i + SUM_j + s_{ij}}{((N_i + N_j)(N_i + N_j - 1))/2}$$

Single Linkage

Update s_{tr} by

$$s_{tr} = \begin{cases} min\,(s_{pr}, s_{qr}) & \text{if S is a dissimilarity matrix} \\ max\,(s_{pr}, s_{qr}) & \text{if S is a similarity matrix} \end{cases}$$

Complete Linkage

Update s_{tr} by

$$s_{tr} = \begin{cases} max\,(s_{pr}, s_{qr}) & \text{if S is a dissimilarity matrix} \\ min\,(s_{pr}, s_{qr}) & \text{if S is a similarity matrix} \end{cases}$$

Centroid Method

Update s_{tr} by

$$s_{tr} = \frac{N_p}{N_p + N_q} s_{pr} + \frac{N_q}{N_p + N_q} s_{qr} - \frac{N_p N_q}{(N_p + N_q)^2} s_{pq}$$

Median Method

Update s_{tr} by

$$s_{tr} = (s_{pr} + s_{qr})/2 - s_{pq}/4$$

Ward's Method

Update s_{tr} by

$$s_{tr} = \frac{1}{(N_t + N_r)} [\,(N_r + N_p)\, s_{rp} + (N_r + N_q)\, s_{rq} - N_r s_{pq}]\,.$$

Update the coefficient W by

$$W = W + .5 s_{pq}$$

Note that for Ward's method, the coefficient given in the agglomeration schedule is really the within-cluster sum of squares at that step. For all other methods, this coefficient represents the distance at which the clusters p and q were joined.

References

Anderberg (1973)

CNLR

General

CNLR is used to estimate the parameters of a function by minimizing a smooth nonlinear loss function (objective function) when the parameters are subject to a set of constraints.

Model

Consider the model

$$f = f(\underset{\sim}{x}, \underset{\sim}{\theta}),$$

where $\underset{\sim}{\theta}$ is a $p \times 1$ parameter vector, $\underset{\sim}{x}$ is an independent variable vector, and f is a function of $\underset{\sim}{x}$ and $\underset{\sim}{\theta}$.

Goal

Find the estimate $\underset{\sim}{\theta}^*$ of $\underset{\sim}{\theta}$ such that $\underset{\sim}{\theta}^*$ minimizes

$$F = F(\underset{\sim}{y}, f)$$

subject to

$$\underset{\sim}{l} \le \left\{ \begin{array}{c} \underset{\sim}{\theta} \\ A_L \underset{\sim}{\theta} \\ C(\underset{\sim}{\theta}) \end{array} \right\} \le \underset{\sim}{u}$$

where F is the smooth loss function (objective function), which can be specified by the user. A_L is an $m_L \times p$ matrix of linear constraints, and $C(\underset{\sim}{\theta})$ is an $m_N \times 1$ vector of nonlinear constraint functions. $\underset{\sim}{l}' = (\underset{\sim}{l}_B', \underset{\sim}{l}_L', \underset{\sim}{l}_N')$, where $\underset{\sim}{l}_B'$, $\underset{\sim}{l}_L'$, and $\underset{\sim}{l}_N'$ represent the lower bounds, linear constraints and nonlinear constraints, respectively. The upper bound $\underset{\sim}{u}$ is defined similarly.

Algorithm

CNLR uses the algorithms proposed and implemented in NPSOL by Gill, Murray, Saunders & Wright. A description of the algorithms can be found in the *User's Guide for NPSOL*, Version 4.0 (1986).

The method used in NPSOL is a sequential quadratic programming (SQP) method. For an overview of SQP methods, see Gill, Murray, & Wright (1981), pp. 237–242.

The basic structure of NPSOL involves major and minor iterations. Based on the given initial value $\underset{\sim}{\theta}^{(0)}$ of $\underset{\sim}{\theta}$, the algorithm first selects an initial working set that includes bounds or general inequality constraints that lie within a crash tolerance (CRSHTOL). At the kth iteration, the algorithm starts with

(I) Minor Iteration

This iteration searches for the direction P_k, which is the solution of a quadratic subproblem, i.e., P_k, is found by minimizing

$$g_k'P + \frac{1}{2}P'H_k P \tag{1}$$

subject to

$$\underset{\sim}{\bar{l}}^{(k)} \le \left\{ \begin{array}{c} P \\ A_L P \\ A_N P \end{array} \right\} \le \underset{\sim}{\bar{u}}^{(k)}$$

where g_k is the gradient of F at $\underset{\sim}{\theta}^{(k)}$, the matrix H_k is a positive-definite quasi-Newton approximation to the Hessian of the Lagrangian function, A_N is the Jacobian matrix of the nonlinear-constraint vector C evaluated at $\underset{\sim}{\theta}^{(k)}$, and

$$\begin{aligned}
\underset{\sim}{\bar{l}}^{(k)} &= (\bar{l}_B', \bar{l}_L, \bar{l}_N') \\
\underset{\sim}{\bar{u}}^{(k)} &= (\bar{u}_B', \bar{u}_L', \bar{u}_N') \\
\bar{l}_B &= l_B - \underset{\sim}{\theta}^{(k)} \\
\bar{l}_L &= l_L - A_L \underset{\sim}{\theta}^{(k)} \\
\bar{l}_N &= l_N - C(\underset{\sim}{\theta}^{(k)}) \\
\bar{u}_B &= u_B - \underset{\sim}{\theta}^{(k)} \\
\bar{u}_L &= u_L - A_L \underset{\sim}{\theta}^{(k)} \\
\bar{u}_N &= u_N - C(\underset{\sim}{\theta}^{(k)}) .
\end{aligned}$$

The linear feasibility tolerance, the nonlinear feasibility tolerance, and the feasibility tolerance are used to decide if a solution of (1) is feasible for linear and nonlinear constraints.

Once the search direction P_k is found, the algorithm goes to the major iteration.

(II) Major Iteration

The purpose of the major iteration is to find a non-negative scalar α_k such that

$$\underset{\sim}{\theta}^{(k+1)} = \underset{\sim}{\theta}^{(k)} + \alpha_k P_k$$

satisfies the following conditions:

- $\underset{\sim}{\theta}^{(k+1)}$ produces a "sufficient decrease" in the augmented Lagrangian merit function

$$L(\underset{\sim}{\theta}, \underset{\sim}{\lambda}, \underset{\sim}{s}) = F(\underset{\sim}{\theta}) - \sum_i \lambda_i (c_i(\underset{\sim}{\theta}) - s_i) + \frac{1}{2}\sum_i \rho\, (c_i(\underset{\sim}{\theta}) - s_i)^2 \tag{2}$$

The summation terms in (2) involve only the nonlinear constraints. The vector λ is an estimate of the Lagrange multipliers for the nonlinear constraints. The non-negative slack variables $\{s_i\}$ allow nonlinear inequality constraints to be treated without introducing discontinuities. The solution of the QP subproblem defined in (1) provides a vector triple that serves as a direction search for $\underset{\sim}{\theta}$, $\underset{\sim}{\lambda}$, and $\underset{\sim}{s}$. The non-negative vector of penalty parameters (ρ) is initialized to zero at the beginning of the first major iteration. Function precision criteria are used as a measure of the accuracy with which the functions F and c_i can be evaluated.

- $\underset{\sim}{\theta}^{(k+1)}$ is close to a minimum of F along P_k. The criterion is

$$|g'(\underset{\sim}{\theta}^{(k+1)})P_k| < -\eta g_k' P_k ,$$

where η is the Line Search Tolerance and $0 \le \eta < 1$. The value of η determines the accuracy with which α_k approximates a stationary point of F along P_k. A smaller value of η produces a more accurate line search.

- The step length is in a certain range, i.e.,

$$\|\underset{\sim}{\theta}^{(k+1)} - \underset{\sim}{\theta}^{(k)}\| = \|\alpha_k P_k\| \le \text{Step Limit}.$$

(III) Convergence Tests

After α_k is determined from the major iteration, the following conditions are checked:

- $k+1 \le$ Maximum number of major iterations

- The sequence $\{\underset{\sim}{\theta}^{(l)}\}$ converged at $\underset{\sim}{\theta}^{(k+1)}$, i.e.,

$$\|\alpha_k P_k\| \le \sqrt{r}(1 + \|\underset{\sim}{\theta}^{(k+1)}\|)$$

- $\underset{\sim}{\theta}^{(k+1)}$ satisfies the Kuhn-Tucker conditions to the accuracy requested, i.e.,

$$\|g_z(\underset{\sim}{\theta}^{(k+1)})\| \le \sqrt{r}(1 + \max(1 + |F(\underset{\sim}{\theta}^{(k+1)})|, \|g(\underset{\sim}{\theta}^{(k+1)})\|))$$

and

- $\|\text{res}_j\| \le \text{FTOL}$, for all j,

where g_z is the projected gradient, g is the gradient of F with respect to the free parameters, res_j is the violation of the jth nonlinear constraint, FTOL is the Nonlinear Feasibility Tolerance, and r is the Optimality Tolerance.

If none of these three conditions are satisfied, the algorithm continues with the Minor Iteration to find a new search direction.

Termination

The following are various termination conditions.

- Underflow. A single underflow will always occur if machine constants are computed automatically. Other floating-point underflows may occur occasionally, but can usually be ignored.

- Overflow. If the printed output before the overflow error contains a warning about serious ill-conditioning in the working set when adding the jth constraint, it may be possible to avoid the difficulty by increasing the magnitude of FTOL, LFTOL, or NFTOL and rerunning the program. If the message recurs after this change, the offending linearly dependent constraint (with index "j") must be removed from the problem.

- Optimal solution found.

- Optimal solution found, but the requested accuracy could not be achieved, NPSOL terminates because no further improvement can be made in the merit function. This is probably caused by requesting a more accurate solution than is attainable with the given precision of the problem (as specified by FPRECISION).

- No point has been found that satisfies the linear constraints. NPSOL terminates without finding a feasible point for the given value of LFTOL. The user should check that there are no constraint redundancies and ensure that the value of LFTOL is greater than the precision of parameter estimates.

- No point has been found which satisfies the nonlinear constraints. There is no feasible point found in QP subproblems. The user should check the validity of constraints. If the user is convinced that a feasible point does exist, NPSOL should be restarted at a different starting point.

- Too many major iterations. If the algorithm appears to be making progress, increase the value of ITER and rerun NPSOL. If the algorithm seems to be "bogged down," the user should check for incorrect gradients.

- Cannot improve on current point. A sufficient decrease in the merit function could not be attained during the final line search. This sometimes occurs because an overly stringent accuracy has been requested, e.g., Optimality Tolerance is too small or a too-small step limit is given when the parameters are measured on different scales.

Notes:

- Unlike the other procedures in SPSS, the weight function is not treated as a case replicate in CNLR.

- When both weight and loss function are specified, the algorithm takes the product of these two functions as the loss function.

- If the loss function is not specified, the default loss function is a squared loss function and the default output in NLR will be printed. However, if the loss function is not a squared loss function, CNLR prints only the final parameter estimates, iteration history, and termination message. In order to obtain estimates of the standard errors of parameter estimates and correlations between parameter estimates, the bootstrapping method can be requested.

Bootstrapping Estimates

Bootstrapping is a nonparametric technique of estimating the standard error of a parameter estimate using repeated samples from the original data. This is done by sampling with replacement. CNLR computes and saves the parameter estimates for each sample generated. This results, for each parameter, in a sample of estimates from which the standard deviation is calculated. This is the estimated standard error.

Mathematically, the bootstrap covariance matrix S for the p parameter estimates is:

$$S = (s_{ij})_{p \times p}$$

where

$$s_{ij} = \sum_{k=1}^{m} (\hat{\theta}_{ik} - \bar{\theta}_i)\,(\hat{\theta}_{jk} - \bar{\theta}_j)$$

$$\bar{\theta}_i = \sum_{k=1}^{m} \hat{\theta}_{ik}/m \,,$$

and $\hat{\theta}_{ik}$ is the CNLR parameter estimate of θ_i for the kth bootstrap sample and m is the number of samples generated by the bootstrap. By default, $m = \dfrac{10p\,(p+1)}{2}$.

The standard error for the jth parameter estimate is estimated by

$$\sqrt{\frac{s_{jj}}{m-1}}$$

and the correlation between the ith and jth parameter estimates is estimated by

$$\frac{s_{ij}}{\sqrt{s_{ii}s_{jj}}}$$

The "95% Trimmed Range" values are the most extreme values that remain after trimming from the set of estimates for a parameter, the g largest, and the g smallest estimates, where g is the largest integer not exceeding $0.025\,m$.

References

Gill, Murray & Wright (1981)

Gill, Murray, Saunders & Wright (1984)

Gill, Murray, Saunders & Wright (1986)

CONJOINT

General

This procedure performs conjoint analysis using ordinary least squares.

Notation

n	The total number of regular cards in the PLAN file.
p	The total number of factors
d	The number of discrete factors
l	The number of linear factors
q	The number of quadratic factors
m_i	The number of levels of the ith discrete factor
a_{ij}	The jth level of the ith discrete factor (i=1,...,d)
x_i	The ith linear factor (i=1,...,l)
z_i	The ith ideal or anti-ideal factor (i=1,...,q)
r_i	The response for the ith card (i=i,...,n)
t	The total number of subjects being analyzed at the same time. (When /SUBJECT is specified, t is usually 1.)

Model

The model for the response r_i for the ith card from a subject is

$$r_i = \beta_0 + \sum_{j=1}^{p} u_{jk_{ji}}$$

where $u_{jk_{ji}}$ is the utility (part worth) associated with the k_{ji}^{th} level of the jth factor on the ith card.

The Design Matrix

A design matrix X is formed from the values in the PLAN file. There is one row for each card in the PLAN file. The columns of the matrix are defined by each of the factor variables in the following manner:

- There is a column of 1s for the constant. This column is used for the estimate of β_0^*.

- For each discrete factor containing m_i levels, $m_i - 1$ columns are formed. Each column represents the deviation of one of the factor levels from the overall mean. There is a 1 in the column if that level of the factor was observed, $a - 1$ if the last level of the factor was observed, or a 0 otherwise. These columns are used to estimate the $m_i - 1$ values of α_{ij}.

- For each linear factor there is one column which is the centered value of that factor $(x_{ij} - \bar{x}_i)$. These columns are used to estimate the values for $\hat{\beta}_i$.

- For each quadratic factor there are two columns, one which contains the centered value of the factor $(z_{ij} - \bar{z}_i)$, the next which contains the square of the centered factor value $(z_{ij} - \bar{z}_i)^2$. These columns are used to estimate the values of $\hat{\gamma}^*$.

Converting Card Numbers to Ranks

If the observations are card numbers, they are converted to ranks. If card number i has a value of k, then $r_i = k$.

Estimation

The estimates

$$(\hat{\beta}_0^* \, \hat{\alpha} \, \hat{\beta} \hat{\gamma}^*)' = (X'X)^{-1} X'y$$

are computed by using a QR decomposition (see MANOVA) where

$$y_i = \begin{cases} r_i & \text{if responses are scores} \\ n - r_i & \text{if responses are ranks} \end{cases}$$

The variance-covariance matrix of these estimates is

$$\hat{\sigma}\,(X'X)^{-1}$$

where

$$\hat{\sigma} = \sum_{i=1}^{t}\sum_{j=1}^{n} (r_{ij} - \hat{r}_{ij})^2 / (nt - d - l - 2q - 1)$$

The values of $\hat{\gamma}$ are computed by

$$\hat{\gamma}_{i1} = \hat{\gamma}_{i1}^* - 2\hat{\gamma}_{i2}^* \bar{z}_i$$

and

$$\hat{\gamma}_{i2} = \hat{\gamma}_{i2}^*$$

with variances

$$Var(\hat{\gamma}_{j1}) = Var(\hat{\gamma}_{j1}^*) - 4\bar{z}_j Cov(\hat{\gamma}_{j1}^*, \hat{\gamma}_{j2}) + 4\bar{z}_j^2 Var(\hat{\gamma}_{j2})$$

and

$$Var(\hat{\gamma}_{j2}) = Var(\hat{\gamma}_{j2}^*)$$

where

$$Cov(\hat{\gamma}_{j1}, \hat{\gamma}_{j2}) = Cov(\hat{\gamma}_{j1}^*, \hat{\gamma}_{j2}) - 2\bar{z}^2 Var(\hat{\gamma}_{j2})$$

The value for $\hat{\beta}_0$ is calculated by

$$\hat{\beta}_0 = \hat{\beta}_0^* - \sum \hat{\beta}_i \bar{x}_i - \sum (\hat{\gamma}_{i1} \bar{z}_i + \hat{\gamma}_{i2} \bar{z}_i^2)$$

with variance

$$Var(\hat{\beta}_0) = a \Sigma_a^{-1} a'$$

where

$$a = (1, -\bar{x}_1, \ldots, -\bar{x}_l, -\bar{z}_1, \bar{z}_1^2, \ldots, -\bar{z}_q, \bar{z}_q^2)$$

and

$$\Sigma_a = \begin{pmatrix} Var\hat{\beta}_0^* & Cov(\hat{\beta}_0^*, \hat{\beta}_1) \ldots & Cov(\hat{\beta}_0^*, \hat{\Upsilon}_{q1}^*) & Cov(\hat{\beta}_0^*, \hat{\Upsilon}_{q2}^*) \\ & Var\hat{\beta}_1 & & \\ & & Var\hat{\Upsilon}_{q1}^* & \\ & & & Var\hat{\Upsilon}_{q2}^* \end{pmatrix}$$

Utility (Part Worth) Values

- Discrete Factors

$$\hat{u}_{jk} = \begin{cases} \hat{a}_{jk} & \text{for } k = 1,\ldots,m_j - 1 \\ -\sum_{j=1}^{m_j - 1} \hat{a}_{jk} & \text{for } k = m_j \end{cases}$$

- Linear Factors

$$\hat{u}_{jk} = \hat{\beta}_j x_k$$

- Ideal or Anti-ideal Factors

$$\hat{u}_{jk} = \hat{\gamma}_{j1} z_{jk} + \hat{\gamma}_{j2} z_{jk}^2$$

Standard Errors of Part Worths

The standard error of part worth $u_{jk} = \sqrt{Var(u_{jk})}$ where $Var(u_{jk})$ is defined below:

- Discrete Factors

$$Var(u_{jk}) = \begin{cases} Var(\hat{\alpha}_{jk}) & \text{for } k = 1, \ldots, m_j - 1 \\ \sum_{i=1}^{m_j - 1} Var(\hat{\alpha}_{jk}) - 2 \sum_{i=1}^{m_j - 1} \sum_{l<i} Cov(\hat{\alpha}_{ji}, \hat{\alpha}_{jl}) & \text{for } k = m_j \end{cases}$$

- Linear Factors

$$Var(u_{jk}) = x_k^2 Var(\hat{\beta}_j)$$

- Ideal and Anti-ideal Factors

$$Var(u_{jk}) = z_k^2 Var(\hat{\gamma}_{j1}) + 2 z_k^3 Cov(\hat{\gamma}_{j1}, \hat{\gamma}_{j2}) + z_k^4 Var(\hat{\gamma}_{j2})$$

Importance Scores

The importance score for factor *i* is

$$IMP_i = 100\frac{RANGE_i}{\sum_{i=1}^{p} RANGE_i}$$

where $RANGE_i$ is the highest minus lowest utility for factor *i*.

Predicted Scores

$$\hat{r}_i = \hat{\beta}_0 + \sum_{j=1}^{p} \hat{u}_{jk_{ji}}$$

where $\hat{u}_{jk_{ji}}$ is the estimated utility (part worth) associated with the k_{ji}^{th} level of the jth factor.

Correlations

Pearson and Kendall correlations are calculated between predicted $(\hat{r}_i)$ and the observed (r_i) responses. See CORRELATIONS and NONPAR CORR chapters for algorithms.

Simulations

Each person is assigned a probability p_i for each simulation *i*. The probabilities are all computed based on the predicted score $(\hat{r}_i)$ for that product. The probabilities are computed as follows:.

- Max Utility

$$p_i = \begin{cases} 1 & \text{if } \hat{r}_i = max(\hat{r}_i) \\ 0 & \text{otherwise} \end{cases}$$

- BTL

$$p_i = \frac{\hat{r}_i}{\sum_j \hat{r}_j}$$

- Logit

$$p_i = \frac{e^{\hat{r}_i}}{\sum_j e^{\hat{r}_j}}$$

Probabilities are averaged across respondents for the grouped simulation results. For the BTL and Logit methods, only subjects having all positive $\hat{r}_i$ values are used.

CORRELATIONS

General

The user-specified treatment for missing values is used for computation of all statistics except, under certain conditions, the means and standard deviations.

Notation

N	number of cases
X_{kl}	value of the variable k for case l
w_l	weight for case l
W_k	sum of weights of cases used in computation of statistics for variable k
W_{kj}	sum of weights of cases used in computation of statistics for variables k and j

Statistics

Means and Standard Deviations

$$\bar{X}_k = \frac{\sum_{l=1}^{N} w_l X_{kl}}{W_k}$$

$$S_k = \sqrt{\left(\sum_{l=1}^{N} w_l X_{kl}^2 - \bar{X}_k^2 W_k\right) / (W_k - 1)}$$

Note: If no treatment for missing values is specified (default is pairwise), means and standard deviations are computed based on all nonmissing values for each variable. If missing values are to be included or listwise is chosen, that option is used for means and standard deviations as well.

Cross-product Deviations and Covariances

The cross-product deviation for variables i and j is

$$C_{ij} = \sum_{l=1}^{N} w_l X_{il} X_{jl} - \left(\sum_{l=1}^{N} w_l X_{il}\right)\left(\sum_{l=1}^{N} w_l X_{jl}\right) / W_{ij}$$

The covariance is

$$S_{ij} = \frac{C_{ij}}{W_{ij} - 1}$$

Pearson Correlation

$$r_{ij} = \frac{C_{ij}}{\sqrt{C_{ii}C_{jj}}}$$

Significance Level of *r*

The significance level for r_{ij} is based on

$$t = r_{ij}\sqrt{\frac{W_{ij} - 2}{1 - r_{ij}^2}}$$

which, under the null hypothesis, is distributed as a *t* with $W_{ij} - 2$ degrees of freedom. By default, the significance level is two-tailed.

References

Blalock (1972)

Cox Regression (COXREG)

Overview

Cox (1972) first suggested the models in which factors related to lifetime have a multiplicative effect on the hazard function. These models are called proportional hazards (PH) models

Under the proportional hazards assumption, the hazard function h of t given X is of the form

$$h(t|x) = h_0(t)e^{x'\beta} \qquad (1)$$

where x is a known vector of regressor variables associated with the individual, β is a vector of unknown parameters, and $h_0(t)$ is the baseline hazard function for an individual with $x = 0$. Hence, for any two covariates sets x_1 and x_2, the log hazard functions $h(t|x_1)$ and $h(t|x_2)$ should be parallel across time.

When a factor does not affect the hazard function multiplicatively, stratification may be useful in model building. Suppose that individuals can be assigned to one of m different strata, defined by the levels of one or more factors. The hazard function for an individual in the jth stratum is defined as

$$h_j(t|x) = h_{0j}(t)e^{x'\beta} \qquad (2)$$

There are two unknown components in the model: The regression parameter β and the baseline hazard function $h_{0j}(t)$. The estimation for the parameters is described below.

Estimation

We begin by considering a nonnegative random variable T representing the lifetimes of individuals in some population. Let $f(t|x)$ denote the probability density function (pdf) of T given a regressor x and let $S(t|x)$ be the survivor function (the probability of an individual surviving until time t). Hence

$$S(t|x) = \int_t^{\infty} f(u|x)\,du \qquad (3)$$

The hazard $h(t|x)$ is then defined by

$$h(t|x) = \frac{f(t|x)}{S(t|x)} \qquad (4)$$

Another useful expression for $S(t|x)$ in terms of $h(t|x)$ derived from equations 3 and 4 is

$$S(t|x) = exp\left(-\int_0^t h(u|x)\,du\right) \qquad (5)$$

Thus

$$lnS(t|x) = -\int_0^t h(u|x)\,du \qquad (6)$$

For some purposes it is also useful to define the cumulative hazard function

$$H(t|x) = \int_0^t h(u|x)\,du = -lnS(t|x) \qquad (7)$$

Assume that the hazard function has the form of equation 1. The survivor function can be written as

$$S(t|x) = [S_0(t)]^{\exp(x'\beta)} \tag{8}$$

where $S_0(t)$ is the baseline survivor function defined by

$$S_0(t) = exp(-H_0(t)) \tag{9}$$

and

$$H_0(t) = \int_0^t h_0(u)\,du$$

Some relationships between $S(t|x)$, $H(t|x)$ and $H_0(t)$, $S_0(t)$ and $h_0(t)$ which will be used later are

$$lnS(t|x) = -H(t|x) = -exp(x'\beta)H_0(t) \tag{10}$$

$$ln(-lnS(t|x)) = x'\beta + lnH_0(t) \tag{11}$$

To estimate the survivor function $S(t|x)$, we can see from equation 8 that there are two components, β and $S_0(t)$, which need to be estimated. The approach we use here is to estimate β from the partial likelihood function and then to maximize the full likelihood for $S_0(t)$.

Estimation of Beta

Assume that

- There are m levels for the stratification variable
- Individuals in the same stratum have proportional hazard functions
- The relative effect of the regressor variables is the same in each stratum.

Let $t_{j1} < \ldots < t_{jk_j}$ be the observed uncensored failure times of the n_j individuals in the jth stratum and $x_{j1} \ldots x_{jk_j}$ be the corresponding covariates. Then the partial likelihood function is defined by

$$L(\beta) = \prod_{j=1}^{m}\prod_{i=1}^{k_j}\frac{e^{S_{ji}'\beta}}{\left(\sum_{l\in R_{ji}} w_l e^{x_l'\beta}\right)^{d_{ji}}} \tag{12a}$$

where d_{ji} is the sum of case weights of individuals whose lifetime is equal to t_{ji} and S_{ji} is the weighted sum of the regression vector x for those d_{ji} individuals, w_l is the case weight of individual l, and R_{ji} is the set of individuals alive and uncensored just prior to t_{ji} in the jth stratum. Thus the log likelihood arising from equation 12a is

$$l = \ln L(\beta) = \sum_{j=1}^{m}\sum_{i=1}^{k_j} S_{ji}'\beta - \sum_{j=1}^{m}\sum_{i=1}^{k_j} d_{ji}\ln\left(\sum_{l\in R_{ji}} w_l e^{x_l'\beta}\right) \tag{12b}$$

and the first derivatives of l are

$$D_{\beta_r} = \frac{\partial l}{\partial \beta_r} = \sum_{j=1}^{m}\sum_{i=1}^{k_j}\left(S_{ji}^{(r)} - d_{ji}\frac{\sum_{l\in R_{ji}} w_l x_{lr} e^{x_l'\beta}}{\sum_{l\in R_{ji}} w_l e^{x_l'\beta}}\right), \quad r = 1, \ldots, p \tag{13}$$

In equation 13, $S_{ji}^{(r)}$ is the rth component of $S_{ji} = (S_{ji}^{(1)}, \ldots, S_{ji}^{(p)})'$. The maximum partial likelihood estimate (MPLE) of β is obtained by setting $\frac{\partial l}{\partial \beta_r}$ equal to zero for $r=1,\ldots,p$, where p is the number of independent variables in the model. The equations $\frac{\partial l}{\partial \beta_r} = 0 \ (r = 1, \ldots, p)$ can usually be solved by using the Newton-Raphson method.

Note that from equation 12a the partial likelihood function $L(\beta)$ is invariant under translation. All the covariates are centered by their corresponding overall mean. The overall mean of a covariate is defined as the sum of the product of weight and covariate for all the censored and uncensored cases in each stratum. For notational simplicity, x_l used in the Estimation Section denotes centered covariates.

Three convergence criteria for the Newton-Raphson method are available:

- Absolute value of the largest difference in parameter estimates between iterations (δ) divided by the value of the parameter estimate for the previous iteration, i.e.,

$$\text{BCON} = \left| \frac{\delta}{\text{parameter estimate for previous iteration}} \right|$$

- Absolute difference of the log likelihood function between iterations divided by the log likelihood function for previous iteration.

- Maximum number of iterations.

The asymptotic covariance matrix for the MPLE $\hat{\beta} = (\hat{\beta}_1, \ldots, \hat{\beta}_p)'$ is estimated by I^{-1} where I is the information matrix containing minus the second partial derivatives of ln$L$. The $(r, s)^{th}$ element of I is defined by

$$I_{rs} = -E\frac{\partial^2}{\partial\beta_r\partial\beta_s}\ln L = \sum_{j=1}^{m}\sum_{i=1}^{k_j} d_{ji}\left[\frac{\sum_{l \in R_{ji}} w_l x_{ls} x_{lr} e^{x_l'\beta}}{\sum_{l \in R_{ji}} w_l e^{x_l'\beta}} - \frac{\left(\sum_{l \in R_{ji}} w_l x_{lr} e^{x_l'\beta}\right)\left(\sum_{l \in R_{ji}} w_l x_{ls} e^{x_l'\beta}\right)}{\left(\sum_{l \in R_{ji}} w_l e^{x_l'\beta}\right)^2}\right] \tag{14}$$

We can also write I in a matrix form as

$$I_{rs} = \sum_{j=1}^{m}\sum_{i=1}^{k_j} d_{ji}(x'(t_{ji}))V(t_{ji})(x(t_{ji}))$$

where $x(t_{ji})$ is a $n_{ji} \times p$ matrix which represents the p covariate variables in the model evaluated at time t_{ji}, n_{ji} is the number of distinct individuals in R_{ji}, and $V(t_{ji})$ is a $n_{ji} \times n_{ji}$ matrix with the lth diagonal element $v_{ll}(t_{ji})$ defined by

$$v_{ll}(t_{ji}) = p_l(t_{ji})w_l - (w_l p_l(t_{ji}))^2$$

$$p_l(t_{ji}) = \frac{\exp(x_l'\hat{\beta})}{\sum_{h \in R_{ji}} w_h \exp(x_h'\hat{\beta})}$$

and the (l, k) element $v_{lk}(t_{ji})$ defined by

$$v_{lk}(t_{ji}) = w_l p_l(t_{ji}) \times w_k p_k(t_{ji})$$

Estimation of the Baseline Function

After the MPLE $\hat{\beta}$ of β is found, the baseline survivor function $S_{0j}(t)$ is estimated separately for each stratum. Assume that, for a stratum, $t_1 < \ldots < t_k$ are the observed lifetimes in the sample. There are n_i at risk and d_i deaths at t_i, and in the interval $[t_{i-1}, t_i)$ there are λ_i censored times. Since $S_0(t)$ is a survivor function, it is nonincreasing and left continuous, and thus $\hat{S}_0(t)$ must be constant except for jumps at the observed lifetimes $t_1 \ldots t_k$.

Further, it follows that

$$\hat{S}_0(t_1) = 1$$

and

$$\hat{S}_0(t_i+) = \hat{S}_0(t_{i+1})$$

Writing $\hat{S}_0(t_i+) = p_i$ (i=1,...,k), the observed likelihood function is of the form

$$L_1 = \prod_{i=1}^{k} \{ \prod_{l \in D_i} (p_{i-1}^{\exp(x_l'\beta)} - p_i^{\exp(x_l'\beta)})^{w_l} \prod_{l \in C_i} (p_{i-1}^{\exp(x_l'\beta)})^{w_l} \} \prod_{l \in C_{k+1}} (p_k^{\exp(x_l'\beta)})^{w_l}$$

where D_i is the set of individuals dying at t_i and C_i is the set of individuals with censored times in $[t_{i-1}, t_i)$. (Note that if the last observation is uncensored, C_{k+1} is empty and p_k=0.)

If we let $\alpha_i = p_i / p_{i-1}$ ($i = 1, \ldots, k$), L_1 can be written as

$$L_1 = \prod_{i=1}^{k} \prod_{l \in D_i} (1 - \alpha_i^{\exp(x_l'\beta)})^{w_l} \prod_{l \in R_i - D_i} \alpha_i^{w_l \exp(x_l'\beta)}$$

Differentiating $\ln L_1$ with respect to $\alpha_1, \ldots, \alpha_k$ and setting the equations equal to zero, we get

$$\sum_{l \in D_i} \frac{w_l exp(x_l'\beta)}{1 - \alpha_i^{exp(x_l'\beta)}} = \sum_{l \in R_i} w_l exp(x_l'\beta) \quad i = 1, \ldots, k \qquad (16)$$

We then plug the MPLE $\hat{\beta}$ of β into equation 16 and solve these k equations separately.

There are two things worth noting:

- If any $|D_i| = 1$, $\hat{\alpha}_i$ can be solved explicitly.

$$\hat{\alpha}_i = \left[1 - \frac{w_i \exp(x_i'\hat{\beta})}{\sum_{l \in R_i} w_l \exp(x_l'\hat{\beta})} \right]^{\exp(-x_i'\hat{\beta})} \qquad (17)$$

- If $|D_i| > 1$, equation 17 must be solved iteratively for $\hat{\alpha}_i$. A good initial value for $\hat{\alpha}_i$ is

$$\hat{\alpha}_i = \exp\left(\frac{-d_i}{\sum_{l \in R_i} w_l \exp(x_l'\hat{\beta})} \right) \qquad (18)$$

where $d_i = \sum_{l \in D_i} w_l$ is the weight sum for set D_i. (See Lawless (1982), p. 361.)

Once the $\hat{\alpha}_i$, $i = 1, \dots, k$ are found, $S_0(t)$ is estimated by

$$\hat{S}_0(t) = \prod_{i:\,(t_i < t)} \hat{\alpha}_i \tag{19}$$

Since the above estimate of $S_0(t)$ requires some iterative calculations when ties exist, Breslow (1974) suggests using equation 18 as an estimate of α_i; however, we will use this as an initial estimate.

The asymptotic variance for $-\ln \hat{S}_0(t)$ can be found in Chapter 4 of Kalbfleisch & Prentice (1980). At a specified time t, it is consistently estimated by

$$\mathrm{Var}\,(-\ln \hat{S}_0(t)) = \sum_{t_i < t} |D_i| \left(\sum_{l \in R_i} w_l \exp(x_l'\hat{\beta}) \right)^{-2} + a'I^{-1}a \tag{20}$$

where a is a $p \times 1$ vector with the jth element defined by

$$\sum_{t_i < t} |D_i| \frac{\sum_{l \in R_i} w_l x_{lj} \exp(x_l'\hat{\beta})}{\left(\sum_{l \in R_i} w_l \exp(x_l'\hat{\beta}) \right)^2}$$

and I is the information matrix. The asymptotic variance of $\hat{S}(t|\,x)$ is estimated by

$$e^{2x'\hat{\beta}} (\hat{S}(t|\,x))^2 \,\mathrm{Var}(-\ln \hat{S}_0(t)) \tag{21}$$

Selection Statistics for Stepwise Methods

COX REGRESSION offers the same methods for variable selection as LOGISTIC REGRESSION. For the details of these methods and stepwise algorithms, see the LOGISTIC REGRESSION chapter. Here we will only define the three removal statistics, Wald, LR, and Conditional, and the Score entry statistic.

Score Statistic

The Score statistic is calculated for every variable not in the model to decide which variable should be added to the model. First we compute the information matrix I for all eligible variables based on the parameter estimates for the variables in the model and zero parameter estimates for the variables not in the model. Then we partition the resulting I into four submatrices as follows:

$$\begin{bmatrix} A_{11} & A_{12} \\ A_{21} & A_{22} \end{bmatrix} \tag{22}$$

where A_{11} and A_{22} are square matrices for variables in the model and variables not in the model, respectively, and A_{12} is the cross-product matrix for variables in and out. The score statistic for variable x_i is defined by

$$D_{x_i}' B_{22,i} D_{x_i}$$

where D_{x_i} is the first derivative of the log likelihood with respect to all the parameters associated with x_i and $B_{22,i}$ is equal to $(A_{22,i} - A_{21,i} A_{11}^{-1} A_{12,i})^{-1}$, and $A_{22,i}$ and $A_{12,i}$ are the submatrices in A_{22} and A_{12} associated with variable x_i.

Wald Statistic

The Wald statistic is calculated for the variables in the model to select variables for removal. The Wald statistic for variable x_j is defined by

$$\hat{\beta}_j' B_{11,j} \hat{\beta}_j$$

where $\hat{\beta}_j$ is the parameter estimate associated with x_j and $B_{11,j}$ is the submatrix of A_{11}^{-1} associated with x_j.

LR (Likelihood Ratio) Statistic

The LR statistic is defined as twice the log of the ratio of the likelihood functions of two models evaluated at their own MPLES. Assume that r variables are in the current model and let us call the current model the full model. Based on the MPLES of parameters for the full model, *l (full)* is defined in equation 12b. For each of r variables deleted from the full model, MPLES are found and the reduced log likelihood function, *l(reduced)*, is calculated. Then LR statistic is defined as

$$-2\,(l\,(reduced) - l\,(full))$$

Conditional Statistic

The conditional statistic is also computed for every variable in the model. The formula for conditional statistic is the same as LR statistic except that the parameter estimates for each reduced model are conditional estimates, not MPLES. The conditional estimates are defined as follows. Let $\hat{\beta} = (\hat{\beta}_1, \ldots, \hat{\beta}_r)'$ be the MPLES for the r variables (blocks) and C be the asymptotic covariance matrix for $\hat{\beta}$. If variable x_i is removed from the model, the conditional estimates for the parameters left in the model given $\hat{\beta}_i$ is

$$\tilde{\beta}_{(i)} = \hat{\beta}_{(i)} - C_{12}^{(i)} (C_{22}^{(i)})^{-1} \hat{\beta}_i$$

where $\hat{\beta}_i$ is the MPLE for the parameter(s) associated with x_i and $\hat{\beta}_{(i)}$ is $\hat{\beta}$ without $\hat{\beta}_i$, $C_{12}^{(i)}$ is the covariance between the parameter estimates left in the model $\hat{\beta}_{(i)}$ and $\hat{\beta}_i$, and $C_{22}^{(i)}$ is the covariance of $\hat{\beta}_i$. Then the conditional statistic for variablex_i is defined by

$$-2\,(l\,(\tilde{\beta}_{(i)}) - l\,(full))$$

where $l\,(\tilde{\beta}_{(i)})$ is the log likelihood function evaluated at $\tilde{\beta}_{(i)}$.

Note that all these four statistics have a chi-square distribution with degrees of freedom equal to the number of parameters the corresponding model has.

Statistics

Initial Model Information

The initial model for the first method is for a model that does not include covariates. The log likelihood function l is equal to

$$l\,(0) = -\sum_{j=1}^{m} \sum_{i=1}^{k_j} d_{ji} \ln\,(n_{ji}^*)$$

where n_{ji}^{*} is the sum of weights of individuals in set R_{ji}.

Model Information

When a stepwise method is requested, at each step, -2 log likelihood function and three chi-square statistics (model chi-square, improvement chi-square, and overall chi-square) and their corresponding degrees of freedom and significance are printed.

- -2 log likelihood

$$-2\sum_{j=1}^{m}\sum_{i=1}^{k_j}\left(s_{ji}'\hat{\beta}-d_{ji}ln\left(\sum_{l\in R_{ji}} w_l exp\,(x_l'\hat{\beta})\right)\right)$$

where $\hat{\beta}$ is the MPLE of β for the current model.

- Improvement chi-square

(-2 log likelihood function for previous model) - (-2 log likelihood for current model).

The previous model is the model from the last step. The degrees of freedom are equal to the absolute value of the difference between the number of parameters estimated in these two models.

- Model chi-square

(-2 log likelihood function for initial model) - (-2 log likelihood function for current model).

The initial model is the final model from the previous method. The degrees of freedom are equal to the absolute value of the difference between the number of parameters estimated in these two models.

Note: The values of the model chi-square and improvement chi-square can be less than or equal to zero. If the degrees of freedom are equal to zero, the chi-square is not printed.

- Overall chi-square

The overall chi square statistic tests the hypothesis that all the regression coefficients for the variables in the model are identically zero. This statistic is defined as

$$u'(0)\,I^{-1}u\,(0)$$

where $u(0)$ represents the vector of first derivatives of the partial log likelihood function evaluated at $\beta = 0$. The elements of u are defined in equation 13 and I is defined in equation 14.

Information for Variables in the Equation

For each of the single variables in the equation, MPLE, SE for MPLE, Wald statistic, and its corresponding df, significance, and partial R are given. For a single variable, R is defined by

$$R = \left[\frac{\text{Wald - 2}}{\text{-2 log likelihood for the initial model}}\right]^{1/2} \times \text{sign of MPLE}$$

if Wald > 2. Otherwise R is set to zero.

For a multiple category variable, only the Wald Statistic, df, significance, and Partial R are printed, where R is defined by

$$R = \left[\frac{\text{Wald-2*df}}{\text{-2 log likelihood for the initial model}}\right]^{1/2}$$

if Wald > 2 df. Otherwise R is set to zero.

Information for the Variables Not in the Equation

For each of the variables not in the equation, the Score statistic is calculated and its corresponding degrees of freedom, significance, and partial R are printed. The partial R for variables not in the equation is defined similarly to the R for the variable in the equation by changing the Wald statistic to the Score statistic.

There is one overall statistic called the residual chi-square. This statistic tests if all regression coefficients for the variables not in the equation are zero. It is defined by

$$u'(\hat{\beta})\, B_{22} u(\hat{\beta})$$

where $u(\hat{\beta})$ is the vector of first derivatives of the partial log likelihood function with respect to all the parameters not in the equation evaluated at MPLE $\hat{\beta}$ and B_{22} is equal to $(A_{22} - A_{21}A_{11}^{-1}A_{12})^{-1}$ and A is defined in equation 22.

Survival Table

For each stratum, the estimates of the baseline cumulative survival (S_0) and hazard (H_0) function and their standard errors are computed. The estimate $\hat{S}_0$ for S_0 has been discussed in equations 16–19. It is easy to see from equation 9 that $H_0(t)$ is estimated by

$$\hat{H}_0(t) = -\ln \hat{S}_0(t)$$

and the asymptotic variance of $\hat{H}_0(t)$ is defined in equation 20. Finally, the cumulative hazard function $H(t|x)$ and survival function $S(t|x)$ are estimated by

$$\hat{H}(t|x) = \exp(X'\hat{\beta})\, \hat{H}_0(t)$$

and, for a given X,

$$\hat{S}(t|x) = [\hat{S}_0(t)]^{\exp(X'\hat{\beta})} = \left[\hat{S}_0^*(t)\right]^{\exp(x'\hat{\beta} - a)}$$

The asymptotic variances are

$$\text{Var}(\hat{H}(t|x)) = \exp(2X'\hat{\beta})\, \text{Var}(\hat{H}_0(t))$$

and

$$\text{Var}(\hat{S}(t|x)) = \exp(2X'\hat{\beta})\, (\hat{S}(t|x))^2\, \text{Var}(\hat{H}_0(t))$$

Diagnostic Statistics

Three casewise diagnostic statistics, Residual, Partial Residual, and DFBETAs, are produced. Both Residual and DFBETA are computed for all distinct individuals. Partial Residuals are calculated only for uncensored individuals.

Assume that there are n_j subjects in stratum j and k_j distinct observed events $t_1 < \ldots < t_{k_j}$. Define the selected probability for the lth individual at time t_i as

$$p_l(t_i) = \begin{cases} \dfrac{\exp(x_l'(t_i)\hat{\beta})}{\sum_{h \in R_i} w_h \exp(x_h'(t_i)\hat{\beta})} & \text{if } l^{th} \text{ individual is in } R_i \\ 0 & \text{otherwise} \end{cases}$$

and

$$u_l = \sum_{i=1}^{k_j} d_i [p_l(t_i) - p_l(t_i)^2]$$

$$y_l(t_i) = \begin{cases} 1 & \text{if } l^{th} \text{ individual is in } D_i \\ 0 & \text{otherwise} \end{cases}$$

$$r_l = \sum_{i=1}^{k_j} [y_l(t_i) - d_i p_l(t_i)]$$

DFBETA

The changes in the maximum partial likelihood estimate of beta due to the deletion of a single observation have been discussed in Cain and Lange (1984) and Storer and Crowley (1985). The estimate of DFBETA computed is derived from augmented regression models. The details can be found in Storer and Crowley (1985). When the lth individual in the jth stratum is deleted, the change $\Delta\beta_j$ is estimated by

$$\Delta\beta_l = -\frac{1}{m_l} I^{-1} v_l r_l$$

where

$$w = \text{diag}(w_1 \ldots w_{n_{ji}})$$

$$v_l - \sum_{i=1}^{k_j} d_i p_l(t_i)(x_l(t_i) - x(t_i) w p(t_i))$$

$$p'(t_i) = (p_1(t_i) \ldots p_{n_{ji}}(t_i))$$

$$m_l = u_l - v_l I^{-1} v_l$$

and $x'(t_i)$ is an $n_{ji} \times p$ matrix which represents the p covariate variables in the model evaluated at t_i, and n_{ji} is the number of individuals in R_{ji}.

Partial Residuals

Partial residuals can only be computed for the covariates which are not time dependent. At time t_i in stratum j, x_g is the $p \times 1$ observed covariate vector for any g^{th} individual in set D_i, where D_i is the set of individuals dying at t_i. The partial residual γ_g is defined by

$$\gamma_g = \begin{pmatrix} \gamma_{g1} \\ \ldots \\ \gamma_{gp} \end{pmatrix} = x_g - p(t_i) x$$

Rewriting the above formula in a univariate form, we get

$$\gamma_{gh} = x_{gh} - \frac{\sum_{l \in R_i} w_l x_{lh} \exp(x_l'\hat{\beta})}{\sum_{l \in R_i} w_l \exp(x_l'\hat{\beta})}, \quad h = 1, \ldots, p, g \in D_i$$

where x_{gh} is the hth component for x_g. For every variable, the residuals can be plotted against times to test the proportional hazards assumption.

Residuals

The residuals e_i are computed by

$$e_i = \hat{H}(t_i | x_i) = \exp(x_i'\hat{\beta})(\hat{H}_0(t_i))$$

which is the same as the estimate of the cumulative hazard function.

Plots

For a specified pattern, the covariate values X_c are determined and $X_c'\hat{\beta}$ is computed. There are three plots available in COXREG.

Survival Plot

For stratum j, $(t_i, \hat{S}_0(t_i | X_c))$, $i = 1, \ldots k_j$ are plotted where

$$\hat{S}(t_i | X_c) = (\hat{S}_0(t_i))^{\exp(x_i'\hat{\beta})}$$

When PATTERN(ALL) is requested, for every uncensored time t_i in stratum j the survival function is estimated by

$$\hat{S}(t_i) = \frac{\sum_{l=1}^{k_j} w_l \tilde{S}(t_i | x_l)}{\sum_{l=1}^{k_j} w_l} = \frac{\sum_{l=1}^{k_j} w_l (\hat{S}_0(t_i))^{\exp(x_l'\hat{\beta})}}{\sum_{l=1}^{k_j} w_l}$$

Then $(t_i, \tilde{S}(t_i))$, $i = 1, \ldots, k_j$ are plotted for stratum j.

Hazard Plot

For stratum j, $(t_i, \hat{H}(t_i | X_c))$, $i = 1, \ldots k_j$ are plotted where

$$\hat{H}(t_i | X_c) = \exp(X_c'\hat{\beta}) \hat{H}_0(t_i)$$

LML Plot

The log minus log plot is used to see whether the stratification variable should be included as a covariate. For stratum j, $(t_i, X'_c\hat{\beta} + \ln \hat{H}_0(t_i))$ $i = 1, \ldots, k_j$ are plotted. If the plot shows parallelism among strata, then the stratum variable should be a covariate.

References

Breslow (1974)

Cair & Lange (1984)

Cox (1972)

Kalbfleisch & Prentice (1980)

Lawless (1982)

Storer & Crowley (1985)

CREATE

General

CREATE produces new series as a function of existing series.

Notation

Existing Series	$X_1, \ldots, X_n$
New Series	$Y_1, \ldots, Y_n$

Cumulative Sum (CSUM(*X*))

$$Y_j = \sum_{i=1}^{j} X_i \qquad j = 1, \ldots, n$$

Differences of Order *m* (DIFF(*X*, *m*))

Define

$$Z_j(k) = Z_j(k-1) - Z_{j-1}(k-1) \qquad k = 1, \ldots, m \qquad j = k+1, \ldots, n$$

with

$$Z_j(0) = X_j \qquad j = 1, \ldots, n$$

then

$$Y_j = \begin{cases} Z_j(m) & j = m+1, \ldots, n \\ \text{SYSMIS} & \text{otherwise} \end{cases}$$

Lag of Order *m* (LAG(X, *m*))

$$Y_j = \begin{cases} X_{j-m} & j = m+1, \ldots, n \\ \text{SYSMIS} & j = 1, \ldots, m \end{cases}$$

Lead of Order *m* (LEAD(*X*, *m*))

$$Y_j = \begin{cases} X_{j+m} & j = 1, \ldots, n-m \\ \text{SYSMIS} & j = n-m+1, \ldots, n \end{cases}$$

Moving Average of Length *m* (MA(*X*, *m*))

If *m* is odd, define

$$q = \frac{m-1}{2}$$

then

$$Y_j = \begin{cases} \sum_{k=-q}^{q} X_{j+k}/m & j = q+1, \ldots, n-q \\ \text{SYSMIS} & \text{otherwise} \end{cases}$$

if m is even, define $q = m/2$ and

$$Z_j = \sum_{k=-q+1}^{q} X_{j+k}/m \qquad j = q, \ldots, n-q$$

then

$$Y_j = \begin{cases} (Z_{j-1} + Z_j)/2 & j = q+1, \ldots, n-q \\ \text{SYSMIS} & \text{otherwise} \end{cases}$$

Running Median of Length *m* (*X*, *m*)

If m is odd,

$$q = \frac{m-1}{2}$$

$$Y_j = \begin{cases} \text{median } (X_{j-q}, X_{j-q+1}, \ldots, X_j, X_{j+1}, \ldots, X_{j+q}) & j = q+1, \ldots, n-q \\ \text{SYSMIS} & \text{otherwise} \end{cases}$$

If m is even, define

$$Z_j = \text{median } (X_{j-q+1}, \ldots, X_j, X_{j+1}, \ldots, X_{j+q}) \qquad j = q, \ldots, n-q$$

then

$$Y_j = \begin{cases} (Z_{j-1} + Z_j)/2 & j = q+1, \ldots, n-q \\ \text{SYSMIS} & \text{otherwise} \end{cases}$$

where median $(a_1, \ldots, a_k)$

$$Y_j = \begin{cases} a_{(l)} & \text{if } k \text{ is odd} \\ (a_{(l)} + a_{(l+1)})/2 & \text{if } k \text{ is even} \end{cases}$$

$$l = \begin{cases} (k+1)/2 & \text{if } k \text{ is odd} \\ k/2 & \text{if } k \text{ is even} \end{cases}$$

and $a_{(1)} < a_{(2)} < \ldots < a_{(k)}$ is the ordered sample of $a_1, \ldots, a_k$.

Seasonal Differencing of Order *m* and Period *p* (SDIFF(*X*, *m*, *p*))

Define

$$Z_j(k) = Z_j(k-1) - Z_{j-p}(k-1) \qquad k = 1, \ldots, m \qquad j = p*k+1, \ldots, n$$

where

$$Z_j(0) = X_j \qquad j = 1, \ldots, n$$

then

$$Y_j = Z_j(m) \qquad j = m*p+1, \ldots, n$$

The T4253H Smoothing Function (T4253H(X))

The original series is smoothed by a compound data smoother. The smoother starts with:

- A running median of 4:

Let Z be the smoothed series, then

$$Z_{j+1/2} = \text{median } (X_{j-1}, X_j, X_{j+1}, X_{j+2}) \qquad j = 2, ..., n-2$$

and

$$Z_{0.5}^{(1)} = X_1 \qquad Z_{1.5}^{(1)} = \text{median } (X_1, X_2) = \frac{1}{2}(X_1 + X_2)$$

$$Z_{n-1/2}^{(1)} = \text{median } (X_{n-1}, X_n) = \frac{1}{2}(X_{n-1} + X_n) \qquad Z_{n+1/2}^{(1)} = X_n$$

- A running median of Z:

$$Z_1^{(1)} = Z_{0.5} \qquad Z_n^{(1)} = Z_{n+1/2}$$

and

$$Z_j^{(1)} = \frac{1}{2}(Z_{j-1/2} + Z_{j+1/2}) \qquad j = 2, ..., n-1.$$

- A running median of 5 on $Z_1^{(1)}, ..., Z_n^{(1)}$ from the previous step:

Let $Z^{(2)}$ be the resulting series, then

$$Z_1^{(2)} = Z_1^{(1)} \qquad Z_n^{(2)} = Z_n^{(1)}$$

$$Z_2^{(2)} = \text{median } (Z_1^{(1)}, Z_2^{(1)}, Z_3^{(1)})$$

$$Z_{n-1}^{(2)} = \text{median } (Z_{n-2}^{(1)}, Z_{n-1}^{(1)}, Z_n^{(1)})$$

and

$$Z_j^{(2)} = \text{median } (Z_{j-2}^{(1)}, Z_{j-1}^{(1)}, Z_j^{(1)}, Z_{j+1}^{(1)}, Z_{j+2}^{(2)}) \qquad j = 3, ..., n-2.$$

- A running median of 3 on $Z_1^{(2)}, ..., Z_n^{(2)}$ from the previous step:

Let $Z^{(3)}$ be the resulting series, then

$$Z_j^{(3)} = \text{median } (Z_{j-1}^{(2)}, Z_j^{(2)}, Z_{j+1}^{(2)}) \qquad j = 2, 3, ..., n-1$$

$$Z_1^{(3)} = \text{median } (3Z_2^{(3)} - 2Z_3^{(3)}, Z_1^{(2)}, Z_2^{(3)})$$

$$Z_n^{(3)} = \text{median } (3Z_{n-1}^{(3)} - 2Z_{n-2}^{(3)}, Z_n^{(2)}, Z_{n-1}^{(3)})$$

- Hanning (Running Weighted Averages):

$$Z_j^{(4)} = \frac{1}{4}Z_{j-1}^{(3)} + \frac{1}{2}Z_j^{(3)} + \frac{1}{4}Z_{j+1}^{(3)} \qquad j = 2, \ldots, n-1$$

$$Z_1^{(4)} = Z_1^{(3)}, \quad Z_n^{(4)} = Z_n^{(3)}$$

- Residual:

$$D_i = X_i - Z_i^{(4)} \qquad i = 1, \ldots, n$$

- Repeat the previous steps on the residuals $D_1, \ldots, D_n$:

- Let $D_1^{(4)}, \ldots, D_n^{(4)}$ be the final result.

- Final Smooth:

$$Y_i = Z_i^{(4)} + D_i^{(4)} \qquad i = 1, \ldots, n$$

Prior Moving Averages of Length *m* (PMA(*X, m*))

$$Y_i = \begin{cases} \sum_{j=i-m}^{i-1} X_j/m & i = m+1, \ldots, n \\ \text{SYSMIS} & i = 1, \ldots, m \end{cases}$$

Fast Fourier Transform (FFT(X))

The discrete Fourier transform of a sequence $X=\{X_1, \ldots, X_n\}$ is defined as

$$\begin{aligned} Y_k &= \frac{1}{n}\sum_{t=1}^{n} X_t \exp\{-i2\pi f_k(t-1)\} \\ &= \frac{1}{n}\sum_{t=1}^{n} X_t[\cos(2\pi f_k(t-1)) - i\sin(2\pi f_k(t-1))] \\ &= \frac{1}{n}\sum_{t=1}^{n} X_t\cos(2\pi f_k(t-1)) + i\left[-\frac{1}{n}\sum_{t=1}^{n} X_t\sin(2\pi f_k(t-1))\right] \\ &= a_k + ib_k \end{aligned}$$

Thus a, b are two sequences generated by FFT and they are called real and imaginary, respectively.

$$a_k = \frac{1}{n}\sum_{t=1}^{n} X_t\cos(2\pi f_k(t-1)) \qquad k = 1, \ldots, r$$

$$b_k = -\frac{1}{n}\sum_{t=1}^{n} X_t\sin(2\pi f_k(t-1)) \quad k = 1, \ldots, r$$

where

$$r = \begin{cases} (n-1)/2 & \text{if } n \text{ is odd} \\ n/2 & \text{if } n \text{ is even} \end{cases}$$

and

$$a_0 = \bar{X} \qquad b_0 = \frac{1}{n}\sum_{t=1}^{n} X_t \cos(\pi(t-1))$$

Inverse Fast Fourier Transform of Two Series (IFFT(*a, b*))

The inverse Fourier Transform of two series $\{a, b\}$ is defined as

$$X_t = a_0 - b_0 \cos(\pi(t-1)) + 2\left[\sum_{k=1}^{q} a_k \cos(2\pi f_k(t-1)) - \sum_{k=1}^{q} b_k \sin(2\pi f_k(t-1))\right]$$

References

Brigham (1974)

Monro (1975)

Monro & Branch (1977)

Velleman & Hoaglin (1981)

CROSSTABS

General

The notation and statistics refer to bivariate subtables defined by a row variable X and a column variable Y, unless specified otherwise. By default, CROSSTABS deletes cases with missing values on a table-by-table basis.

Notation

X_i	distinct values of row variable arranged in ascending order: $X_1 < X_2 < \ldots < X_R$
Y_j	distinct values of column variable arranged in ascending order: $Y_1 < Y_2 < \ldots < Y_C$
f_{ij}	sum of cell weights for cases in cell (i, j)
c_j	$\sum_{i=1}^{R} f_{ij}$, the jth column subtotal
r_i	$\sum_{j=1}^{C} f_{ij}$, the ith row subtotal
W	$\sum_{j=1}^{C} c_j = \sum_{i=1}^{R} r_i$, the grand total

Marginal and Cell Statistics

- Count

  $\text{count} = f_{ij}$

- Expected count

  $$E_{ij} = \frac{r_i c_j}{W}$$

- Row percent

  $\text{row percent} = 100 \times (f_{ij}/r_i)$

- Column percent

  $\text{column percent} = 100 \times (f_{ij}/c_j)$

- Total percent

  total percent = $100 \times (f_{ij}/W)$

- Residual

  $$R_{ij} = f_{ij} - E_{ij}$$

- Standardized residual

  $$SR_{ij} = \frac{R_{ij}}{\sqrt{E_{ij}}}$$

- Adjusted residual

  $$AR_{ij} = \frac{R_{ij}}{\sqrt{E_{ij}\left(1 - \frac{r_i}{W}\right)\left(1 - \frac{c_j}{W}\right)}}$$

Chi-square Statistics

- Pearson's

  $$\chi_P^2 = \sum_{ij} \frac{(f_{ij} - E_{ij})^2}{E_{ij}}$$

  The degrees of freedom are $(R\text{-}1)(C\text{-}1)$.

- Likelihood ratio

  $$\chi_{LR}^2 = -2\sum_{ij} f_{ij}\ ln\ (E_{ij}/f_{ij})$$

  The degrees of freedom are $(R\text{-}1)(C\text{-}1)$.

- Fisher's exact test

  If the table is a 2×2 table, not resulting from a larger table with missing cells, with at least one expected cell count less than 5, then the Fisher exact test is calculated. See Appendix 5 for details.

- Yates continuity corrected for 2×2 tables

  $$\chi_c^2 = \begin{cases} \dfrac{W\left(|f_{11}f_{22} - f_{12}f_{21}| - 0.5W\right)^2}{r_1 r_2 c_1 c_2} & \text{if } |f_{11}f_{22} - f_{12}f_{21}| > 0.5W \\ 0 & \text{otherwise} \end{cases}$$

  The degrees of freedom are 1.

- Mantel-Haenszel test of linear association

  $$\chi_{MH}^2 = (W - 1)\, r^2$$

  where r is the Pearson correlation coefficient to be defined later. The degrees of freedom are 1.

Other Measures of Association

- Phi coefficient

$$\varphi = \sqrt{\frac{\chi_p^2}{W}}$$

- Coefficient of contingency

$$CC = \left(\frac{\chi_p^2}{\chi_p^2 + W}\right)^{1/2}$$

- Cramer's V

$$V = \left(\frac{\chi_p^2}{W(q-1)}\right)^{1/2}$$

where $q = \min\{R,C\}$.

Measures of Proportional Reduction in Predictive Error

- Lambda

Let f_{im} and f_{mj} be the largest cell count in row i and column j, respectively. Also, let r_m be the largest row subtotal and c_m the largest column subtotal. Define $\lambda_{Y|X}$ as the proportion of relative error in predicting an individual's Y category that can be eliminated by knowledge of the X category. $\lambda_{Y|X}$ is computed as

$$\lambda_{Y|X} = \frac{\sum_{i=1}^{R} f_{im} - c_m}{W - c_m}$$

The standard errors are

$$ASE_0 = \frac{\sqrt{\sum_{i=1}^{R}\sum_{j=1}^{C} f_{ij}(\delta_{ij} - \delta_j)^2 - \left(\sum_{i=1}^{R} f_{im} - c_m\right)^2 / W}}{W - c_m}$$

$$ASE_1 = \frac{\sqrt{\sum_{i=1}^{R}\sum_{j=1}^{C} f_{ij}(\delta_{ij} - \delta_j + \lambda\delta_j)^2 - W\lambda_{Y|X}}}{W - c_m}$$

where

$$\delta_{ij} = \begin{cases} 1 & \text{if } j \text{ is column index for } f_{im} \\ 0 & \text{otherwise} \end{cases}$$

$$\delta_j = \begin{cases} 1 & \text{if } j \text{ is index for } c_m \\ 0 & \text{otherwise} \end{cases}$$

Lambda for predicting X from Y, $\lambda_{X|Y}$, is obtained by permuting the indices in the above formulae.

The two asymmetric lambdas are averaged to obtain the symmetric lambda.

$$\lambda = \frac{\sum_{i=1}^{R} f_{im} + \sum_{j=1}^{C} f_{mj} - c_m - r_m}{2W - r_m - c_m}$$

The standard errors are

$$ASE_0 = \frac{\sqrt{\sum_{i=1}^{R}\sum_{j=1}^{C} f_{ij}(\delta_{ij}^r + \delta_{ij}^c - \delta_i^r - \delta_j^c)^2 - \left[\left(\sum_{i=1}^{R} f_{im} + \sum_{j=1}^{C} f_{mj} - c_m - r_m\right)^2 / W\right]}}{2W - r_m - c_m}$$

$$ASE_1 = \frac{\sqrt{\sum_{i=1}^{R}\sum_{j=1}^{C} f_{ij}[\delta_{ij}^r + \delta_{ij}^c - \delta_i^r - \delta_j^c + \lambda(\delta_i^r + \delta_j^c)]^2 - 4W\lambda^2}}{2W - r_m - c_m}$$

where

$$\delta_{ij}^r = \begin{cases} 1 & \text{if } i \text{ is row index for } f_{mj} \\ 0 & \text{otherwise} \end{cases}$$

$$\delta_i^r = \begin{cases} 1 & \text{if } i \text{ is index for } r_m \\ 0 & \text{otherwise} \end{cases}$$

and where

$$\delta_{ij}^c = \begin{cases} 1 & \text{if } j \text{ is column index for } f_{im} \\ 0 & \text{otherwise} \end{cases}$$

$$\delta_i^c = \begin{cases} 1 & \text{if } j \text{ is index for } c_m \\ 0 & \text{otherwise} \end{cases}$$

Goodman and Kruskal Tau

Similarly defined are Goodman and Kruskal's τ:

$$\tau_{Y|X} = \frac{W\sum_{i,j}(f_{ij}^2/r_i) - \sum_{j=1}^{C} c_j^2}{W^2 - \sum_{j=1}^{C} c_j^2}$$

with standard error

$$ASE_1 = \sqrt{\frac{4}{\delta^4}\sum_{i,j} f_{ij}\left\{(v-\delta)\left(\frac{1}{r_i}\sum_{j=1}^{C} f_{ij}c_j - c_j\right) - W\delta\left(\frac{1}{r_i^2}\sum_{j=1}^{C} f_{ij}^2 - \frac{1}{r_i}f_{ij}\right)\right\}^2}$$

in which

$$\delta = W^2 - \sum_{j=1}^{C} c_j^2 \quad \text{and} \quad v = W\sum_{i,j} f_{ij}^2/r_i - \sum_{j=1}^{C} c_j^2$$

$\tau_{X|Y}$ and its standard error can be obtained by interchanging the roles of X and Y.

The significance level is based on the chi-square distribution, since

$$(W-1)\,(C-1)\,\tau_{Y|X} \sim \chi^2_{(R-1)\,(C-1)}$$

$$(W-1)\,(R-1)\,\tau_{X|Y} \sim \chi^2_{(R-1)\,(C-1)}$$

Uncertainty Coefficient

Let $U_{Y|X}$ be the proportional reduction in the uncertainty (entropy) of Y that can be eliminated by knowledge of X. It is computed as

$$U_{Y|X} = \frac{U(X) + U(Y) - U(XY)}{U(Y)}$$

where

$$U(X) = -\sum_{i=1}^{R} \frac{r_i}{W} \ln\left(\frac{r_i}{W}\right)$$

$$U(Y) = -\sum_{j=1}^{C} \frac{c_j}{W} \ln\left(\frac{c_j}{W}\right)$$

and

$$U(XY) = -\sum_{i,j} \frac{f_{ij}}{W} \ln\left(\frac{f_{ij}}{W}\right), \text{ for } f_{ij} > 0.$$

The asymptotic standard errors are

$$ASE_1 = \frac{1}{WU(Y)^2}\sqrt{\sum_{i,j} f_{ij}\left\{U(Y)\ln\left(\frac{f_{ij}}{r_i}\right) + [U(X) - U(XY)]\ln\left(\frac{c_j}{W}\right)\right\}^2}$$

$$ASE_0 = \frac{\sqrt{P - W[U(X) + U(Y) - U(XY)]^2}}{[WU(Y)]}$$

where

$$P = \sum_{i,j} f_{ij} ln\left(\frac{c_j r_i}{Wf_{ij}}\right)^2$$

The formulas for $U_{X|Y}$ can be obtained by interchanging the roles of X and Y.

A symmetric version of the two asymmetric uncertainty coefficients is defined as follows:

$$U = 2\left[\frac{U(X) + U(Y) - U(XY)}{U(X) + U(Y)}\right]$$

with asymptotic standard errors

$$ASE_1 = \frac{2}{W[U(X) + U(Y)]^2}\sqrt{\sum_{i,j} f_{ij}\left\{U(XY)\, ln\left(\frac{r_i c_j}{W^2}\right) - [U(X) + U(Y)]\, ln\left(\frac{f_{ij}}{W}\right)\right\}^2}$$

or

$$ASE_0 = \frac{2}{W[U(X) + U(Y)]}\sqrt{P - [U(X) + U(Y) - U(XY)]^2 / W}$$

Cohen's Kappa

Cohen's kappa κ, defined only for square table (R=C), is computed as

$$\kappa = \frac{W\sum_{i=1}^{R} f_{ii} - \sum_{i=1}^{R} r_i c_i}{W^2 - \sum_{i=1}^{R} r_i c_i}$$

with variance

$$VAR_1 = W\left\{\frac{(\sum f_{ii})(W-\sum f_{ii})}{(W^2-\sum r_i c_i)^2} + \frac{2(W-\sum f_{ii})(2\sum f_{ii}\sum r_i c_i - W\sum f_{ii}(r_i+c_i))}{(W^2-\sum r_i c_i)^3}\right.$$

$$\left. + \frac{(W-\sum f_{ii})^2\left[W\sum_{i,j} f_{ij}(r_j+c_i)^2 - 4(\sum r_i c_i)^2\right]}{(W^2-\sum r_i c_i)^4}\right\}$$

$$VAR_0 = \frac{1}{W(W^2-\sum_i r_i c_i)^2}\left[W^2(\sum_i r_i c_i) + (\sum_i r_i c_i)^2 - W\sum_i r_i c_i(r_i+c_i)\right]$$

Kendall's Tau-b and Tau-c

Define

$$D_r = W^2 - \sum_{i=1}^{R} r_i^2$$

$$D_c = W^2 - \sum_{j=1}^{C} c_j^2$$

$$C_{ij} = \sum_{h<i}\sum_{k<j} f_{hk} + \sum_{h>i}\sum_{k>j} f_{hk}$$

$$D_{ij} = \sum_{h<i}\sum_{k>j} f_{hk} + \sum_{h>i}\sum_{k<j} f_{hk}$$

$$P = \sum_{i,j} f_{ij} C_{ij}$$

$$Q = \sum_{i,j} f_{ij} D_{ij}$$

- Kendall's τ_b is

$$\tau_b = \frac{P-Q}{\sqrt{D_r D_c}}$$

with standard error

$$ASE_1 = \frac{1}{(D_r D_c)}\sqrt{\sum_{i,j} f_{ij}(2\sqrt{D_r D_c}(C_{ij}-D_{ij}) + \tau_b v_{ij})^2 - W^3\tau_b^2(D_r+D_c)^2}$$

where

$$v_{ij} = r_i D_c + c_j D_r$$

Under the independence assumption, the standard error is

$$ASE_0 = 2\sqrt{\frac{\sum_{i,j} f_{ij}(C_{ij}-D_{ij})^2 - \frac{1}{W}(P-Q)^2}{D_r D_c}}$$

- Kendall's τ_c is

$$\tau_c = \frac{q(P-Q)}{W^2(q-1)}$$

with standard error

$$ASE_1 = \frac{2q}{(q-1)W^2}\sqrt{\sum_{i,j} f_{ij}(C_{ij}-D_{ij})^2 - (P-Q)^2/W}$$

or, under the independence assumption,

$$ASE_0 = \frac{2q}{(q-1)W^2}\sqrt{\sum_{i,j} f_{ij}(C_{ij}-D_{ij})^2 - (P-Q)^2/W}$$

where

$$q = \min\{R, C\}$$

Gamma

Gamma γ is estimated by

$$G = \frac{P-Q}{P+Q}$$

with standard error

$$ASE_1 = \frac{4}{(P+Q)^2}\sqrt{\sum_{i,j} f_{ij}(QC_{ij}-PD_{ij})^2}$$

or, under the hypothesis of independence,

$$ASE_0 = \frac{2}{(P+Q)}\sqrt{\sum_{i,j} f_{ij}(C_{ij}-D_{ij})^2 - \frac{1}{W}(P-Q)^2}$$

Somers' *D*

Somers' d with row variable X as the independent variable is calculated as

$$D_{Y|X} = \frac{P-Q}{D_r}$$

with standard error

$$ASE_1 = \frac{2}{D_R^2}\sqrt{\sum_{i,j} f_{ij}\{D_R(C_{ij}-D_{ij}) - (P-Q)(W-R_i)\}^2}$$

or, under the hypothesis of independence,

$$ASE_0 = \frac{2}{D_R}\sqrt{\sum_{i,j} f_{ij}(C_{ij}-D_{ij})^2 - \frac{1}{W}(P-Q)^2}$$

By interchanging the roles of X and Y, the formulas for Somers' d with X as the dependent variable can be obtained.

Symmetric version of Somers' d is

$$d = \frac{(P-Q)}{\frac{1}{2}(D_c + D_r)}$$

The standard error is

$$ASE_1 = \frac{2\sigma^2_{\tau_b}}{(D_r + D_c)} \sqrt{D_r D_c}$$

where $\sigma^2_{\tau_b}$ is the variance of Kendall's tau-b,

$$ASE_0 = \frac{4}{(D_c + D_r)} \sqrt{\sum_{ij} f_{ij} (C_{ij} - D_{ij})^2 - \frac{1}{W}(P-Q)^2}$$

Pearson's *r*

The Pearson's product moment correlation r is computed as

$$r = \frac{COV(X,Y)}{\sqrt{S(X)\,S(Y)}} \equiv \frac{S}{T}$$

where

$$COV(X,Y) = \sum_{i,j} X_i Y_j f_{ij} - \left(\sum_{i=1}^{R} X_i r_i\right)\left(\sum_{j=1}^{C} Y_j c_j\right) / W$$

$$S(X) = \sum_{i=1}^{R} X_i^2 r_i - \left(\sum_{i=1}^{R} X_i r_i\right)^2 / W$$

and

$$S(Y) = \sum_{j=1}^{C} Y_j^2 c_j - \left(\sum_{j=1}^{C} Y_j c_j\right)^2 / W$$

The variance of r is

$$VAR_1 = \frac{1}{T^4} \sum_{i,j} f_{ij} \{ T(X_i - \bar{X})(Y_j - \bar{Y}) - \frac{S}{2T} [(X_i - \bar{X})^2 S(Y)$$

$$+ (Y_j - \bar{Y})^2 S(X)\,]\,\}^2$$

If the null hypothesis is true,

$$VAR_0 = \frac{\sum_{i,j} f_{ij} X_i^2 Y_j^2 - \left(\sum_{i,j} f_{ij} X_i Y_j\right)^2 / W}{\left(\sum_i r_i X_i^2\right)\left(\sum_j c_j Y_j^2\right)}$$

where

$$\bar{X} = \sum_{i=1}^{R} X_i r_i / W$$

and

$$\bar{Y} = \sum_{j=1}^{C} Y_j c_j / W.$$

Under the hypothesis that $\rho = 0$,

$$t = \frac{r\sqrt{W-2}}{\sqrt{1-r^2}}$$

is distributed as a t with W-2 degrees of freedom.

Spearman Correlation

The Spearman's rank correlation coefficient r_s is computed by using rank scores R_i for X_i and C_i for Y_j. These rank scores are defined as follows:

$$R_i = \sum_{k<i} r_k + (r_i + 1)/2 \quad \text{for } i = 1, 2, \ldots, R$$

$$C_j = \sum_{h<j} c_h + (c_j + 1)/2 \quad \text{for } j = 1, 2, \ldots, C$$

The formulas for r_s and its asymptotic variance can be obtained from the Pearson formulas by substituting R_i and C_j for X_i and Y_j, respectively.

Eta

Asymmetric η with the column variable Y as dependent is

$$\eta_Y = \sqrt{1 - \frac{S_{YW}}{S(Y)}}$$

where

$$S_{YW} = \sum_{i,j} Y_j^2 f_{ij} - \sum_{i=1}^{R} \frac{1}{r_i} \left(\sum_{j=1}^{C} Y_j f_{ij} \right)^2$$

Relative Risk

Consider a 2×2 table (i.e., R=C=2). In a case-control study, the relative risk is estimated as

$$R_0 = \frac{f_{11} f_{22}}{f_{12} f_{21}}$$

The $100(1-\alpha)$ percent CI for the relative risk is obtained as

$$\left[R_0 \exp(-z_{1-\alpha/2} v), \qquad R_0 \exp(z_{1-\alpha/2} v) \right]$$

where

$$v = \left(\frac{1}{f_{11}} + \frac{1}{f_{12}} + \frac{1}{f_{21}} + \frac{1}{f_{22}} \right)^{1/2}$$

The relative risk ratios in a cohort study are computed for both columns. For column 1, the risk is

$$R_1 = \frac{f_{11}(f_{21}+f_{22})}{f_{21}(f_{11}+f_{12})}$$

and the corresponding $100(1-\alpha)$ percent *CI* is

$$[R_1 \exp(-z_{1-\alpha/2}v), \quad R_1 \exp(z_{1-\alpha/2}v)]$$

where

$$v = \left(\frac{f_{12}}{f_{11}(f_{11}+f_{12})} + \frac{f_{22}}{f_{21}(f_{21}+f_{22})}\right)^{1/2}$$

The relative risk for column 2 and the confidence interval are computed similarly.

References

Bishop, Feinberg & Holland (1975)

Brown (1975)

Brown & Benedetti (1977)

Goodman & Kruskal (1972)

CURVEFIT

General

Eleven models can be selected to fit times series and produce forecasts, forecast errors and confidence limits. In all of the models, the observed series is some function of time.

Notation

Y_t observed series; $t = 1, \ldots, n$.

$E(Y_t)$ expected value of Y_t.

$\hat{Y}_t$ predicted value for Y_t.

Models

CURVEFIT allows the user to specify a model with or without a constant term designated by β_0. If this constant term is excluded, simply set it zero or one depending upon whether it appears in an additive or multiplicative manner in the models listed below.

(1) Linear $E(Y_t) = \beta_0 + \beta_1 t$

(2) Logarithmic $E(Y_t) = \beta_0 + \beta_1 ln(t)$

(3) Inverse $E(Y_t) = \beta_0 + \beta_1 / t$

(4) Quadratic $E(Y_t) = \beta_0 + \beta_1 t + \beta_2 t^2$

(5) Cubic $E(Y_t) = \beta_0 + \beta_1 t + \beta_2 t^2 + \beta_3 t^3$

(6) Compound $E(Y_t) = \beta_0 \beta_1^t$

(7) Power $E(Y_t) = \beta_0 t^{\beta^1}$

(8) S $E(Y_t) = exp(\beta_0 + \beta_1 / t)$

(9) Growth $E(Y_t) = exp(\beta_0 + \beta_1 t)$

(10) Exponential $E(Y_t) = \beta_0 e^{\beta_1 t}$

(11) Logistic $E(Y_t) = (\frac{1}{u} + \beta_0 \beta_1^t)^{-1}$

Assumption

We assume that nonlinear models (6) to (11) can be expressed in linear model form by logarithmic transformation. So, for models (6) to (10),

$$ln(Y_t) = ln(E(Y_t)) + \varepsilon_t$$

and for model (11),

$$ln\left(\frac{1}{Y_t} - \frac{1}{u}\right) = ln\left(\frac{1}{E(Y_t)} - \frac{1}{u}\right) + \varepsilon_t$$

with ε_t, $t = 1, \ldots, n$ being independently distributed $N(0, \sigma^2)$.

Application of Regression

Each of the models is expressed in linear form and computational techniques described in the REGRESSION procedure are applied. The dependent variable and independent variables for each model are listed as follows:

Model	Dependent Variable	Independent Variables	Coefficients
(1)	Y	t	β_0, β_1
(2)	Y	$ln(t)$	β_0, β_1
(3)	Y	$1/t$	β_0, β_1
(4)	Y	t, t^2	$\beta_0, \beta_1, \beta_2$
(5)	Y	t, t^2, t^3	$\beta_0, \beta_1, \beta_2, \beta_3$
(6)	$ln(Y)$	t	β_0^*, β_1^*
(7)	$ln(Y)$	$ln(t)$	β_0^*, β_1
(8)	$ln(Y)$	$1/t$	β_0, β_1
(9)	$ln(Y)$	t	β_0, β_1
(10)	$ln(Y)$	t	β_0^*, β_1
(11)	$ln\left(\frac{1}{Y} - \frac{1}{u}\right)$	t	β_0^*, β_1^*

where $\beta_0^* = ln(\beta_0)$ and $\beta_1^* = ln(\beta_1)$.

The ANOVA table, coefficient estimates and their standard errors, t-values, and significance levels are computed as in the REGRESSION procedure. Note that for the nonlinear models (6) to (11), we have

$$SE(\hat{\beta}_0) \approx exp(\hat{\beta}_0^*) \times SE(\hat{\beta}_0^*)$$

and

$$SE(\hat{\beta}_1) \approx exp(\hat{\beta}_1^*) \times SE(\hat{\beta}_1^*)$$

Predicted Values and Confidence Intervals

The regression coefficients for model (1) to (5) are used to obtain the predicted values. For the transformed models, more computations are required to obtain the predicted values for the original model. The formulas are listed below:

(1) $\hat{Y}_t = \hat{\beta}_0 + \hat{\beta}_1 t$

(2) $\hat{Y}_t = \hat{\beta}_0 + \hat{\beta}_1 ln(t)$

(3) $\hat{Y}_t = \hat{\beta}_0 + \hat{\beta}_1 / t$

(4) $\hat{Y}_t = \hat{\beta}_0 + \hat{\beta}_1 t + \hat{\beta}_2 t^2$

(5) $\hat{Y}_t = \hat{\beta}_0 + \hat{\beta}_1 t + \hat{\beta}_2 t^2 + \hat{\beta}_3 t^3$

(6) $\hat{Y}_t^* = \hat{\beta}_0^* + \hat{\beta}_1^* t$

(7) $\hat{Y}_t^* = \hat{\beta}_0^* + \hat{\beta}_1 ln(t)$

(8) $\hat{Y}_t^* = \hat{\beta}_0 + \hat{\beta}_1 / t$

(9) $\hat{Y}_t^* = \hat{\beta}_0 + \hat{\beta}_1 t$

(10) $\hat{Y}_t^* = \hat{\beta}_0^* + \hat{\beta}_1 t$

(11) $\hat{Y}_t^* = \hat{\beta}_0^* + \hat{\beta}_1^* t$

where $\hat{Y}_t^* = ln(\hat{Y}_t)$ in models (5) to (10), and $\hat{Y}_t^* = ln\left(\frac{1}{\hat{Y}_t} - \frac{1}{u}\right)$ in model (11).

The 95% prediction interval for an observation at time t is constructed as follows:

For models (1) to (5):

$\hat{Y}_t \pm t_{0.025}\sqrt{MSE(1 + h_t + \frac{1}{n})}$ if constant term is included

$\hat{Y}_t \pm t_{0.025}\sqrt{MSE(1 + h_t)}$ otherwise

For models (6) to (10):

$$exp(\hat{Y}_t^* \pm t_{0.025}\sqrt{MSE(1 + h_t + \frac{1}{n})})$$

and for model (11):

$$\frac{1}{exp(\hat{Y}_t^* \pm t_{0.025}\sqrt{MSE(1 + h_t + \frac{1}{n})}) + \frac{1}{u}}$$

where MSE is the mean square error obtained by fitting the linear model, $t_{0.025}$ is the 97.5 percentage point from Student t-distribution with MSE degrees of freedom, and h_t is the leverage (computational detail in the REGRESSION procedure).

DESCRIPTIVES

Notation

X_i	value of the variable for case i
w_i	weight for case i
N	number of cases
W_i	sum of the weights for the first i cases
$\bar{X}_i$	mean for the first i cases

Moments

Moments about the mean are calculated recursively using a provisional means algorithm (Spicer (1972)):

$$W_j = \sum_{i=1}^{j} w_i$$

$$v_j = \frac{w_j}{W_j}(X_j - \bar{X}_{j-1})$$

$$M_j^4 = M_{j-1}^4 - 4v_j M_{j-1}^3 + 6v_j^2 M_{j-1}^2 + \left(\frac{W_j^2 - 3w_j W_{j-1}}{w_j^3}\right) v_j^4 W_{j-1} W_j$$

$$M_j^3 = M_{j-1}^3 - 3v_j M_{j-1}^2 + \frac{W_j W_{j-1}}{w_j^2}(W_j - 2w_j)\, v_j^3$$

$$M_j^2 = M_{j-1}^2 + \frac{W_j W_{j-1}}{w_j} v_j^2$$

$$\bar{X}_j = \bar{X}_{j-1} + v_j$$

$$W_0 = \bar{X}_0 = M_0^2 = M_0^3 = M_0^4 = 0$$

After the last observation has been processed,

W_N = sum of weights for all cases

$\bar{X}_N$ = mean

$$M_N^r = \sum_{i=1}^{N} w_i (X_i - \bar{X})^r$$

Basic Statistics

- Mean

  $\bar{X}_N$

- Variance

$$S^2 = M_N^2 / (W_N - 1)$$

- Standard deviation

$$S = \sqrt{S^2}$$

- Standard error

$$S_{\bar{X}} = \frac{S}{\sqrt{W_N}}$$

- Minimum

$$\min_j X_j$$

- Maximum

$$\max_j X_j$$

- Sum

$$\bar{X}_N W_N$$

- Skewness and standard error of skewness

$$g_1 = \frac{W_N M_N^3}{(W_N - 1)(W_N - 2) S^3} \qquad SE(g_1) = \sqrt{\frac{6 W_N (W_N - 1)}{(W_N - 2)(W_N + 1)(W_N + 3)}}$$

If $W_N \le 2$, or $S^2 < 1 \times 10^{-20}$, g_1 and its standard error are not calculated.

- Kurtosis (Bliss, (1967), p. 144) and standard error of kurtosis

$$g_2 = \frac{W_N (W_N + 1) M_N^4 - 3 M_N^2 M_N^2 (W_N - 1)}{(W_N - 1)(W_N - 2)(W_N - 3) S^4} \qquad SE(g_2) = \frac{4 (W_N^2 - 1) SE(g_1)^2}{(W_N - 3)(W_N + 5)}$$

If $W_N \le 3$, or $S^2 < 1 \times 10^{-20}$, g_2 and its standard error are not calculated.

- Z-scores

$$Z_i = \left(\frac{X_i - \bar{X}_N}{S}\right)$$

If X_i is missing or $S \le 0$, Z_i is set to the system-missing value.

References

Bliss (1967)
Spicer (1972)

DISCRIMINANT

General

No analysis is done for any subfile group for which the number of non-empty groups is less than 2 or the number of cases or sum of weights fails to exceed the number of non-empty groups. An analysis may be stopped if no variables are selected during variable selection or the eigenanalysis fails.

Notation

g	number of groups
p	number of variables
q	number of variables selected
X_{ijk}	the value of variable i for case k in group j
f_{jk}	the case weights for case k in group j
m_j	the number of cases in group j
n_j	the sum of case weights in group j
n	the total sum of weights

Basic Statistics

- Means

$$\bar{X}_{ij} = \left(\sum_{k=1}^{m_j} f_{jk} X_{ijk}\right) / n_j \qquad \text{(variable } i \text{ in group } j\text{)}$$

$$\bar{X}_{i.} = \left(\sum_{j=1}^{g} \sum_{k=1}^{m_j} f_{jk} X_{ijk}\right) / n \qquad \text{(variable } i\text{)}$$

- Variances

$$S_{ij}^2 = \frac{\left(\sum_{k=1}^{m_j} f_{jk} X_{ijk}^2 - n_j \bar{X}_{ij}^2\right)}{(n_j - 1)} \qquad \text{(variable } i \text{ in group } j\text{)}$$

$$S_{i.}^2 = \frac{\left(\sum_{j=1}^{g} \sum_{k=1}^{m_j} f_{jk} X_{ijk}^2 - n \bar{X}_{i}^2\right)}{(n - 1)} \qquad \text{(variable } i\text{)}$$

- Within-groups sums of squares and crossproduct matrix (W)

$$w_{il} = \sum_{j=1}^{g}\sum_{k=1}^{m_j} f_{jk}X_{ijk}X_{ljk} - \sum_{j=1}^{g}\left(\sum_{k=1}^{m_j} f_{jk}X_{ijk}\right)\left(\sum_{k=1}^{m_j} f_{jk}X_{ljk}\right)/n_j$$

$$i, l = 1, ..., p$$

- Total sums of squares and crossproduct matrix (T)

$$t_{il} = \sum_{j=1}^{g}\sum_{k=1}^{m_j} f_{jk}X_{ijk}X_{ljk} - \left(\sum_{j=1}^{g}\sum_{k=1}^{m_j} f_{jk}X_{ijk}\right)\left(\sum_{j=1}^{g}\sum_{k=1}^{m_j} f_{jk}X_{ljk}\right)/n$$

- Within-groups covariance matrix

$$C = \frac{W}{(n-g)} \qquad n > g$$

- Individual group covariance matrices $(C^{(j)})$

$$c_{il}^{(j)} = \frac{\left(\sum_{k=1}^{m_j} f_{jk}X_{ijk}X_{ljk} - \bar{X}_{ij}\bar{X}_{lj}n_j\right)}{(n_j - 1)}$$

- Within-groups correlation matrix (R)

$$r_{il} = \begin{cases} \dfrac{w_{il}}{\sqrt{w_{ii}w_{ll}}} & \text{if } w_{ii}w_{ll} > 0 \\ \text{SYSMIS} & \text{otherwise} \end{cases}$$

- Total covariance matrix

$$T' = \frac{T}{n-1}$$

- Univariate F and Λ for variable i

$$F_i = \frac{(t_{ii} - w_{ii})\,(n-g)}{w_{ii}\,(g-1)}$$

with g-1 and n-g degrees of freedom

$$\Lambda_i = \frac{w_{ii}}{t_{ii}}$$

with 1, g-1 and n-g degrees of freedom.

Rules of Variable Selection

Both direct and stepwise variable entry are possible. Multiple inclusion levels may also be specified.

Method = Direct

For direct variable selection, variables are considered for inclusion in the order they are written on the ANALYSIS = list. A variable is included in the analysis if, when it is included, no variable in the analysis will have a tolerance less than the specified tolerance limit (default = 0.001).

Stepwise Variable Selection

At each step, the following rules control variable selection:

- Eligible variables with higher inclusion levels are entered before eligible variables with lower inclusion levels.

- The order of entry of eligible variables with the same even inclusion level is determined by their order on the ANALYSIS = specification.

- The order of entry of eligible variables with the same odd level of inclusion is determined by their value on the entry criterion. The variable with the "best" value for the criterion statistic is entered first.

- When level-one processing is reached, prior to inclusion of any eligible variables, all already-entered variables which have level one inclusion numbers are examined for removal. A variable is considered eligible for removal if its F-to-remove is less than the F value for variable removal, or, if probability criteria are used, the significance of its F-to-remove exceeds the specified probability level. If more than one variable is eligible for removal, that variable is removed which leaves the "best" value for the criterion statistic for the remaining variables. Variable removal continues until no more variables are eligible for removal. Sequential entry of variables then proceeds as described previously, except that, after each step, variables with inclusion numbers of one are also considered for exclusion as described before.

- A variable with a zero inclusion level is never entered, although some statistics for it are printed.

Ineligibility for Inclusion

A variable with an odd inclusion number is considered ineligible for inclusion if:

- The tolerance of any variable in the analysis (including its own) drops below the specified tolerance limit if it is entered, or

- Its F-to-enter is less than the F-value for a variable to enter value, or

- If probability criteria are used, the significance level associated with its F-to-enter exceeds the probability to enter.

A variable with an even inclusion number is ineligible for inclusion if the first condition above is met.

Computations During Variable Selection

During variable selection, the matrix W is replaced at each step by a new matrix $W*$ using the symmetric sweep operator described by Dempster (1969). If the first q variables have been included in the analysis, W may be partitioned as:

$$\begin{bmatrix} W_{11} & W_{12} \\ W_{21} & W_{22} \end{bmatrix}$$

where W_{11} is $q \times q$. At this stage, the matrix $W*$ is defined by

$$W* = \begin{bmatrix} -W_{11}^{-1} & W_{11}^{-1} W_{12} \\ W_{21} W_{11}^{-1} & W_{22} - W_{21} W_{11}^{-1} W_{12} \end{bmatrix} = \begin{bmatrix} W_{11}^* & W_{12}^* \\ W_{21}^* & W_{22}^* \end{bmatrix}$$

In addition, when stepwise variable selection is used, T is replaced by the matrix $T*$, defined similarly.

The following statistics are computed:

- Tolerance

$$\mathrm{TOL}_i = \begin{cases} 0 & \text{if } w_{ii} = 0 \\ w_{ii}^* / w_{ii} & \text{if variable i is not in the analysis and } w_{ii} \neq 0 \\ -1/(w_{ii}^* w_{ii}) & \text{if variable i is in the analysis and } w_{ii} \neq 0. \end{cases}$$

If a variable's tolerance is less than or equal to the specified tolerance limit, or its inclusion in the analysis would reduce the tolerance of another variable in the equation to or below the limit, the following statistics are not computed for it or any set including it.

- F to Remove

$$F_i = \frac{(w_{ii}^* - t_{ii}^*)(n - q - g + 1)}{t_{ii}^*(g - 1)}$$

with degrees of freedom g-1 and n-q-g+1.

- F to Enter

$$F_i = \frac{(t_{ii}^* - w_{ii}^*)(n - q - g)}{w_{ii}^*(g - 1)}$$

with degrees of freedom g-1 and n-q-g.

- Wilks' lambda for testing the equality of group means

$$\Lambda = |W_{11}| / |T_{11}|$$

with degrees of freedom q, g-1, and n-g.

- The approximate F test for lambda (the "overall F"), also known as Rao's R (Tatsuoka,

1971).

$$F = \frac{(1-\Lambda^s)\,(r/s+1-qh/2)}{\Lambda^s qh}$$

where

$$s = \begin{cases} \sqrt{\dfrac{q^2+h^2-5}{q^2h^2-4}} & \text{if } q^2+h^2 \neq 5 \\ 1 & \text{otherwise} \end{cases}$$

$$r = n-1-(q+g)/2$$
$$h = g-1$$

with degrees of freedom qh and $r/s + 1 - qh/2$. The approximation is exact if q or h is 1 or 2.

- Rao's V (Lawley-Hotelling trace) (Rao, 1952, Morrison, 1976)

$$V = -(n-g)\sum_{i=1}^{q}\sum_{l=1}^{q} w^*_{il}(t_{il}-w_{il})$$

When n-g is large, V, under the null hypothesis, is approximately distributed as χ^2 with $q(g$-1) degrees of freedom. When an additional variable is entered, the change in V, if positive, has approximately a χ^2 distribution with g-1 degrees of freedom.

- The squared Mahalanobis distance (Morrison, 1976) between groups a and b

$$D^2_{ab} = -(n-g)\sum_{i=1}^{q}\sum_{l=1}^{q} w^*_{il}(\bar{X}_{ia}-\bar{X}_{ib})\,(\bar{X}_{la}-\bar{X}_{lb})$$

- The F value for testing the equality of means of groups a and b

$$F_{ab} = \frac{(n-q-g+1)\,n_a n_b}{q\,(n-q)\,(n_a+n_b)} D^2_{ab}$$

- The sum of unexplained variations (Dixon, 1973)

$$R = \sum_{a=1}^{g-1}\sum_{b=a+1}^{g} 4/(4+D^2_{ab})$$

Classification Functions

Once a set of q variables has been selected, the classification functions (also known as Fisher's linear discriminant functions) can be computed using

$$b_{ij} = (n-g)\sum_{l=1}^{q} w_{il}^{*}\bar{X}_{lj} \qquad i = 1, 2...., q \qquad j = 1, 2...., g$$

for the coefficients, and

$$a_j = \log p_j - \frac{1}{2}\sum_{i=1}^{q} b_{ij}\bar{X}_{ij} \qquad j = 1, 2...., q$$

for the constant, where p_j is the prior probability of group j.

Canonical Discriminant Functions

The canonical discriminant function coefficients are determined by solving the general eigenvalue problem

$$(T-W)V = \lambda WV$$

where V is the unscaled matrix of discriminant function coefficients and λ is a diagonal matrix of eigenvalues. The eigensystem is solved as follows:

The Cholesky decomposition

$$W = LU$$

is formed, where L is a lower triangular matrix, and $U = L'$.

The symmetric matrix $L^{-1}BU^{-1}$ is formed and the system

$$(L^{-1}(T-W)U^{-1} - \lambda I)(UV) = 0$$

is solved using tridiagonalization and the QL method. The result is m eigenvalues, where $m = \min(q, g-1)$ and corresponding orthonormal eigenvectors, UV. The eigenvectors of the original system are obtained as

$$V = U^{-1}(UV)$$

For each of the eigenvalues, which are ordered in descending magnitude, the following statistics are calculated:

Percentage of between-groups variance accounted for

$$\frac{100\lambda_k}{\sum_{k=1}^{m}\lambda_k}$$

Canonical correlation

$$\sqrt{\lambda_k/(1+\lambda_k)}$$

Wilks' Lambda

Testing the significance of all the discriminating functions after the first k:

$$\Lambda_k = \prod_{i=k+1}^{m} 1/(1+\lambda_i) \qquad k = 0, 1, ..., m-1$$

The significance level is based on

$$\chi^2 = -(n-(q+g)/2-1)\ln\Lambda_k,$$

which is distributed as a χ^2 with $(q-k)(g-k-1)$ degrees of freedom.

The standardized canonical discriminant coefficient matrix *D*

The standard canonical discriminant coefficient matrix D is computed as

$$D = S_{11}^{-1} V$$

where

S = diag $(\sqrt{w_{11}}, \sqrt{w_{22}}, ..., \sqrt{w_{pp}})$

S_{11} = partition containing the first q rows and columns of S

V = matrix of eigenvectors such that

$V' W_{11} V = I$

The correlations between the canonical discriminant functions and the discriminating variables

The correlations between the canonical discriminant functions and the discriminating variables are given by

$$R = S_{11}^{-1} W_{11} V$$

If some variables were not selected for inclusion in the analysis $(q<p)$, the eigenvectors are implicitly extended with zeroes to include the nonselected variables in the correlation matrix. Variables for which $w_{ii} = 0$ are excluded from S and W for this calculation; p then represents the number of variables with non-zero within-groups variance.

The unstandardized coefficients

The unstandardized coefficients are calculated from the standardized ones using

$$B = \sqrt{(n-g)}\, S_{11}^{-1} D$$

The associated constants are:

$$a_k = -\sum_{i=1}^{q} b_{ik}\bar{X}_{i.}$$

The group centroids are the canonical discriminant functions evaluated at the group means:

$$\bar{f}_{kj} = a_k + \sum_{i=1}^{q} b_{ik}\bar{X}_{ij}$$

Tests For Equality Of Variance

Box's M is used to test for equality of the group covariance matrices.

$$M = (n-g)\log|C'| - \sum_{j=1}^{g}(n_j-1)\log\left|C^{(j)}\right|$$

where

C' = pooled within-groups covariance matrix excluding groups with singular covariance matrices

$C^{(j)}$ = covariance matrix for group j.

Determinants of C' and $C^{(j)}$ are obtained from the Cholesky decomposition. If any diagonal element of the decomposition is less than 10^{-11}, the matrix is considered singular and excluded from the analysis.

$$\log|C^{(j)}| = 2\sum_{i=1}^{p} \log l_{ii} - p \log(n_j - 1)$$

where l_{ii} is the ith diagonal entry of L such that $(n_j - 1)C^{(j)} = L^T L$.

Similarly,

$$\log|C'| = 2\sum_{i=1}^{p} \log l_{ii} - p \log(n' - g)$$

where

$(n' - g)C' = L'L$

n' = sum of weights of cases in all groups with nonsingular covariance matrices

The significance level is obtained from the F distribution with t_1 and t_2 degrees of freedom using (Cooley and Lohnes, 1971)

$$F = \begin{cases} M/b & \text{if } e_2 > e_1^2 \\ \dfrac{t_2 M}{t_1(b - M)} & \text{if } e_2 < e_1^2 \end{cases}$$

where

$$e_1 = \left(\sum_{j=1}^{g} \frac{1}{n_j - 1} - \frac{1}{n - g}\right)\frac{2p^2 + 3p - 1}{6(g-1)(p+1)}$$

$$e_2 = \left(\sum_{j=1}^{g} \frac{1}{(n_j - 1)^2} - \frac{1}{(n - g)^2}\right)\frac{(p-1)(p+2)}{6(g-1)}$$

$$t_1 = (g-1)p(p+1)/2$$

$$t_2 = (t_1 + 2)/|e_2 - e_1^2|$$

$$b = \begin{cases} \dfrac{t_1}{1 - e_1 - t_1/t_2} & \text{if } e_2 > e_1^2 \\ \dfrac{t_2}{1 - e_1 + 2/t_2} & \text{if } e_2 < e_1^2 \end{cases}$$

If $e_1^2 - e_2$ is zero, or much smaller than e_2, t_2 cannot be computed or cannot be computed accurately. If

$$e_2 = e_2 + 0.0001\,(e_2 - e_1^2)$$

the program uses Bartlett's χ^2 statistic rather than the F statistic:

$$\chi^2 = M\,(1 - e_1)$$

with t_1 degrees of freedom.

For testing the group covariance matrix of the canonical discriminant functions, the procedure is similar. The covariance matrices $C^{(j)}$ and C' are replaced by D_j and D', where

$$D_j = B'\,C^{(j)}\,B$$

is the group covariance matrix of the discriminant functions.

The pooled covariance matrix in this case is an identity, so that

$$D' = (n-g)\,I_m - \sum_j (n_j - 1)\,D_j$$

where the summation is only over groups with singular D_j.

Classification

The basic procedure for classifying a case is as follows:

- If $\underset{\sim}{X}$ is the $1 \times q$ vector of discriminating variables for the case, the $1 \times m$ vector of canonical discriminant function values is

$$\underset{\sim}{f} = \underset{\sim}{X}B + \underset{\sim}{a}$$

- A chi-square distance from each centroid is computed

$$\chi_j^2 = (\underset{\sim}{f} - \bar{\underset{\sim}{f}}_j)\,D_j^{-1}\,(\underset{\sim}{f} - \bar{\underset{\sim}{f}}_j)'$$

where D_j is the covariance matrix of canonical discriminant functions for group j and $\bar{\underset{\sim}{f}}_j$ is the group centroid vector. If the case is a member of group j, χ_j^2 has a χ^2 distribution with m degrees of freedom. $P\,(\underset{\sim}{X}\,|\,G)$ is the significance level of such a χ_j^2.

- The classification, or posterior probability $P\,(G_j\,|\,\underset{\sim}{X})$, is

$$P\,(G_j\,|\,\underset{\sim}{X}) = \frac{P_j |D_j|^{-1/2} e^{-\chi_j^2/2}}{\sum_{j=1}^{g} P_j |D_j|^{-1/2} e^{-\chi_j^2/2}}$$

where p_j is the prior probability for group j. A case is classified into the group for which $P\,(G_j\,|\,\underset{\sim}{X})$ is highest.

The actual calculation of $P(G_j | \underset{\sim}{X})$ is

$$g_j = \log P_j - \frac{1}{2}(\log |D_j| + \chi_j^2)$$

$$P(G_j | \underset{\sim}{X}) = \begin{cases} \dfrac{\exp(g_j - \max_j g_j)}{\sum_{j=1}^{g} \exp(g_j - \max_j g_j)} & \text{if } g_j - \max_j g_j > -46 \\ 0 & \text{otherwise} \end{cases}$$

If individual group covariances are not used in classification, the pooled within-groups covariance matrix of the discriminant functions (an identity matrix) is substituted for D_j in the above calculation, resulting in considerable simplification.

If any D_j is singular, a pseudo-inverse of the form

$$\begin{bmatrix} D_{j11}^{-1} & 0 \\ 0 & 0 \end{bmatrix}$$

replaces D_j^{-1} and $|D_{j11}|$ replaces $|D_j|$. D_{j11} is a submatrix of D_j whose rows and columns correspond to functions not dependent on preceding functions. That is, function 1 will be excluded only if the rank of $D_j = 0$, function 2 will be excluded only if it is dependent on function 1, and so on. This choice of the pseudo-inverse is not optimal for the numerical stability of D_{j11}^{-1}, but maximizes the discrimination power of the remaining functions.

Rotations

Varimax rotations may be performed on either the matrix of canonical discriminant function coefficients or on that of the correlation between the canonical discriminant functions and the discrimination variables (the structure matrix). The actual algorithm for the rotation is described in FACTOR.

For the Kaiser normalization

$$h_i^2 = \begin{cases} 1 + 1/w_{ii}w^*_{ii} & \text{if coefficients rotated} \\ \text{(squared multiple correlation)} & \\ \sum_{k=1}^{m} r_{ik}^2 & \text{if correlations rotated.} \end{cases}$$

The unrotated structure matrix is

$$R = S_{11}^{-1} W_{11} V$$

If the rotation transformation matrix is represented by K, the rotated standardized coefficient matrix D_R is given by

$$D_R = DK$$

The rotated matrix of pooled within-groups correlations between the canonical discriminant functions and the discriminating variables R_R is

$$R_R = RK$$

The eigenvector matrix V satisfies

$$V'(T - W)V = \Lambda = \text{diag}(\lambda_1, \lambda_2, \ldots., \lambda_m)$$

where the λ_k are the eigenvalues. The equivalent matrix for the rotated coefficient V_R

$$(V_R)'(T-W)\,V_R$$

is not diagonal, meaning the rotated functions, unlike the unrotated ones, are correlated for the original sample, although their within-groups covariance matrix is an identity. The diagonals of the above matrix may still be interpreted as the between-groups variances of the functions. They are the numerators for the proportions of variance printed with the transformation matrix. The denominator is their sum. After rotation, the columns of the transformation are exchanged, if necessary, so that the diagonals of the matrix above are in descending order.

References

Anderson (1958)

Cooley & Lohnes (1971)

Dempster (1969)

Dixon (1973)

Tatsuoka (1971)

EXAMINE

UNIVARIATE STATISTICS

Notation

Let $y_1 < \ldots < y_m$ be m distinct ordered observations for the sample and $c_1, \ldots, c_m$ be the corresponding caseweights. Then

$$cc_i = \sum_{k=1}^{i} c_k = \text{cumulative frequency up to and including } y_i$$

and

$$W = cc_m = \sum_{k=1}^{m} c_k = \text{total sum of weights.}$$

Descriptive Statistics

- Minimum and Maximum

  min = y_1, max = y_m

- Range

  range = $y_m - y_1$

- Mean $(\bar{y})$

$$\bar{y} = \frac{\sum_{i=1}^{m} c_i y_i}{W}$$

- Median

  The median is the 50th percentile, which is calculated by the method requested. The default method is HAVERAGE.

- Interquartile Range (IQR)

  IQR = 75th percentile - 25th percentile, where the 75th and 25th percentiles are calculated by the method requested for percentiles.

- Variance (s^2)

$$s^2 = \frac{1}{W-1} \sum_{i=1}^{m} c_i (y_i - \bar{y})^2$$

- Standard Deviation

$$s = \sqrt{s^2}$$

- Standard Error

$$SE = \frac{s}{\sqrt{W}}$$

- Skewness (g_1) and SE of Skewness

$$g_1 = \frac{WM_3}{(W-1)(W-2)s^3}$$

$$SE(g_1) = \sqrt{\frac{6W(W-1)}{(W-2)(W+1)(W+3)}}$$

$$M_3 = \sum_{i=1}^{m} c_i (y_i - \bar{y})^3$$

- Kurtosis (g_2) and SE of Kurtosis

$$g_2 = \frac{W(W+1)M_4 - 3M_2^2(W-1)}{(W-1)(W-2)(W-3)s^4}$$

$$M_2 = \sum_{i=1}^{m} c_i (y_i - \bar{y})^2$$

$$M_4 = \sum_{i=1}^{m} c_i (y_i - \bar{y})^4$$

$$SE(g_2) = \sqrt{\frac{4(W^2-1)SE^2(g_1)}{(W-3)(W+5)}}$$

- 5% Trimmed Mean $T_{0.9}$

$$T_{0.9} = \frac{1}{0.9W}\left\{ (cc_{k_1+1} - tc)\, y_{k_1+1} + (W - cc_{k_2-1} - tc)\, y_{k_2} + \sum_{i=k_1+2}^{k_2-1} c_i y_i \right\}$$

where k_1 and k_2 satisfy the following conditions

$$cc_{k_1} < tc \le cc_{k_1+1}, \quad W - cc_{k_2} < tc \le W - cc_{k_2-1}$$

and

$$tc = 0.05W$$

Note: If $k_1 + 1 = k_2$, then $T_{0.9} = y_{k_2}$

Percentiles

There are five methods for computation of percentiles. Let

$$tc_1 = Wp, \quad tc_2 = (W+1)p$$

where p is the requested percentile divided by 100, and k_1 and k_2 satisfy

$$cc_{k_1} \le tc_1 < cc_{k_1+1}$$
$$cc_{k_2} \le tc_2 < cc_{k_2+1}$$

Then

$$g_1 = \frac{(tc_1 - cc_{k_1})}{c_{k_1+1}}, \quad g_1^* = tc_1 - cc_{k_1}$$
$$g_2 = \frac{(tc_2 - cc_{k_2})}{c_{k_2+1}}, \quad g_2^* = tc_2 - cc_{k_2}$$

Let x be the *pth* percentile; the five definitions are as follows:

- Waverage (Weighted Average at y_{tc_1})

If $g_1^* \ge 1$,

$$x = y_{k_1+1}$$

If $g_1^* < 1$ and $c_{k_1+1} \ge 1$, then

$$x = (1 - g_1^*)\, y_{k_1} + g_1^*\, y_{k_1+1}$$

If $g_1^* < 1$ and $c_{k_1+1} < 1$, then

$$x = (1 - g_1)\, y_{k_1} + g_1 y_{k_1+1}$$

- Round (Observation Closest to tc_1)

If $c_{k_1+1} \ge 1$, then

$$x = \begin{cases} y_{k_1} & \text{if } g_1^* < \frac{1}{2} \\ y_{k_1+1} & \text{if } g_1^* \ge \frac{1}{2} \end{cases}$$

If $c_{k_1+1} < 1$, then

$$x = \begin{cases} y_{k_1} & \text{if } g_1 < \frac{1}{2} \\ y_{k_1+1} & \text{if } g_1 \ge \frac{1}{2} \end{cases}$$

- Empirical (Empirical Distribution Function)

$$x = \begin{cases} y_{k_1} & \text{if } g_1^* = 0 \\ y_{k_1+1} & \text{if } g_1^* > 0 \end{cases}$$

- Haverage (Weighted Average at y_{tc_2})

If $g_2^* \ge 1$, then

$$x = y_{k_2+1}$$

If $g_2^* < 1$ and $c_{k_2+1} \geq 1$, then

$$x = (1-g_2^*)\, y_{k_2} + g_2^*\, y_{k_2+1}$$

If $g_2^* < 1$ and $c_{k_2+1} < 1$, then

$$x = (1-g_2)\, y_{k_2} + g_2 y_{k_2+1}$$

- Aempirical (Empirical Distribution Function with Averaging)

$$x = \begin{cases} (y_{k_1} + y_{k_1+1})/2 & \text{if } g_1^* = 0 \\ y_{k_1+1} & \text{if } g_1^* > 0 \end{cases}$$

Note: If either the 25th, 50th, or 75th percentiles is requested, Tukey Hinges will also be printed.

- Tukey Hinges

Let Q_1, Q_2, and Q_3 be the 25th, 50th, and 75th percentiles. If $c^* \geq 1$, where $c^* = \min(c_1, \ldots, c_m)$, define

$$d = \frac{\text{greatest integer} \leq ((W+3)/2)}{2}$$

$$L_1 = d$$
$$L_2 = W/2 + 1/2$$
$$L_3 = W + 1 - d$$

Otherwise

$$d = \frac{\text{greatest integer} \leq (W/c^* + 3)/2}{2}$$

and

$$L_1 = dc^*$$
$$L_2 = W/2 + c^*/2$$
$$L_3 = W + c^* - dc^*$$

Then for every i, $i = 1,2,3$, find h_i such that

$$cc_{h_i} \leq L_i < cc_{h_i+1}$$

and

$$Q_i = \begin{cases} (1-a_i^*)\, y_{h_i} + a_i^*\, y_{h_i+1} & \text{if } a_i^* < 1 \text{ and } c_{h_i+1} \geq 1 \\ (1-a_i)\, y_{h_i} + a_i\, y_{h_i+1} & \text{if } a_i^* < 1 \text{ and } c_{h_i+1} < 1 \\ y_{h_i+1} & \text{if } a_i^* \geq 1 \end{cases}$$

where

$$a_i^* = L_i - cc_{h_i}$$

$$a_i = \frac{a_i^*}{c_{h_i+1}}$$

- M-Estimation (Robust Location Estimation)

The M-estimator T of location is the solution of

$$\sum_{i=1}^{m} c_i \Psi\left(\frac{y_i - T}{s}\right) = 0$$

where Ψ is an odd function and s is a measure of the spread.

An alternative form of M-estimation is

$$\sum_{i=1}^{m} c_i \left(\frac{y_i - T}{s}\right) \omega\left(\frac{y_i - T}{s}\right) = 0$$

where

$$\omega(u) = \frac{\Psi(u)}{u}$$

After rearranging the above equation, we get

$$T = \frac{\sum_{i=1}^{m} c_i y_i \omega\left(\frac{y_i - T}{s}\right)}{\sum_{i=1}^{m} c_i \omega\left(\frac{y_i - T}{s}\right)}$$

Therefore, the algorithm to find M-estimators is defined iteratively by

$$T_{k+1} = \frac{\sum_{i=1}^{m} c_i y_i \omega\left(\frac{y_i - T_k}{s}\right)}{\sum_{i=1}^{m} c_i \omega\left(\frac{y_i - T_k}{s}\right)}$$

The algorithm stops when either

$|T_{k+1} - T_k| \le \varepsilon [(T_{k+1} + T_k)/2]$, where $\varepsilon = 0.005$

or the number of iterations exceeds 30.

- M-Estimators

Four M-estimators (Huber, Hampel, Andrew, and Tukey) are available. Let

$$u_i = \frac{y_i - T}{s}$$

where

s = median of $\tilde{y}_1, \ldots, \tilde{y}_m$ with caseweights $c_1, \ldots, c_m$

and

$\tilde{y}_i = |y_i - \tilde{y}|$, where $\tilde{y}$ is the median.

- Huber (k), $k > 0$

$$\omega(u_i) = \begin{cases} 1 & \text{if } |u_i| \le k \\ \frac{k}{u_i} sgn(u_i) & \text{if } |u_i| > k \end{cases}$$

The default value of $k = 1.339$

- Hampel (a, b, c), $0 < a \le b \le c$

$$\omega(u_i) = \begin{cases} 1 & \text{if} \quad |u_i| \le a \\ \dfrac{a}{u_i} sgn\,(u_i) & \text{if} \quad a < |u_i| \le b \\ \dfrac{a}{u_i}\dfrac{c - |u_i|}{c - b}\,\text{sgn}\,(u_i) & \text{if} \quad b < |u_i| \le c \\ 0 & \text{if} \quad |u_i| > c \end{cases}$$

By default, $a = 1.7$, $b = 3.4$, and $c = 8.5$

- Andrew's Wave (c), $c > 0$

$$\omega(u_i). = \begin{cases} \dfrac{c}{\pi u_i}\sin\dfrac{\pi u_i}{c} & \text{if } |u_i| \le c \\ 0 & \text{if } |u_i| > c \end{cases}$$

By default, $c = 1.34\pi$

- Tukey's biweight (c)

$$\omega(u_i) = \begin{cases} \left(1 - \dfrac{u_i^2}{c^2}\right)^2 & \text{if } |u_i| \le c \\ 0 & \text{if } |u_i| > c \end{cases}$$

By default, $c = 4.685$.

Tests of Normality

- Shapiro-Wilk Statistic (W)

Since the W statistic is based on the order statistics of the sample, the caseweights have to be restricted to integers. Hence, before W is calculated, all the caseweights are rounded to the closest integer and the series is expanded. Let c_i^* be the closest integer to c_i; then

$$cc_i^* = \sum_{k=1}^{i} c_k^*\,, \qquad W_s = cc_m^* = \sum_{k=1}^{m} c_k^*$$

The original series $y = \{y_1, \ldots, y_m\}$ is expanded to

$$x = \{x_1, \ldots, x_{w_s}\}$$

where

$$x_{cc_{i-1}^* + 1} = \ldots = x_{cc_i^*} = y_i, \ i = 1, \ldots, m$$

Then the W statistic is defined as

$$W = \frac{\left(\sum_{i=1}^{W_s} a_i x_i\right)^2}{\sum_{i=1}^{W_s} (x_i - \bar{x})^2}$$

where

$$\bar{x} = \frac{\sum_{i=1}^{W_s} x_i}{W_s}$$

$$a_1^2 = a_{W_s}^2 = \begin{cases} \dfrac{\Gamma(W_s/2)}{\sqrt{2}\Gamma\left[\dfrac{(W_s+1)}{2}\right]} & \text{if } 5 \le W_s \le 20 \\[2ex] \dfrac{\Gamma(\frac{W_s+1}{2})}{\sqrt{2}\Gamma(\frac{W}{2}+1)} & \text{if } W_s > 20 \end{cases}$$

$$a_1 = -\sqrt{a_1^2}\,,\; a_{W_s} = \sqrt{a_{W_s}^2}$$

$$a_i = \frac{2}{c}m_i,\quad i = 2, \ldots, W_s - 1$$

$$m_i = \psi^{-1}\left(\frac{i-\alpha}{W_s - 2\alpha + 1}\right), \text{ where } \psi \text{ is the c.d.f. of a standard normal distribution}$$

$$\alpha = 0.314195 + 0.063336\beta - 0.010895\beta^2$$

$$\beta = \log_{10} W_s$$

$$c^2 = 4\sum_{i=1}^{W_s-1} \frac{m_i^2}{(1-2a_i^2)}$$

Based on the computed W statistic, the significance is calculated by linearly interpolating within the range of simulated critical values given in Shapiro & Wilk (1965).

The Shapiro and Wilk statistic is calculated only if $W_s \le 50$ and

$$\frac{W_s a_1^2}{(W_s - 1)} \le W \le 1$$

If $W > w_{0.99}$, the critical value of 99th percentile, the significance is reported as >0.99. Similarly, if $W < w_{0.01}$, the critical value of first percentile, the significance is reported as <0.01.

- Kolmogorov-Smirnov Statistic with Lilliefors' Significance

Lilliefors (1967) presented a table for testing normality using the Kolmogorov-Smirnov statistic when the mean and variance of the population are unknown. This statistic is

$$D_a = \max_{y_i} \mid S(y_i) - F^*(y_i) \mid$$

where $S(y_i)$ is the sample cumulative distribution function and $F^*(y_i)$ is the cumulative normal distribution whose mean and variance are estimated from the sample.

Dallal & Wilkinson (1986) corrected the critical values for testing normality reported by Lilliefors. With the corrected table they derived an analytic approximation to the upper tail probabilities of D_a for probabilities less than 0.1.

The following formula is used to estimate the critical value D_c for probability 0.1.

$$D_c = \frac{(-b - \sqrt{b^2 - 4ac})}{2a}$$

where, if $W \leq 100$,

$$a = -7.01256\,(W+2.78019)$$
$$b = 2.99587\sqrt{(W+2.78019)}$$
$$c = 2.1804661 + \frac{0.974598}{\sqrt{W}} + \frac{1.67997}{W}$$

If $W > 100$

$$a = -7.9028898\,W^{0.98}$$
$$b = 3.1803686\,W^{0.49}$$
$$c = 2.2947256$$

The Lilliefors significance p is calculated as follows:

If $D_a = D_c$, $p = 0.1$

If $D_a > D_c$, $p = \exp\{aD_a^2 + bD_a + c - 2.3025851\}$

If $D_{0.2} \leq D_a < D_c$, linear interpolation between $D_{0.2}$ and D_c where $D_{0.2}$ is the critical value for probability 0.2 is done.

If $D_a > D_{0.2}$, p is reported as >0.2.

Group Statistics

Assume that there are $k\ (k \geq 2)$ combinations of grouping factors. For every combination $i, i = 1, 2, ..., k$, let $\{y_{i1}, \ldots, y_{im_i}\}$ be the sample observations with the corresponding caseweights $\{c_{i1}, \ldots, c_{im_i}\}$.

Spread versus Level

If a transformation value, a, is given, the spread(s) and level(l) are defined based on the transformed data. Let x be the transformed value of y; for every $i = 1, ..., k, j = 1, ..., m_i$

$$x_{ij} = \begin{cases} \ln y_{ij} & \text{if } a=0 \\ y_{ij}^a & \text{otherwise} \end{cases}$$

Then the spread (s_i) and the level (l_i) are respectively defined as the Interquartile Range and the median of $\{x_{i1}, \ldots, x_{im_i}\}$ with corresponding caseweights $\{c_{i1}, \ldots, c_{im_i}\}$. However, if a is not specified, the spread and the level are natural logarithms of the Interquartile Range and of the median of the original data. Finally, the slope is the regression coefficient of s on l, which is defined as

$$\frac{\sum_{i=1}^{k} (l_i - \bar{l})(s_i - \bar{s})}{\sum_{i=1}^{k} (l_i - \bar{l})^2}$$

In some situations, the transformations cannot be done. The spread versus level plot and Levene statistic will not be produced if

- a is a negative integer and at least one of the data is zero
- a is a negative non-integer and at least one of the data is less than or equal to zero
- a is a positive non-integer and at least one of the data is less than zero
- a is not specified and the median or the spread is less than or equal to zero

Levene Test of Homogeneity of Variances

The Levene test statistic is based on the transformed data and is defined by

$$L_a = \left(\frac{W-k}{k-1}\right)\frac{\sum_{i=1}^{k} w_i(\bar{z}_i-\bar{z})^2}{\sum_{i=1}^{k}\sum_{l=1}^{m_i} c_{il}(z_{il}-\bar{z}_i)^2}$$

where

$$w_i = \sum_{l=1}^{m_i} c_{il}$$

$$\bar{x}_i = \frac{\sum_{l=1}^{m_i} c_{il}x_{il}}{w_i}$$

$$z_{il} = |x_{il}-\bar{x}_i|$$

$$\bar{z}_i = \sum_{l=1}^{m_i}\frac{c_{il}z_{il}}{w_i}$$

$$\bar{z} = \sum_{i=1}^{k}\frac{w_i\bar{z}_i}{W}$$

The significance of L_a is calculated from the F distribution with degrees of freedom k-1 and W-k.

Groups with zero variance are included in the test.

Plots

Normal Probability Plot (NPPLOT)

For every distinct observation y_i, R_i is the rank (the mean of ranks is assigned to ties). The normal score NS_i is calculated by

$$NS_i = \Psi^{-1}\left(\frac{R_i}{W+1}\right)$$

where Ψ^{-1} is the inverse of the standard normal cumulative distribution function. The NPPLOT is the plot of $(y_1, NS_1), \ldots, (y_m, NS_m)$.

Detrended Normal Plot

The detrended normal plot is the scatterplot of $(y_1, D_1), \dots (y_m, D_m)$, where D_i is the difference between the Z-score and normal score, which is defined by

$$D_i = Z_i - NS_i$$

and

$$Z_i = \frac{y_i - \bar{y}}{s}$$

where $\bar{y}$ is the average and s is the standard deviation.

Boxplot

The boundaries of the box are Tukey's hinges. The length of the box is the interquartile range based on Tukey's hinges. That is

$$IQR = Q_3 - Q_1$$

Define

$$STEP = 1.5\ IQR$$

A case is an outlier if

$$Q_3 + STEP \le y_i < Q_3 + 2STEP$$

or

$$Q_1 - 2STEP < y_i \le Q_1 - STEP$$

A case is an extreme if

$$y_i \ge Q_3 + 2STEP$$

or

$$y_i \le Q_1 - 2STEP$$

References

Dallal & Wilkinson (1986)

Frigge, Hoaglin & Iglewicz (1987)

Haoglin, Mosteller & Tukey (1985)

Hoaglin, Mosteller & Tukey (1983)

Lilliefors (1967)

Tukey (1977)

Velleman & Hoaglin (1981)

Exponential Smoothing (EXSMOOTH)

General

EXSMOOTH produces one period ahead forecasts for different models.

Notation

X_t	observed series, $t = 1, ..., n$
$\hat{X}_t$	forecast of one period ahead from time t
p	the number of periods
k	the number of complete cycles ($[n/p]$)
e_t	the tth residual $(X_t - \hat{X}_{t-1})$
S_0	initial value for series
T_0	initial value for trend
$I_{1-p}, ..., I_0$	initial values for seasonal factors
m_l	the mean for the lth cycle, $\sum_{i=(l-1)p+1}^{lp} X_i/p$

Note:

(1) $I_{1-p}, ..., I_0$ are obtained from the SEASON procedure with MA = EQUAL if p is even; otherwise MA = CENTERED is used for both multiplicative and additive models.

(2) The index for the fitted series starts with zero.

(3) The value saved in the FIT variable for the tth case is $\hat{X}_{t-1}$.

Models

- No Trend, No Seasonality Model

$$X_t = b + \varepsilon_t$$

Initial value

$$S_0 = \bar{X}$$

then

$$\hat{X}_0 = S_0 \ , \quad e_1 = X_1 - \hat{X}_0$$
$$S_t = S_{t-1} + \alpha e_t$$
$$\hat{X}_t = S_t$$

- No Trend, Additive Seasonality Model

$$X_t = b + I_t + \varepsilon_t$$

Initial value

$$S_0 = \frac{\sum_{i=1}^{k} m_i}{k}$$

then

$$\hat{X}_0 = S_0 + I_{1-p}$$

$$e_1 = X_1 - \hat{X}_0$$

$$S_t = S_{t-1} + \alpha e_t$$

$$I_t = I_{t-p} + \delta (1 - \alpha) e_t$$

$$\hat{X}_t = S_t + I_{t-p+1}$$

- No Trend, Multiplicative Seasonality Model

$$X_t = bI_t + \varepsilon_t$$

Initial value

$$S_0 = \frac{\sum_{i=1}^{k} m_i}{k}$$

then

$$\hat{X}_0 = S_0 I_{1-p}$$

$$e_1 = X_1 - \hat{X}_0$$

$$S_t = S_{t-1} + \alpha e_t / I_{t-p}$$

$$I_t = I_{t-p} + \delta (1 - \alpha) e_t / S_t$$

$$\hat{X}_t = S_t I_{t-p+1}$$

- Linear Trend, No Seasonality Model

$$X_t = b_0 + b_1 t + \varepsilon_t$$

Initial values

$$T_0 = \frac{X_n - X_1}{n-1}$$

$$S_0 = X_1 - \frac{1}{2}T_0$$

then

$$\hat{X}_0 = S_0 + T_0$$

$$e_1 = X_1 - \hat{X}_0$$

$$S_t = S_{t-1} + T_{t-1} + \alpha e_t$$

$$T_t = T_{t-1} + \alpha\gamma e_t$$

$$\hat{X}_t = S_t + T_t$$

- Linear Trend, Additive Seasonality Model

$$X_t = b_0 + b_1 t + I_t + \varepsilon_t$$

Initial values

$$T_0 = \frac{m_k - m_1}{(k-1)p}$$

$$S_0 = X_1 - \frac{p}{2}T_0$$

then

$$\hat{X}_0 = S_0 + T_0 + I_{1-p}$$

$$S_t = S_{t-1} + T_{t-1} + \alpha e_t$$

$$T_t = T_{t-1} + \alpha\gamma e_t$$

$$I_t = I_{t-p} + \delta(1-\alpha)e_t$$

$$\hat{X}_t = S_t + T_t + I_{t-p+1}$$

- Linear Trend, Multiplicative Seasonality Model

$$X_t = (b_0 + b_1 t) I_t + \varepsilon_t$$

Initial values

$$T_0 = \frac{m_k - m_1}{(k-1)p}$$

$$S_0 = m_1 - \frac{p}{2}T_0$$

then

$$\hat{X}_0 = (S_0 + T_0)\, I_{1-p}$$

$$S_t = S_{t-1} + T_{t-1} + \alpha (2-\alpha)\, e_t / I_{t-p}$$

$$T_t = T_{t-1} + \alpha^2 e_t / I_{t-p}$$

$$I_t = I_{t-p} + \delta [1 - \alpha (2-\alpha)]\, e_t / S_t$$

$$\hat{X}_t = (S_t + T_t)\, I_{t-p+1}$$

- Exponential Trend, No Season Model

$$X_t = b_0 b_1^t + \varepsilon_t$$

Initial values

$$T_0 = \exp\{\ln X_2 - \ln X_1\} = \frac{X_2}{X_1}$$

$$S_0 = \exp\{\ln X_1 - \frac{1}{2}\ln T_0\} = \frac{X_1}{\sqrt{T_0}}$$

then

$$\hat{X}_0 = S_0 T_0$$

$$S_t = S_{t-1} T_{t-1} + \alpha e_t$$

$$T_t = T_{t-1} + \alpha\gamma e_t / S_{t-1}$$

$$\hat{X}_t = S_t T_t$$

- Exponential Trend, Additive Seasonal Model

$$X_t = b_0 b_1^t + I_t + \varepsilon_t$$

Initial values

$$T_0 = \exp\{(\ln m_2 - \ln m_1)/p\}$$

$$S_0 = \exp\{\ln m_1 - \frac{p}{2}\ln T_0\}$$

then

$$\hat{X}_0 = S_0 T_0 + I_{1-p}$$

$$S_t = S_{t-1} T_{t-1} + \alpha e_t$$

$$T_t = T_{t-1} + \alpha\gamma e_t / S_{t-1}$$

$$I_t = I_{t-p} + \delta(1-\alpha)\, e_t$$

$$\hat{X}_t = S_t T_t + I_{t-p+1}$$

- Exponential Trend, Multiplicative Seasonality Model

$$X_t = (b_0 b_1^t)\, I_t + \varepsilon_t$$

Initial values

$$T_0 = \exp\{(\ln m_2 - \ln m_1) / (k-1)\}$$

$$S_0 = \exp\{\ln m_1 - \frac{p}{2} \ln T_0\}$$

then

$$\hat{X}_0 = (S_0 T_0)\, I_{1-p}$$

$$S_t = S_{t-1} T_{t-1} + \alpha e_t / I_{t-p}$$

$$T_t = T_{t-1} + \alpha\gamma e_t / (I_{t-p} S_{t-1})$$

$$I_t = I_{t-p} + \delta(1-\alpha)\, e_t / S_t$$

$$\hat{X}_t = (S_t T_t)\, I_{t-p+1}$$

- Damped Trend, No Seasonality Model

$$X_t = b_0 + \phi b_1 t + \varepsilon_t$$

Initial values

$$T_0 = \frac{X_n - X_1}{(n-1)\,\phi}$$

$$S_0 = X_1 - \frac{1}{2} T_0$$

then

$$\hat{X}_0 = S_0 + \phi T_0$$

$$S_t = S_{t-1} + \phi T_{t-1} + \alpha e_t$$

$$T_t = \phi T_{t-1} + \alpha\gamma e_t$$

$$\hat{X}_t = S_t + \phi T_t$$

- Damped Trend, Additive Seasonality Model

$$X_t = b_0 + \phi b_1 t + I_t + \varepsilon_t$$

Initial values

$$T_0 = \frac{m_k - m_1}{(k-1)p\phi}$$

$$S_0 = m_1 - \frac{p}{2}T_0$$

then

$$\hat{X}_0 = S_0 + \phi T_0 + I_{-p+1}$$

$$S_t = S_{t-1} + \phi T_{t-1} + \alpha(2-\alpha)e_t$$

$$T_t = \phi T_{t-1} + \alpha(\alpha - \phi + 1)e_t$$

$$I_t = I_{t-p} + \delta[1 - \alpha(2-\alpha)]e_t$$

$$\hat{X}_t = S_t + \phi T_t + I_{t-p+1}$$

- Damped Trend, Multiplicative Seasonality Model

$$X_t = (b_0 + b_1\phi t)I_t + \varepsilon_t$$

Initial values

$$T_0 = \frac{m_k - m_1}{(k-1)p\phi}$$

$$S_0 = m_1 - \frac{p}{2}T_0\phi$$

then

$$\hat{X}_0 = (S_0 + \phi T_0) I_{1-p}$$

$$S_t = S_{t-1} + \phi T_{t-1} + \alpha (2 - \alpha) e_t / I_{t-p}$$

$$T_t = \phi T_{t-1} + \alpha (\alpha - \phi + 1) e_t / I_{t-p}$$

$$I_t = I_{t-p} + \delta [1 - \alpha (2 - \alpha)] e_t / S_t$$

$$\hat{X}_t = (S_t + \phi T_t) I_{t-p+1}$$

References

Abraham & Ledolter (1983)

Gardner (1985)

Ledolter & Abraham (1984)

Makridakis, Wheelwright & McGee (1983)

FACTOR

Extraction of Initial Factors

Principal Components Extraction (PC)

The matrix of factor loadings based on factor m is

$$\Lambda_m = \Omega_m \Gamma_m^{1/2}$$

where

$$\Omega_m = (\underline{\omega}_1, \underline{\omega}_2, \ldots, \underline{\omega}_m)$$

$$\Gamma_m = diag(|\gamma_1|, |\gamma_2|, \ldots, |\gamma_m|)$$

$\gamma_1 \geq \gamma_2 \geq \ldots \geq \gamma_m$ are the eigenvalues and $\underline{\omega}_i$ are the corresponding eigenvectors of R, where R is the correlation matrix.

The communality of variable i is given by

$$h_i = \sum_{j=1}^{m} |\gamma_j| \omega_{ij}^2$$

Principal Axis Factoring

An iterative solution for communalities and factor loadings is sought. At iteration i, the communalities from the preceding iteration are placed on the diagonal of R, and the resulting R is denoted by R_i. The eigenanalysis is performed on R_i and the new communality of variable j is estimated by

$$h_{j(i)} = \sum_{j=1}^{m} |\gamma_{k(i)}| \omega_{jk(i)}^2$$

The factor loadings are obtained by

$$\Lambda_{m(i)} = \Omega_{m(i)} \Gamma_{m(i)}^{1/2}$$

Iterations continue until the maximum number (default 25) is reached or until the maximum change in the communality estimates is less than the convergence criterion (default 0.001).

Maximum Likelihood (ML)

The maximum likelihood solutions of Λ and ψ^2 are obtained by minimizing

$$F = tr\left[(\Lambda\Lambda' + \psi^2)^{-1} R\right] - \log\left|(\Lambda\Lambda' + \psi^2)^{-1} R\right| - p$$

with respect to Λ and ψ, where p is the number of variables, Λ is the factor loading matrix, and ψ^2 is the diagonal matrix of unique variances.

The minimization of F is performed by way of a two-step algorithm. First, the conditional minimum of F for a given ψ is found. This gives the function $f(\psi)$, which is minimized numerically using the Newton-Raphson procedure. Let $x^{(s)}$ be the column vector containing the logarithm of the diagonal elements of ψ at the sth iteration; then

$$\underline{x}^{(s+1)} = \underline{x}^{(s)} - \underline{d}^{(s)}$$

where $d^{(s)}$ is the solution to the system of linear equations

$$\underline{H}^{(s)}\underline{d}^{(s)} = \underline{h}^{(s)}$$

and where

$$H^{(s)} = (\partial^2 f(\psi)/\partial x_i \partial x_j)$$

and $\underline{h}^{(s)}$ is the column vector containing $\partial f(\psi)/\partial x_i$. The starting point $\underline{x}^{(1)}$ is

$$x_i^{(1)} = \begin{cases} \log[(1-m/2p)/r^{ii}] & \text{for ML and GLS} \\ [(1-m/2p)/r^{ii}]^{1/2} & \text{for ULS} \end{cases}$$

where m is the number of factors and r^{ii} is the ith diagonal element of R^{-1}.

The values of $f(\psi)$, $\partial f/\partial x_i$, and $\partial^2 f/\partial x_i \partial x_j$ can be expressed in terms of the eigenvalues

$$\gamma_1 \le \gamma_2 \le \ldots \le \gamma_p$$

and corresponding eigenvectors

$$\underline{\omega}_1, \underline{\omega}_2, \ldots, \underline{\omega}_p$$

of matrix $\psi R^{-1}\psi$. That is,

$$f(\psi) = \sum_{k=m+1}^{p} (\log\gamma_k + \gamma_k^{-1} - 1)$$

$$\frac{\partial f}{\partial x_i} = \sum_{k=m+1}^{p} (1-\gamma_k^{-1})\,\omega_{ik}^2$$

$$\frac{\partial^2 f}{\partial x_i \partial x_j} = -\delta_{ij}\frac{\partial f}{\partial x_i} + \sum_{k=m+1}^{p} \omega_{ik}\omega_{jk}\left(\sum_{n=1}^{m} \frac{\gamma_k+\gamma_n-2}{\gamma_k-\gamma_n}\omega_{in}\omega_{jn} + \delta_{ij}\right)$$

where

$$\delta_{ij} = \begin{cases} 1 \text{ if } i=j \\ 0 \text{ if } i \ne j \end{cases}$$

The approximate second-order derivatives

$$\frac{\partial^2 f}{\partial x_i \partial x_j} \cong \left(\sum_{k=m+1}^{p} \omega_{ik}\omega_{jk}\right)^2$$

are used in the initial step and when the matrix of the exact second-order derivatives is not positive definite or when all elements of the vector $\underline{d}$ are greater than 0.1. If $\partial^2 f/\partial x_i^2 < 0.05$ (Heywood variables), the diagonal element is replaced by 1 and the rest of the elements of that column and row are set to 0. If the value of $f(\psi)$ is not decreased by step $\underline{d}$, the step is halved and halved again until the value of $f(\psi)$ decreases or 25 halvings fail to produce a decrease. (In this case, the computations are terminated.) Stepping continues until the largest absolute value of the elements of $\underline{d}$ is less than the criterion value (default 0.001) or until the maximum number of iterations (default 25) is reached. Using the converged value of ψ (denoted by $\hat{\psi}$), the eigenanalysis is performed on the matrix $\hat{\psi}R^{-1}\hat{\psi}$. The factor loadings are computed as

$$\hat{\Lambda}_m = \hat{\psi}\Omega_m(\Gamma_m^{-1} - I_m)^{1/2}$$

where

$$\Gamma_m = \text{diag}\,(\gamma_1, \gamma_2, \ldots, \gamma_m)$$
$$\Omega_m = (\underline{\omega}_1, \underline{\omega}_2, \ldots, \underline{\omega}_m)$$

Unweighted and Generalized Least Squares (ULS, GLS)

The same basic algorithm is used in ULS and GLS methods as in maximum likelihood, except that

$$f(\psi) = \begin{cases} \sum_{k=m+1}^{p} \frac{\gamma_k^2}{2} & \text{for ULS} \\ \sum_{k=m+1}^{p} \frac{(\gamma_k - 1)^2}{2} & \text{for GLS} \end{cases}$$

for the ULS method, the eigenanalysis is performed on the matrix $R - \psi^2$, where $\gamma_1 \geq \gamma_2 \geq \ldots \geq \gamma_p$ are the eigenvalues. In terms of the derivatives, for ULS

$$\frac{\partial f}{\partial x_i} = 2x_i \sum_{k=m+1}^{p} \gamma_k \omega_{ik}^2$$

$$\frac{\partial^2 f}{\partial x_i \partial x_j} = 4\left[x_i x_j \sum_{k=m+1}^{p} \omega_{ik}\omega_{jk} \sum_{n=1}^{m} \frac{\gamma_k + \gamma_n}{\gamma_k - \gamma_n} \omega_{ik}\omega_{jk} + \delta_{ij} \sum_{k=m+1}^{p} (x_i^2 - \frac{\gamma_k}{2})\, \omega_{ik}^2\right]$$

and

$$\frac{\partial^2 f}{\partial x_i \partial x_j} = 4x_i x_j \left(\sum_{k=m+1}^{p} \omega_{ik}\omega_{jk}\right)^2$$

For GLS

$$\frac{\partial f}{\partial x_i} = \sum_{k=m+1}^{p} (\gamma_k^2 - \gamma_k)\, \omega_{ik}^2$$

$$\frac{\partial^2 f}{\partial x_i \partial x_j} = \delta_{ij} \frac{\partial f}{\partial x_i} + \sum_{k=m+1}^{p} \gamma_k \omega_{ik} \omega_{jk} \left(\sum_{n=1}^{m} \gamma_n \frac{\gamma_k + \gamma_n - 2}{\gamma_k - \gamma_n} \omega_{in}\omega_{jn} + r^{ij} \exp\,[\,(x_i + x_j)\,/2]\right)$$

and

$$\frac{\partial^2 f}{\partial x_i \partial x_j} = \left(\sum_{k=m+1}^{p} \omega_{ik}\omega_{jk}\right)^2$$

Also, the factor loadings of the ULS method are obtained by

$$\hat{\Lambda}_m = \Omega_m \Gamma_m^{1/2}$$

The chi-square statistics for m factors for the ML and GLS methods is given by

$$\chi_m^2 = (W - 1 - \frac{2p+5}{6} - \frac{2m}{3}) f(\hat{\psi})$$

with $((p-m)^2 - p - m)/2$ degrees of freedom.

Alpha (Harman (1976))

Iteration for communalities

At each iteration i:

- The eigenvalues $(r_{(i)})$ and eigenvectors $(\Omega_{(i)})$ of $H_{(i-1)}^{-1/2}(R-I)H_{(i-1)}^{-1/2}+I$ are computed.

- The new communalities are

$$h_{k(i)}\left(\sum_{j=1}^{m}|\gamma_{j(i)}|\,\omega_{kj(i)}^{2}\right)h_{k(i-1)}$$

The initial values of the communalities, H_0, are

$$h_{io}=\begin{cases}1-1/r^{ii} & |R|\geq 10^{-8}\text{ and all } 0\leq h_{io}\leq 1\\ \max\limits_{j}|r_{ij}| & \text{otherwise}\end{cases}$$

where r^{ii} is the ith diagonal entry of R^{-1}.

If $|R|\geq 10^{-8}$ and all r^{ii} are equal to one, the procedure is terminated. If for some i,

$\max\limits_{j}|r_{ij}|>1$, the procedure is terminated.

- Iteration stops if any of the following are true:

$$\max_{k}|h_{k(i)}-h_{k(i-1)}|<\text{EPS}$$

$$i=\text{MAX}$$

$$h_{k(i)}=0\text{ for any }k$$

Final Communalities and Factor Pattern Matrix

The communalities are the values when iteration stops, unless the last termination criterion is true, in which case the procedure terminates. The factor pattern matrix is

$$F_m=H_{(f)}^{1/2}\Omega_{m(f)}\Gamma_{m(f)}^{1/2}$$

where f is the final iteration.

Image (Kaiser (1963))

- Eigenvalues and eigenvectors of $S^{-1}RS^{-1}$ are found.

$$S^2=\text{diag}\,(1/r^{11},\ldots,1/r^{nn})$$

$$r^{ii}=i^{th}\text{ diagonal element of }R^{-1}$$

- The factor pattern matrix is

$$F_m=S\Omega_m(\Lambda_m-I_m)\Lambda_m^{-1/2}$$

where Ω_m and Λ_m correspond to the m eigenvalues greater than 1.

If $m = 0$, the procedure is terminated.

- The communalities are

$$h_i = \sum_{j=1}^{m} (\gamma_j - 1)^2 \omega_{ij}^2 / (\gamma_j r^{ij})$$

- The image covariance matrix is

$$R + S^2 R^{-1} S^2 - 2S^2$$

- The anti-image covariance matrix is

$$S^2 R^{-1} S^2$$

Factor Rotations

Orthogonal Rotations (Harman (1976))

Rotations are done cyclically on pairs of factors until the maximum number of iterations is reached or the convergence criterion is met. The algorithm is the same for all orthogonal rotations, differing only in computations of the tangent values of the rotation angles.

- The factor pattern matrix is normalized by the square root of communalities:

$$\Lambda_m^* = H^{-1/2} \Lambda_m$$

where

$\Lambda_m = (\underline{\lambda}_1, \ldots, \underline{\lambda}_m)$ is the factor pattern matrix
$H = \mathrm{diag}\,(h_1, \ldots, h_n)$ is the diagonal matrix of communalities.

- The transformation matrix T is initialized to I_m

- At each iteration i

(1) The convergence criterion is

$$SV_{(i)} = \sum_{j=1}^{m} \left(n \sum_{k=1}^{n} \lambda_{kj(i)}^{*4} - \left(\sum_{k=1}^{n} \lambda_{kj(i)}^{*2} \right)^2 \right) / n^2$$

where the initial value of $\Lambda_{m(1)}^*$ is the original factor pattern matrix. For subsequent iterations the initial value is the final value of $\Lambda_{m(i-1)}^*$ when all factor pairs have been rotated.

(2) For all pairs of factors (λ_j, λ_k) where $k > j$, the following are computed:

(a) Angle of rotation

$$P = 1/4 \tan^{-1} (X/Y)$$

where

$$X = \begin{cases} D - 2AB/n & \text{Varimax} \\ D - mAB/n & \text{Equimax} \\ D & \text{Quartimax} \end{cases}$$

$$Y = \begin{cases} C - (A^2 - B^2)/n & \text{Varimax} \\ C - m(A^2 - B^2)/2n & \text{Equimax} \\ C & \text{Quartimax} \end{cases}$$

$$u_{p(i)} = f^{*2}_{pj(i)} - f^{*2}_{pk(i)} \qquad v_{p(i)} = 2f^{*}_{pj(i)} f^{*}_{pk(i)} \qquad p = 1, \ldots, n$$

$$A = \sum_{p=1}^{n} u_{p(i)} \qquad B = \sum_{p=1}^{n} v_{p(i)}$$

$$C = \sum_{p=1}^{n} [u^2_{p(i)} - v^2_{p(i)}] \quad D = \sum_{p=1}^{n} 2u_{p(i)} v_{p(i)}$$

If $|\sin(P)| \le 10^{-15}$, no rotation is done on the pair of factors.

(b) New rotated factors

$$(\tilde{\underline{\lambda}}_{j(i)}, \tilde{\underline{\lambda}}_{k(i)}) = (\underline{\lambda}^*_{j(i)}, \underline{\lambda}^*_{k(i)}) \begin{vmatrix} \cos(P) & -\sin(P) \\ \sin(P) & \cos(P) \end{vmatrix}$$

where $\underline{\lambda}^*_{j(i)}$ are the last values for factor j calculated in this iteration.

(c) Accrued rotation transformation matrix

$$(\tilde{t}_j, \tilde{t}_k) = (t_j, t_k) \begin{vmatrix} \cos(P) & -\sin(P) \\ \sin(P) & \cos(P) \end{vmatrix}$$

where t_j and t_k are the last calculated values of the jth and k^{th} columns of T.

(d) Iteration is terminated when

$$|SV_{(i)} - SV_{(i-1)}| \le 10^{-5}$$

or the maximum number of iterations is reached.

(e) Final rotated factor pattern matrix

$$\tilde{\Lambda}_m = H^{1/2} \Lambda^*_{m(f)}$$

where

$\dot{\Lambda}^*_{m(f)}$ is the value of the last iteration.

(f) Reflect factors with negative sums

If

$$\sum_{i=1}^{n} \tilde{\lambda}_{ij(f)} < 0$$

then

$$\tilde{\underline{\lambda}}_j = -\tilde{\underline{\lambda}}_{j(f)}$$

(g) Rearrange the rotated factors such that

$$\sum_{j=1}^{n} \tilde{\lambda}_{j1}^{2} \geq \ldots \geq \sum_{j=1}^{n} \tilde{\lambda}_{jm}^{2}$$

(h) The communalities are

$$h_j = \sum_{i=1}^{m} \tilde{\lambda}_{ji}^{2}$$

Oblique Rotations

The direct oblimin method (Jennrich and Sampson (1966)) is used for oblique rotation. The user can choose the parameter δ. The default value is $\delta = 0$.

(a) The factor pattern matrix is normalized by the square root of the communalities

$$\Omega_m^* = H^{-1/2} \Lambda_m$$

where

$$h_j = \sum_{k=1}^{m} \lambda_{jk}^{2}$$

If no Kaiser is specified, this normalization is not done.

(b) Initializations

The factor correlation matrix C is initialized to I_m. The following are also computed:

$$s_k = \begin{cases} 1 & \text{if Kaiser} \\ h_k & \text{if no Kaiser} \end{cases} \qquad k = 1, \ldots, n$$

$$u_i = \sum_{j=1}^{n} \lambda_{ji}^{*2} \qquad i = 1, \ldots, m$$

$$v_i = \sum_{j=1}^{n} \lambda_{ji}^{*4}$$

$$x_i = v_i - (\delta/n)\, u_i^2$$

$$D = \sum_{i=1}^{m} u_i$$

$$G = \sum_{i=1}^{m} x_i$$

$$H = \sum_{k=1}^{n} s_i^2 - (\delta/n)\, D^2$$

$$FO = H - G$$

(c) At each iteration, all possible factor pairs are rotated. For a pair of factors $\underline{\lambda}_p^*$ and $\underline{\lambda}_q^*$ $(p \neq q)$, the following are computed:

$$D_{pq} = D - u_p - u_q$$
$$G_{pq} = G - x_p - x_q$$
$$s_{pq,i} = s_i - \lambda_{ip}^{*2} - \lambda_{iq}^{*2}$$
$$y_{pq} = \sum_{i=1}^{n} \lambda_{ip}^{*} \lambda_{iq}^{*}$$
$$z_{pq} = \sum_{i=1}^{n} \lambda_{ip}^{*2} \lambda_{iq}^{*2}$$
$$T = \sum_{i=1}^{n} \lambda_{ip}^{*2} s_{pq,i} - (\delta / n)\, u_p D_{pq}$$
$$Z = \sum_{i=1}^{n} s_{pq,i} \lambda_{ip}^{*} \lambda_{iq}^{*} - (\delta / n)\, y_{pq} D_{pq}$$
$$P = \sum_{i=1}^{n} \lambda_{ip}^{*3} \lambda_{iq}^{*} - (\delta / n)\, u_p y_{pq}$$
$$R = z_{pq} - (\delta / n)\, u_p u_q$$
$$P' = \frac{3}{2}(c_{pq} - P / x_p)$$
$$Q' = \frac{1}{2}(x_p - 4c_{pq}P + R + 2T) / x_p$$
$$R' = (\frac{1}{2}(c_{pq}(T + R) - P - Z)) / x_p$$

- A root, a, of the equation

$$b^3 + P'b^2 + Q'b + R' = 0$$

is computed, as well as:

$$A = 1 + 2c_{pq}a + a^2$$
$$t_1 = |A|^{1/2}$$
$$t_2 = a / t_1$$

- The rotated pair of factors is

$$(\tilde{\underline{\lambda}}_p^{*}, \tilde{\underline{\lambda}}_q^{*}) = (\underline{\lambda}_p^{*}, \underline{\lambda}_q^{*}) \begin{vmatrix} t_1 & -a \\ 0 & 1 \end{vmatrix}$$

These replace the previous factor values.

- New values are computed for

$$\tilde{u}_p = |A|\, u_p$$
$$\tilde{x}_p = A^2 x_p$$
$$\tilde{v}_q = \sum_{i=1}^{n} \tilde{\lambda}_{iq}^{*4}$$
$$\tilde{u}_q = \sum_{i=1}^{n} \tilde{\lambda}_{iq}^{*2}$$

$$\tilde{x}_q = \tilde{v}_q - (\delta/n)\,\tilde{u}_q^2$$
$$\tilde{S}_k = S_{pq,k} + \tilde{\lambda}_{kp}^{*2} + \tilde{\lambda}_{kq}^{*2}$$
$$\tilde{D} = D_{pq} + \tilde{u}_p + \tilde{u}_q$$
$$\tilde{G} = G_{pq} + \tilde{x}_p + \tilde{x}_q$$

All values designated as $\tilde{V}$ replaces V and are used in subsequent calculations.

- The new factor correlations with factor p are

$$\tilde{c}_{ip} = t_1^{-1} c_{ip} + t_2 c_{iq} \qquad (i \neq p)$$
$$\tilde{c}_{pi} = \tilde{c}_{ip}$$
$$\tilde{c}_{pp} = 1$$

- After all factor pairs have been rotated, iteration is terminated if

MAX iterations have been done

or

$$\left| F1_{(i)} - F1_{(i-1)} \right| < (FO)\,(EPS)$$

where

$$F1_{(i)} = \tilde{H} - \tilde{G}$$
$$\tilde{H} = \sum_{k=1}^{n} \tilde{s}_k^2 - (\delta/n)\,\tilde{D}^2$$
$$F1_{(0)} = FO$$

Otherwise, the factor pairs are rotated again.

- The final rotated factor pattern matrix is

$$\tilde{\lambda}_m = H^{1/2} \tilde{\lambda}_m^*$$

where $\tilde{\lambda}_m$ is the value in the final iteration.

- The factor structure matrix is

$$S = \tilde{\Lambda}_m \tilde{C}_m$$

where $\tilde{C}_m$ is the factor correlation matrix in the final iteration.

Factor Score Coefficients (Harman (1976))

Regression

$$W = \begin{cases} \Lambda_m \Gamma_m^{-1} & \text{PC without rotation} \\ S_m (S'_m S_m)^{-1} & \text{PC with rotation} \\ R^{-1} S_m & \text{otherwise} \end{cases}$$

where

S_m = factor structure matrix

$S_m = \Lambda_m$ for orthogonal rotations

For PA1 without rotation if any $|\gamma_i| \leq 10^{-8}$, factor score coefficients are not computed. For PC with rotation if the determinant of $S'_m S_m$ is less than 10^{-8}, the coefficients are not computed. Otherwise, if R is singular, factor score coefficients are not computed.

Bartlett

$$W = J^{-1} \Lambda' U^{-2}$$

where

$$J = \Lambda' U^{-2} \Lambda$$

$$U^2 = R - \hat{R}$$

Anderson Rubin

$$W = (\Lambda' U^{-2} R U^{-2} \Lambda)^{-1/2} \Lambda' U^{-2}$$

where the symmetric square root of the parenthetical term is taken.

Optional Statistics (Dziubin & Shirkey (1974))

- The anti-image covariance matrix $A = (a_{ij})$ is given by

$$a_{ij} = \frac{r^{ij}}{r^{ii} r^{jj}}$$

- The chi-square value for Bartlett's test of sphericity is

$$\chi^2 = -(W - 1 - \frac{2p+5}{6}) \log|R|$$

with $p(p-1)/2$ degrees of freedom.

- The Kaiser-Mayer-Olkin measure of sampling adequacy is

$$KMO_j = \frac{\sum_{i \neq j} r_{ij}^2}{\sum_{i \neq j} r_{ij}^2 + \sum_{i \neq j} a_{ij}^{2*}} \qquad KMO = \frac{\Sigma\Sigma_{i \neq j}\, r_{ij}^2}{\Sigma\Sigma_{i \neq j}\, r_{ij}^2 + \Sigma\Sigma_{i \neq j}\, a_{ij}^{*\,2}}$$

where a_{ij}^* is the anti-image correlation coefficient.

References

Dziubin & Shirkey (1974)
Harman (1976)
Jöreskog (1977)
Kaiser (1963)
Rummel (1970)

FIT

General

Procedure FIT displays a variety of descriptive statistics computed from the residual series as an aid in evaluating the goodness of fit of one or more models.

Notation

DFH	hypothesis degrees of freedom
DFE	error degrees of freedom
$e_1, \ldots, e_n$	residual (error) series
$X_1, \ldots, X_n$	observed series
n	number of cases

The Statistics Computed in FIT

- Mean Error (ME)

$$ME = \sum_{i=1}^{n} e_i/n$$

- Mean Percent Error (MPE)

$$MPE = \frac{100}{n}\sum_{i=1}^{n} e_i/X_i$$

- Mean Absolute Error (MAE)

$$MAE = \sum_{i=1}^{n} |e_i|/n$$

- Mean Absolute Percent Error (MAPE)

$$MAPE = \frac{100}{n}\sum_{i=1}^{n} |e_i/X_i|$$

- Sum of Square Error (SSE)

$$SSE = \sum_{i=1}^{n} e_i^2$$

- Mean Square Error (MSE)

$$MSE = \begin{cases} SSE/n & \text{, if none of DFE and DFH is specified} \\ SSE/DFE & \text{, if DFE is specified or DFH is specified; then DFE = n-DFH.} \end{cases}$$

- Root Mean Square Error (RMS)

$$RMS = \sqrt{MSE}$$

- Durbin-Watson Statistics (DW)

$$DW = \frac{\sum_{i=1}^{n-1} (e_i - e_{i+1})^2}{\sum_{i=1}^{n} e_i^2}$$

FREQUENCIES

General

If the absolute value of any observation is greater than 10^{13}, no calculations are done. The GENERAL and INTEGER versions of this routine differ in the computation of the median, as well as the need to sort the observations. (See Appendix 6.)

Notation

X_k	value of the variable for case k
w_k	weight for case k
NV	number of distinct values the variable assumes
N	number of cases
W	sum of weights of the cases

Basic Statistics

The values are sorted into ascending order (GENERAL mode only) and the following calculated:

- Sum of weights of cases having each value of X

$$f_j = \sum_{i=1}^{N} w_i k_i \qquad j = 1, 2, \ldots, NV$$

where

$$k_i = \begin{cases} 1 & \text{if } X_i = X_j \\ 0 & \text{otherwise} \end{cases}$$

where X_j is the jth largest distinct value of X.

- Relative frequency (percentage) for each value of X

$$Rf_j = \left(\frac{f_j}{W'}\right) 100$$

where

$$W' = \sum_{i=1}^{NV} f_i \quad \text{(sum over all categories including those declared as missing values)}$$

- Adjusted frequency (percentage)

$$Af_j = \left(\frac{f_j}{W}\right) 100$$

where

$$W = \sum_{i=1}^{NV} f_i k_i \qquad \text{(sum over nonmissing categories)}$$

and

$$k_i = \begin{cases} 0 & \text{if } X_i \text{ has been declared missing} \\ 1 & \text{otherwise} \end{cases}$$

For all X_j declared missing, an adjusted frequency is not printed.

- Cumulative frequency (percentage)

$$Cf_j = \sum_{i=1}^{j} f_i$$

- Minimum

$$\min_k X_k$$

- Maximum

$$\max_k X_k$$

- Mode

Value of X_j which has the largest observed frequency. If several are tied, the smallest value is selected.

- Range

Maximum-Minimum

- The pth percentile

Find the first score interval ($x2$) containing more than tp cases.

$$p^{th} \text{ percentile} = \begin{cases} x_2 & \text{if } tp - cp_1 \geq 100/W \\ \{1 - [(W+1)p/100 - cc_1]x_1\} + [(W+1)p/100 - cc_1]x_2 & \text{if } tp - cp_1 < 100/W \end{cases}$$

where

$tp = (W+1)p/W$

$cp_1 < tp < cp_2$

x_1 and x_2 are the values corresponding to cp_1 and cp_2, respectively

cc_1 is the cumulative frequency up to x_1

cp_1 is the cumulative percent up to x_1

- Mean

$$\bar{X} = \frac{\sum_{j=1}^{NV} f_j X_j}{W}$$

- Moments about the mean are calculated as

$$M_j = \sum_{i=1}^{NV} f_i (X_i - \bar{X})^j \qquad j = 2, 3, 4$$

- Variance

$$S^2 = \frac{M_2}{(W-1)}$$

- Standard deviation

$$S = \sqrt{S^2}$$

- Standard error of the mean

$$SEM = \frac{S}{\sqrt{W}}$$

- Skewness (computed if $W \geq 3$ and $S^2 > 0$) (Bliss (1967), p. 144)

$$g_1 = \frac{WM_3}{(W-1)(W-2)S^3} \qquad SE(g_1) = \sqrt{\frac{6W(W-1)}{(W-2)(W+1)(W+3)}}$$

- Kurtosis (computed if $W \geq 4$ and $S^2 > 0$)

$$g_2 = \frac{\left[\frac{(W+1)M_4}{W} - \frac{3(W-1)M_2^2}{W^2}\right]W^2}{(W-1)(W-2)(W-3)S^4} \qquad SE(g_2) = \sqrt{\frac{(4W^2-1)SE(g_1)^2}{(W-3)(W+5)}}$$

References

Blalock (1972)

Bliss (1967)

HILOGLINEAR

The Model Minimum Configuration

Consider an $I \times J \times K$ table. Let n_{ijk} be the observed frequency and m_{ijk} the expected frequency for cell (*i,j,k*). A simple way to construct a linear model in the natural logarithms of the expected cell frequencies is by analogy with analysis of variance (ANOVA) models:

$$L_{ijk} \equiv \log(m_{ijk}) = u + u_i^A + u_j^B + u_k^C + u_{ij}^{AB} + u_{ik}^{AC} + u_{jk}^{BC} + u_{ijk}^{ABC} \tag{1}$$

where $1 \le i \le I$, $1 \le j \le J$, and $1 \le k \le K$. In general, each of the seven subscripted *u-terms* sums to zero over each lettered subscript.

It can be shown (Bishop et al. (1975), p. 65) that, under the commonly encountered sampling plans, the log-likelihood is

$$\Phi + Nu + \sum_i n_{i++} u_i^A + \sum_j n_{+j+} u_j^B + \sum_k n_{++k} u_k^C + \sum_{i,j} n_{ij+} u_{ij}^{AB} +$$

$$\sum_{i,k} n_{i+k} u_{ik}^{AC} + \sum_{j,k} n_{+jk} u_{jk}^{BC} + \sum_{i,j,k} n_{ijk} u_{ijk}^{ABC}$$

where Φ is independent of any parameters and N is total number of observations. Also, the n-terms adjacent to the unknown parameters are the sufficient statistics. The formulation of the above log likelihood is based on the saturated model (1). When we consider unsaturated models, terms drop out and those that remain give the sufficient statistics. For instance, if we assume that there is no three-factor effect, that is, $u_{ijk}^{ABC} = 0$ for all i, j, and k, or more briefly $u_{ijk} = 0$, then

$$\log(m_{ijk}) = u + u_i^A + u_j^B + u_k^C + u_{ij}^{AB} + u_{ik}^{AC} + u_{jk}^{BC} \tag{2}$$

and n_{i++}, n_{+j+}, n_{++k}, n_{ij+}, n_{i+k}, and n_{+jk} are the sufficient statistics for this reduced model. These statistics can be considered as *tables of sums configurations* and denoted by C with proper subscripts. For example, $\{n_{ij+}\}$ is the configuration C_{12} and $\{n_{++k}\}$ is the configuration C_3. Note that $\{n_{i++}\}$, $\{n_{+j+}\}$, and $\{n_{++k}\}$ can be obtained from $\{n_{ij+}\}$, $\{n_{i+k}\}$, and $\{n_{+jk}\}$. We then call the last three configurations C_{12}, C_{13}, and C_{23} *minimal configurations* or *minimal statistics.*

Notation for Unlimited Number of Dimensions

To generalize results, we denote the complete set of subscripts by a single symbol θ. Thus, n_θ is the observed frequency in an elementary cell and w_θ is the cell weight. We add a subscript to θ to denote a reduced dimensionality so that $n_{\theta i}$ is the observed sum in a cell of $C_{\theta i}$. We use the second subscript, *i*, solely to distinguish between different configurations.

Iterative Proportional Fitting Procedure (IPFP)

We can obtain MLEs for the elementary cells under any hierarchical model by iterative fitting of the minimal sufficient configurations. To illustrate the algorithm, we consider model (2). The MLEs must fit the configurations C_{12}, C_{13}, and C_{23}. The basic IPFP chooses an initial table $m_{ijk}^{(0)}$ and then sequentially adjusts the preliminary estimates to fit C_{12}, C_{13}, and C_{23}. Fitting to C_{12} gives

$$\hat{m}_{ijk}^{(1)} = \hat{m}_{ijk}^{(0)} \frac{n_{ij+}}{\hat{m}_{ij+}^{(0)}}$$

Subsequent fitting to C_{13} gives

$$\hat{m}_{ijk}^{(2)} = \hat{m}_{ijk}^{(1)} \frac{n_{i+k}}{\hat{m}_{i+k}^{(1)}}$$

and similarly, after fitting C_{23} we have

$$\hat{m}_{ijk}^{(3)} = \hat{m}_{ijk}^{(2)} \frac{n_{+jk}}{\hat{m}_{+jk}^{(2)}}$$

We repeat this three-step cycle until convergence to the desired accuracy is attained. The extension of the above procedure to the general procedure for fitting s configurations is straightforward. Let the minimal configurations be $C_{\theta i}$ for $i = 1, 2, \ldots, s$, with cell entries n_{θ_i}, respectively. The procedure is as follows:

- Initial Cell Estimates

To start the iterations, set

$$m_{\theta}^{(0)} = \begin{cases} 1 & \text{if } n_{\theta} > 0 \\ 0.5 & \text{if } n_{\theta} = 0 \\ 0 & \text{otherwise} \end{cases}$$

- Intermediate Computations

After obtaining the initial cell estimates, the algorithm proceeds to fit each of these configurations in turn. After r cycles, the relations are

$$\hat{m}_{\theta}^{(sr+i)} = \hat{m}_{\theta}^{(sr+i-1)} \frac{n_{\theta_i}}{\hat{m}_{\theta_i}^{(sr+i-1)}} \qquad \text{for } 1 \le i \le s; r \ge 0$$

- Convergence Criteria

The computations stop either when a complete cycle, which consists of s steps, does not cause any cell to change by more than a preset amount ε; that is,

$$\left|\hat{m}_{\theta}^{(sr)} - \hat{m}_{\theta}^{(sr-s)}\right| < \varepsilon \text{ for all } \theta$$

or the number of cycles is larger than a preset integer *max*. Both ε and *max* can be specified. The default for ε is

$$\varepsilon = \max_{\theta} \{0.25; \frac{n_{\theta} w_{\theta}}{1000}\}$$

and the default for *max* is 20.

Goodness of Fit Tests

The Pearson chi-square statistic is

$$\chi^2 = \sum_{\theta} \frac{(n_\theta - \hat{m}_\theta)^2}{\hat{m}_\theta}$$

and the likelihood-ratio chi-square statistic is

$$L^2 = 2\sum_{\theta} n_\theta \ln (n_\theta / \hat{m}_\theta)$$

where the first summation is done over the cells with nonzero estimated cell frequencies while the second summation is done over cells with positive observed and estimated cell frequencies. The degrees of freedom for the above two statistics are computed as follows:

- Adjusted Degrees of Freedom

Let T_c be the total number of the cells and P the number of parameters in the model. Also, let z_c be the number of cells such that $\hat{m}_\theta = 0$. The adjusted degrees of freedom is

$$\text{adjusted df} = T_c - P - z_c$$

- Unadjusted Degrees of Freedom

$$\text{unadjusted df} = T_c - P$$

Parameter Estimates and Standard Errors

If a saturated model is fitted and neither $n_\theta + \delta$ nor w_θ is equal to 0 for all cells, then the parameter estimates and their standard errors will be computed. Each estimate of the parameters in the saturated model can be expressed as a linear combination of the logarithms of the observed cell frequencies plus user-specified δ, where the coefficients used in the linear combination add to zero. We discuss the rule of obtaining the coefficients. Consider, in general case, a $J_1 \times J_2 \times \ldots \times J_M$ frequency table with defining variables $X_1, \ldots, X_M$. Let $u_{j_{s1}, \ldots, j_{s1}}^{X_{s1}, \ldots, X_{sL}}$ denote an L-term interaction involving $X_{s1}, \ldots, X_{sL}$ at level $j_{s1}, \ldots, j_{sL}$ respectively. Denote A as a vector that is constructed in the way that its nonzero components correspond to the variables in the parameter to be estimated and are set to the level of the variable. Let $C_{j_1, \ldots, j_M}$ be a M-dim vector with components equal to cell IDs. That is,

$$C_{j_1, \ldots, j_M} = (j_1, \ldots, j_M)\,;\, 1 \le j_1 \le J_1,\ 1 \le i \le M$$

The coefficient $\beta_{j_1, \ldots, j_M}$ is determined through the comparison of the components of A and $C_{j_1, \ldots, j_M}$. Let s be the number of nonzero components of A that do not match (equal) the corresponding components of $C_{j_1, \ldots, j_M}$. Also, let matching occur at component $i_1, \ldots, i_K$. Then the coefficient for cell $(j_1, \ldots, j_M)$ is

$$\beta_{j_1, \ldots, j_M} = (-1)^s (J_{i_1} - 1) \times \ldots \times (J_{i_K} - 1)$$

The estimate $\hat{u}_{j_{s1}, \ldots, j_{s1}}^{X_{s1}, \ldots, X_{sL}}$ of $u_{j_{s1}, \ldots, j_{s1}}^{X_{s1}, \ldots, X_{sL}}$ is then

$$\hat{u}_{j_{s1}, \ldots, j_{s1}}^{X_{s1}, \ldots, X_{sL}} = \sum_{j_1, \ldots, j_M} \beta_{j_1, \ldots, j_M} \ln (n_{j_1, \ldots, j_M} + \delta) \qquad (3)$$

The large-sample variance of the estimate (3) is

$$\sum_{j_1, \ldots, j_M} \beta^2_{j_1, \ldots, j_M} [\ln (n_{j_1, \ldots, j_M} + \delta)]^{-1} \quad (4)$$

For a large sample, estimate (3) approximately follows a normal distribution with mean $u^{X_{s1}, \ldots, X_{sL}}_{j_{s1}, \ldots, j_{s1}}$ and variance (4) if the sampling model follows a Poisson, multinomial, or product-multinomial distribution. The confidence interval for the parameter can be computed based on the asymptotic normality.

Raw Residuals and Standardized Residuals

Two different residuals are computed:

- Raw Residual

  raw residual = $n_\theta - \hat{m}_\theta$

- Standardized Residual

  standardized residual = $(n_\theta - \hat{m}_\theta) / \sqrt{\hat{m}_\theta}$

where $\hat{m}_\theta$ must be greater than 0.

Partial Associations and Partial Chi-squares

Partial associations of effects can be requested when a saturated model is specified. Let $\chi^2(k)$ be the chi-square for the model that contains the effects up to and including the *k*-interaction terms. The test of the significance of the *k*th-order interaction can be based on

$$\chi^2(k-1) - \chi^2(k)$$

Degrees of freedom are obtained by subtracting the degrees of freedom for the corresponding models.

Model Selection Via Backward Elimination

The selection process starts with the model specified (either via DESIGN or MAXORDER subcommand). The partial chi-square is calculated for every term in the generating class. Any term with zero partial chi-square is deleted, then the effect with the largest observed significance level for the change in chi-square is deleted, provided the significance level is larger than 0.05, the default. With the removal of a highest-order term, a new model with new generating class is generated. The above process of removing a term is repeated for the new model and is continued until no remaining terms in the model can be deleted.

References

Bishop et al. (1975)

Fienberg (1977)

HOMALS

The iterative HOMALS algorithm is a modernized version of Guttman (1941). The treatment of missing values, described below, is based on setting weights in the loss function equal to zero, and was first described in De Leeuw and Van Rijckevorsel (1980). Other possibilities do exist and can be accomplished by recoding the data (Gifi, 1981; Meulman, 1982).

Notation

n	number of cases (objects)
m	number of variables
p	number of dimensions.

For variable j, $j = 1, \ldots, m$

h_j	n-vector with categorical observations
k_j	number of valid categories (distinct values) of variable j
G_j	indicator matrix for variable j, of order $n \times k_j$

$$g_{(j)ir} = \begin{cases} 1 \text{ when the } i^{th} \text{ object is in the } r^{th} \text{ category of variable } j \\ 0 \text{ when the } i^{th} \text{ object is not in the } r^{th} \text{ category of variable } j \end{cases}$$

M_j binary, diagonal $n \times n$ matrix, with diagonal elements defined as

$$m_{(j)ii} = \begin{cases} 1 \text{ when the } i^{th} \text{ observation is within the range } [1, k_j] \\ 0 \text{ when the } i^{th} \text{ observation is outside the range } [1, k_j] \end{cases}$$

D_j diagonal matrix containing the univariate marginals, i.e., the column sums of G_j.

The quantification matrices are

X	object scores, of order $n \times p$
Y_j	category quantifications, of order $k_j \times p$
Y	concatenated category quantification matrices, of order $\sum_j k_j \times p$.

Note: the matrices G_j M_j and D_j are exclusively notational devices; they are stored in reduced form, and the program fully profits from their sparseness by replacing matrix multiplications with selective accumulation.

Objective Function Optimization

The HOMALS objective is to find object scores X and a set of Y_j (for $j = 1, ..., m$) so that the function

$$\sigma(X;Y) = 1/m \sum_j \operatorname{tr} (X - G_j Y_j)' M_j (X - G_j Y_j)$$

is minimal, under the normalization restriction $X' M_* X = mnI$, where the matrix $M_* = \sum_j M_j$, and I is the $p \times p$ identity matrix. The inclusion of M_j in $\sigma(X;Y)$ ensures that there is no influence of data values outside the range $[1, k_j]$, which may be really missing or merely regarded as such; M_* contains the number of "active" data values for each object. The object scores are also centered; i.e., they satisfy $u' M_* X = 0$, with u denoting an n-vector with ones.

Optimization is achieved through the following iteration scheme:

1. Initialization
2. Update object scores
3. Orthonormalization
4. Update category quantifications
5. Convergence test: repeat 2–4 or continue
6. Rotation

These steps are explained below.

1. Initialization

The object scores X are initialized with random numbers, which are normalized so that $u' M_* X = 0$ and $X' M_* X = mnI$, yielding $\tilde{X}$. Then the first category quantifications are obtained as $\tilde{Y}_j = D_j^{-1} G_j' \tilde{X}$.

2. Update object scores

First the auxiliary score matrix Z is computed as

$$Z \leftarrow \sum_j M_j G_j \tilde{Y}_j$$

and centered with respect to M_*:

$$\tilde{Z} \leftarrow \{M_* - (M_* u u' M_* / u' M_* u)\} Z.$$

These two steps yield locally the best updates when there are no orthogonality constraints.

3. Orthonormalization

The orthonormalization problem is to find an M_*-orthonormal X^+ that is closest to $\tilde{Z}$ in the least squares sense. In HOMALS this is done by setting

$$X^+ \leftarrow m^{1/2} M_*^{-1/2} \text{GRAM} (M_*^{-1/2} \tilde{Z}),$$

which is equal to the genuine least squares estimate up to a rotation. The notation GRAM ( ) is used to denote the Gram-Schmidt transformation (Björk and Golub, 1973).

4. Update category quantifications

For $j = 1, ..., m$ the new category quantifications are computed as:

$$Y_j^+ = D_j^{-1} G_j' \tilde{X}$$

5. Convergence test

The difference between consecutive loss function values $\sigma(\tilde{X};\tilde{Y}) - \sigma(X^+;Y^+)$ is compared with the user-specified convergence criterion ε—a small positive number. Steps 2 to 4 are repeated as long as the loss difference exceeds ε.

6. Rotation

As indicated in 3, during iteration the orientation of X and Y with respect to the coordinate system is not necessarily correct; this also reflects the fact that $\sigma(X;Y)$ is invariant under simultaneous rotations of X and Y. From theory it is known that solutions in different dimensionality should be nested; i.e., the p-dimensional solution should be equal to the first p columns of the $(p+1)$-dimensional solution. Nestedness is achieved by computing the eigenvectors of the matrix $1/m \sum_j Y'_j D_j Y_j$. The corresponding eigenvalues are printed after the convergence message of the program. The calculation involves tridiagonalization with Householder transformations followed by the implicit QL algorithm (Wilkinson, 1965).

Diagnostics

- Maximum rank (may be issued as a warning when exceeded)

The maximum rank p_{max} indicates the maximum number of dimensions that can be computed for any data set. In general we have:

$$p_{max} = \min\{(n-1), ((\textstyle\sum_j k_j) - \max(m_1, 1))\},$$

where m_1 is the number of variables with no missing values. Although the number of nontrivial dimensions may be less than p_{max} when $m = 2$, HOMALS does allow dimensionalities all the way up to p_{max}.

- Marginal frequencies

The frequencies table gives the univariate marginals and the number of missing values (i.e., values that are regarded as out of range for the current analysis) for each variable. These are computed as the column sums of D_j and the total sum of M_j.

- The discrimination measure

These are the dimensionwise variances of the quantified variables. For variable j and dimension s, we have:

$$\eta^2_{js} = y_{(j)s}' D_j y_{(j)s} / n,$$

where $y_{(j)s}$ is the sth column of Y_j, corresponding to the sth quantified variable $G_j y_{(j)s}$.

- Eigenvalues

The computation of the eigenvalues that are reported after convergence is discussed in 6. With the HISTORY option, the sum of the eigenvalues is reported during iteration under the heading "total fit." Due to the fact that the sum of the eigenvalues is equal to the trace of the original matrix, the sum can be computed as $1/m\sum_j\sum_s\eta_{js}^2$. The value of $\sigma(X;Y)$ is equal to $p-1/m\sum_j\sum_s\eta_{js}^2$.

References

Björk& Golub (1973)

De Leeuw& Van Rijckevorsel (1980)

Gifi (1981)

Guttman (1941)

Meulman (1982)

Wilkinson(1965)

Kaplan-Meier (KM)

General

This procedure estimates the survival function for time to occurence of an event. Some of the times may be "censored" in that the event does not occur during the observation period, or contact is lost with participants (loss to follow-up).

If the subjects are divided into treatment groups, KM produces a survival function for each treatment group (factor level) and a test of equality of the survival functions across treatment groups. The survival functions across treatment groups can also be compared while controlling for categories of a stratification variable.

Notation

p	number of levels (strata) for the stratification variable
g	number of levels (treatment groups) for the factor variable

Estimation and SE for Survival Distribution

Suppose that for a given combination of the stratification and factor variables, a random sample of n individuals yields a sample with k distinct observed failure times (uncensored). Let $t_1 < \ldots < t_k$ represent the observed life times and T_L be the largest observation in the sample. (Note that $T_L = t_k$ if the largest observation is uncensored). Define

n_i = Number of subjects who are at risk at time t_i.

d_i = Number of failures (deaths) at t_i.

λ_i = Number of censorings in interval $[t_i, t_{i+1})$

Note :

$$n_0 = n$$
$$n_{i+1} = n_i - d_i - \lambda_i,\ i = 0, 1, \ldots, k-1$$
$$t_0 = 0$$
$$t_{k+1} = \infty$$
$$d_0 = 0$$
$$\lambda_0 = 0$$

The Kaplan-Meier estimate $\hat{S}(t)$ for the survival function is computed as

$$\hat{S}(t) = \prod_{t_i < t} \left(1 - \frac{d_i}{n_i}\right)$$

Note that

$$\hat{S}(t_l^+) = \prod_{i=1}^{l}(1-\frac{d_i}{n_i}),\ l = 1, 2, \ldots, k.$$

$$\hat{S}(t_0^+) = 1$$

$$\hat{S}(t_{l+1}^+) = \hat{S}(t_l^+)\left(1-\frac{d_{l+1}}{n_{l+1}}\right)$$

$$\hat{S}(t_k^+) = 0 \text{ if } n_k = d_k\ (T_l = t_k \text{ and } \lambda_k = 0), \text{ otherwise}$$

$$\hat{S}(t_k^+) = \prod_{l=1}^{k}(1-\frac{d_l}{n_l}),\ T_L \ge t \ge t_k$$

$\hat{S}(t_1^+), \ldots, \hat{S}(t_k^+)$ are the survival functions shown in the table.

The asymptotic standard error for $\hat{S}(t_l^+)$ is computed as the square root of

$$Var(\hat{S}(t_l^+)) = [\hat{S}(t_l^+)]^2\sum_{i=1}^{l}\frac{d_i}{n_i(n_i-d_i)},\ l = 1, \ldots, k.$$

Note: When $n_k = d_k$ ($T_L = t_k$ and $\lambda_k = 0$), $\hat{S}(t_k^+) = 0$ and $Var(\hat{S}(t_k^+)) = 0$.

Estimation of Mean Survival Time and Standard Error

$$\hat{\mu} = \begin{cases} \sum_{i=0}^{k-1}\hat{S}(t_i^+)(t_{i+1}-t_i) & \text{if } T_L = t_k \\ \sum_{i=0}^{k-1}\hat{S}(t_i^+)(t_{i+1}-t_i) + \hat{S}(t_k^+)(T_L-t_k) & \text{otherwise} \end{cases}$$

The variance of the mean survival time is

$$Var(\hat{\mu}) = \sum_{i=1}^{k}\frac{a_i^2 d_i}{n_i(n_i-d_i)}$$

$$a_i = \sum_{l=i}^{k-1}\hat{S}(t_l^+)(t_{l+1}-t_l) + \hat{S}(t_k^+)(T_L-t_k)$$

$$d = \sum_{i=1}^{k}d_i$$

unless there are both censored and uncensored occurrences of the largest survival time. In that case,

$$Var(\hat{\mu}) = \frac{d}{d-1}\sum_{i=1}^{k-1}\frac{a_i^2 d_i}{n_i(n_i-d_i)}$$

$$a_i = \sum_{l=i}^{k-1}\hat{S}(t_l^+)(t_{l+1}-t_l)$$

The standard error is the square root of the variance.

Plots

- Survival Functions vs. Time
  The survival function $\hat{S}(t)$ is plotted against *t*.

- Log Survival Functions vs. Time
  $ln(\hat{S}(t))$ is plotted against *t*.

- Cumulative Hazard Functions vs. Time
  $-ln(\hat{S}(t))$ is plotted against *t*.

Estimation of Percentiles and Standard Error

100p percentile of the survival time, where *p* is between 0 and 1, is computed as

$$t_p = inf\{t_i | (\hat{S}(t_i) \le p)\}$$

The asymptotic variance of t_p is estimated by

$$Var(t_p) = \frac{Var(\hat{S}(t_p))}{(\hat{f}(t_p))^2}$$

where $\hat{f}(t_p)$ is computed as

$$\hat{f}(t_p) = \frac{\hat{S}(u_{p+0.05}) - \hat{S}(t_{p-0.05})}{t_{p-0.05} - u_{p+0.05}}$$

where $u_q = sup\{t_i | (\hat{S}(t_i) \ge q)\}$.

Testing the Equality of the Survival Functions

Three statistics are computed to test the equality of survival distributions in the presence of arbitrary right censorship. These statistics are the logrank(Mantel-Cox), the modified Wilcoxon test statistic (Breslow), and an alternative test statistic proposed by Tarone and Ware (1977). Using the regression model proposed by Cox (1972), all three test statistics have been modified for testing monotonic trend in hazard functions.

- Test Statistics

Let $n^{(s)}$ be the number of subjects in stratum *s*. Let

$$t_1^{(s)} < \ldots < t_{m_s}^{(s)}$$

be the observed failure times (responses) and

$n_{li}^{(s)}$ = In stratum s the number of individuals in group l at risk just prior to $t_i^{(s)}$

$d_{li}^{(s)}$ = number of deaths at $t_i^{(s)}$ in group l

and

$$d_i^{(s)} = \sum_{l=1}^{g} d_{li}^{(s)}$$

$$n_i^{(s)} = \sum_{l=1}^{g} n_{li}^{(s)}$$

Hence, the expected number of events in group l at time $t_i^{(s)}$ is given by

$$E_{li}^{(s)} = \frac{d_i^{(s)} n_{li}^{(s)}}{n_i^{(s)}}$$

Define

$$U_s = (U_1^{(s)}, \ldots, U_{g-1}^{(s)})'$$

with

$$U_l^{(s)} = \sum_{i=1}^{m_s} w_i^{(s)} (d_{li}^{(s)} - E_{li}^{(s)}) \quad \text{for } l = 1, \ldots, g-1.$$

Also, let V_s be a $(g-1) \times (g-1)$ covariance matrix with

$$V_{jl}^{(s)} = \sum_{i=1}^{m_s} (w_i^{(s)})^2 \frac{d_i^{(s)} (n_i^{(s)} - d_i^{(s)})}{n_i^{(s)} - 1} \frac{n_{ji}^{(s)}}{n_i^{(s)}} \left(\delta_{jl} - \frac{n_{li}^{(s)}}{n_i^{(s)}} \right) \quad \text{for } j, l = 1, \ldots, g-1$$

where

$$w_i^{(s)} = 1 \quad \text{for log-rank test}$$

$$w_i^{(s)} = n_i^{(s)} \quad \text{for Breslow test}$$

$$w_i^{(s)} = \sqrt{n_i^{(s)}} \quad \text{for Tarone Ware test}$$

and

$$\delta_{jl} = \begin{cases} 1 & \text{if } j = l \\ 0 & \text{otherwise} \end{cases}$$

Define

$$U = \sum_{s=1}^{p} U_s$$

and

$$V = \sum_{s=1}^{p} V_s$$

The test statistic for the equality of the g survival functions is defined by

$$\chi^2 = U'V^{-1}U$$

χ^2 has an asymptotic chi-square distribution with $(g-1)$ degrees of freedom.

- Test Statistic for Trend

Let

$$t = (t_1, \ldots, t_g)'$$

be a vector with t_j = trend weighting coefficient for group *j*. Form the vector

$$U_{(s)} = (U_1^{(s)}, \ldots, U_g^{(s)})'$$

$U_{(s)}$ differs from U_s only in the last component.

Let $V^{(s)}$ be a $g \times g$ matrix with element $V_{lj}^{(s)}$ for $1 \le l, j \le g$. The test statistic is defined by

$$\chi_t^2 = \frac{(t'U)^2}{t'Vt}$$

where

$$U = \sum_{s=1}^{p} U_{(s)}$$

$$V = \sum_{s=1}^{p} V_{(s)}$$

The logrank, Breslow, and Tarone Ware tests may involve trend. Each of the test statistics has a chi-square distribution with one degree of freedom.

The default trend is defined as follows:

$$t = \begin{cases} (-(g-1), \ldots, -3, -1, 1, 3, \ldots, (g-1)) & \text{if } g \text{ is even} \\ (-\frac{(g-1)}{2}, \ldots, -1, 0, 1, \ldots, \frac{(g-1)}{2}) & \text{otherwise} \end{cases}$$

References

Cox (1972)

Tarone & Ware (1977)

Tarone (1975)

LOGLINEAR

General

The LOGLINEAR procedure models cell frequencies using the multinomial response model and produces maximum likelihood estimates of parameters by the Newton-Raphson method. The contingency tables are converted to two-way $I \times J$ tables, with I and J being the dimensions of the independent and dependent categorical variables respectively.

Notation

n_{ij}	Observed frequency of cell (i, j)
I	Dimension of the row variable, associated with independent variables
J	Dimension of the column variable, associated with dependent variable
w_{ij}	Weight of cell (i, j)
β_k	Coefficients in the loglinear model; $1 \le k \le p$
$\beta_k^{(l)}$	Estimate of β_k at the lth iteration
$\hat{\beta}_k$	Final estimate of β_k
m_{ij}	Expected values of n_{ij}
$m_{ij}^{(l)}$	Estimate of m_{ij} at the lth iteration
$\hat{m}_{ij}$	Estimate of m_{ij} at the final iteration
$\hat{M}_{i.}$	$\sum_{j=1}^{J} \hat{m}_{ij}$
$\hat{M}_{.j}$	$\sum_{i=1}^{I} \hat{m}_{ij}$
M	$\sum_{j=1}^{J} \sum_{i=1}^{I} \hat{m}_{ij}$

Model

In the general LOGLINEAR model, the logarithms of the cell frequencies are formulated as a linear function of the parameters. The actual form of the model is determined by the contrast and the effects specified. The model has the form

$$y_{ij} \equiv ln\left(\frac{m_{ij}}{w_{ij}}\right) = \lambda_i + \sum_{k=1}^{p} \beta_k x_{ijk} \quad 1 \le i \le I,\ 1 \le j \le J$$

where λ_i are chosen so that $\sum_j m_{ij} = \sum_j n_{ij}$, and x_{ijk} are the independent variables in the linear model.

Contrasts

The values of x_{ijk} are determined by the types of contrasts specified in the procedure. The default contrast is DEVIATION.

Computational Algorithm

To estimate the coefficients, a series of weighted regressions is used for iterative calculations. The iterative process is outlined (also see Haberman, 1978) as follows:

(1) Obtain initial approximations $y_{ij}^{(0)}$ and use them to obtain $\beta_k^{(0)}$

(2) Obtain the next approximations $y_{ij}^{(1)}$ and $m_{ij}^{(1)}$

(3) Use the updated $y_{ij}^{(1)}$ in (2) to obtain the next approximations $\beta_k^{(1)}$

(4) Repeat (2) and (3), replacing $\beta_k^{(l)}$ with $\beta_k^{(l+1)}$. Continue repeating this until convergence is achieved.

The computations begin with selection of initial approximations $m_{ij}^{(0)} = n_{ij} + \delta$ for m_{ij}. The default for δ is 0.5. If the model is saturated, δ is added to n_{ij} permanently. So, for a saturated model, the observed counts n_{ij} are increased by δ. If the model is not saturated, δ is added to n_{ij} only at the initial step, and is then subtracted at the second step.

The maximum likelihood estimates $\hat{\beta}_k$ of β_k are found by the Newton-Raphson method. Let $\beta^{(l)}$ be the column vector containing the ML estimates at the lth iteration; then

$$\beta^{(0)} = (C^{(0)})^{-1} a^{(0)}$$

$$\beta^{(l+1)} = \beta^{(l)} + (C^{(l+1)})^{-1} a^{(l+1)},\ \text{for } l \ge 0,$$

where the (k,l)-element of $C^{(l)}$ is

$$c_{kl}^{(l)} = \sum_{j=1}^{J} \sum_{i=1}^{I} (x_{ijk} - \theta_{ik}^{(l)})(x_{ijl} - \theta_{il}^{(l)}) m_{ij}^{(l)}$$

with

$$\theta_{ik}^{(l)} = \frac{\sum_j m_{ij}^{(l)} x_{ijk}}{\sum_j m_{ij}^{(l)}} \quad \text{for } 1 \le i \le I,\ 1 \le k \le p$$

and the k-th element of $a^{(0)}$ is

$$a_k^{(0)} = \sum_{i,j} x_{ijk} y_{ij}^{(0)} m_{ij}^{(0)} - \frac{(\sum_{i,j} x_{ijk} m_{ij}^{(0)}) (\sum_{i,j} y_{ij} m_{ij}^{(0)})}{\sum_{i,j} m_{ij}^{(0)}}$$

and the k-th element of $a^{(l)}$ is

$$a_k^{(l)} = \sum_{i,j} x_{ijk} (n_{ij} - m_{ij}^{(l)}) \quad \text{for } l \geq 1.$$

The estimated cell means are updated by

$$m_{ij}^{(l)} = \frac{T w_{ij} exp (v_{ij}^{(l-1)})}{\sum_{i,j} w_{ij} exp (v_{ij}^{(l-1)})} \quad \text{for } l \geq 1$$

where

$$T = \begin{cases} \sum_{i,j} (n_{ij} + \delta) & \text{if the model is saturated} \\ \sum_{i,j} n_{ij} & \text{otherwise} \end{cases}$$

and

$$v_{ij}^{(l-1)} = \sum_{k=1}^{p} x_{ijk} \beta_k^{(l-1)}$$

The iterative process stops when either the maximum number of iterations (default=20) is reached or

$$MAX_{i,j} \left| v_{ij}^{(l+1)} - v_{ij}^{(l)} \right| < \varepsilon \quad (\text{with default } \varepsilon = 0.001).$$

Computed Statistics

- Correlation Matrix of Parameter Estimates

  Let C be the final $C^{(l)}$ and $H = C^{-1}$. The correlation between $\hat{\beta}_i$ and $\hat{\beta}_j$ is computed as

  $$\frac{h_{ij}}{\sqrt{h_{ii} h_{jj}}}$$

- Goodness of Fit

  The Pearson chi-square is computed as

  $$\chi^2 = \sum_{i,j} \frac{(n_{ij} - \hat{m}_{ij})^2}{\hat{m}_{ij}}$$

  and the likelihood-ratio chi-square is

  $$L = 2 \sum_{i,j} n_{ij} ln \left(\frac{n_{ij}}{\hat{m}_{ij}} \right)$$

  The degrees of freedom are $I \times (J-1) - p - E$, where E is the number of cells with $n_{ij} w_{ij} \leq 0$ and p is the number of coefficients in the model.

Residuals

- Residuals

$$residual_{ij} = n_{ij} - \hat{m}_{ij}$$

- Standardized Residuals

$$standard\ residual_{ij} = \frac{n_{ij} - \hat{m}_{ij}}{\sqrt{\hat{m}_{ij}}}$$

- Adjusted Residuals

$$adjusted\ residual_{ij} = \frac{n_{ij} - \hat{m}_{ij}}{\sqrt{s_{ij}}}$$

where

$$s_{ij} = \hat{m}_{ij}\left[1 - \frac{\hat{m}_{ij}}{T} - \hat{m}_{ij}\sum_{k,l}(x_{ijk} - \hat{\theta}_{ik})(x_{ijl} - \hat{\theta}_{il})\,h_{kl}\right]$$

$$\hat{\theta}_{ik} = \frac{\sum_j \hat{m}_{ij}x_{ijk}}{\sum_j \hat{m}_{ij}}$$

Generalized Residuals

Consider a linear combination of the cell counts

$$\sum_{i,j} d_{ij}n_{ij}$$

The estimated expected value is computed as

$$\sum_{i,j} d_{ij}\hat{m}_{ij}$$

Two generalized residuals are computed.

- Residuals

$$residual = \sum_{i,j} d_{ij}n_{ij} - \sum_{i,j} d_{ij}\hat{m}_{ij}$$

- Adjusted Residuals

$$adjusted\ residual = \frac{\sum_{i,j} d_{ij}n_{ij} - \sum_{i,j} d_{ij}\hat{m}_{ij}}{\sqrt{C_1}}$$

where

$$C_1 = \sum_{i,j} d_{ij}^2 \hat{m}_{ij} - \sum_i \left[\frac{\left(\sum_j \hat{m}_{ij} d_{ij}\right)^2}{\sum_j \hat{m}_{ij}} \right] - \sum_{k=1}^{p} \sum_{l=1}^{p} f_k f_l h_{kl}$$

$$f_k = \sum_{i,j} \hat{m}_{ij} d_{ij} (x_{ijk} - \hat{\theta}_{ik})$$

Analysis of Dispersion

Following Haberman (1982), define

$S(Y) =$ Total dispersion

$S(Y|X) =$ Conditional dispersion

$S(X) =$ Dispersion due to fit

$R = \frac{S(X)}{S(Y)} =$ Measure of association.

For entropy

$$S(Y) = -M \sum_{j=1}^{J} \hat{p}_j ln(\hat{p}_j)$$

$$S(Y|X) = -\sum_{i=1}^{I} \hat{M}_{i.} \sum_{j=1}^{J} \hat{p}_{i|j} ln(\hat{p}_{i|j})$$

$$S(X) = S(Y) - S(Y|X)$$

For concentration

$$S(Y) = M \times \left(1 - \sum_{j=1}^{J} \hat{p}_j^2\right)$$

$$S(Y|X) = \sum_{i=1}^{I} \hat{M}_{i.} \left(1 - \sum_{j=1}^{J} \hat{p}_{i|j}^2\right)$$

$$S(X) = S(Y) - S(Y|X)$$

where

$$\hat{p}_j = \frac{\hat{M}_{.j}}{M}$$

$$\hat{p}_{j|i} = \frac{\hat{m}_{ij}}{\hat{M}_{i.}}$$

Haberman (1977) shows that, under the hypothesis that Y and X are independent,

$$\psi_E = 2S(X) \rightarrow \chi^2_{I(J-1)}$$

in the case of entropy, and

$$\psi_C = \frac{M(J-1)S(X)}{S(Y)} \rightarrow \chi^2_{I-1}$$

in the case of concentration.

References

Haberman (1977)

Haberman (1978)
Haberman (1982)

LOGISTIC REGRESSION

General

Logistic regression regresses a dichotomous dependent variable on a set of independent variables. Several methods are implemented for selecting the independent variables.

Notation

Y	Dichotomous dependent variable
X_i	The ith independent variable
l	Likelihood function
L	Log likelihood function
I	Information matrix

Model

The linear logistic model assumes a dichotomous dependent variable Y with mean μ, whose dependence on the k explanatory variables $X = (X_1, \ldots, X_k)'$ takes the form

$$\mu = \frac{exp(\eta)}{1 + exp(\eta)},$$

with $\eta = \beta_0 + \beta_1 X_1 + \ldots + \beta_k X_k$.

That is,

$$P(Y = 1) = \frac{exp(\eta)}{1 + exp(\eta)},$$

or

$$ln\left(\frac{\mu}{1-\mu}\right) = \eta = \beta_0 + \beta_1 X_1 + \ldots + \beta_k X_k.$$

Hence, the likelihood function l for n observations $y_1, \ldots, y_n$, with means $\mu_1, \ldots, \mu_n$ and case weights $c_1, \ldots, c_n$, can be written as

$$l = \prod_{i=1}^{n} \mu_i^{c_i y_i} (1 - \mu_i)^{c_i (1 - y_i)},$$

where

$$\mu_i = \frac{exp(\eta_i)}{1 + exp(\eta_i)}$$

and

$$\eta_i = \beta_0 + \beta_1 x_{i1} + \ldots + \beta_k x_{ik}.$$

It follows that the logarithm of l is

$$L = ln(l) = \sum_{i=1}^{n} (c_i y_i ln(\mu_i) + c_i (1-y_i) ln(1-\mu_i))$$

and the derivative of L with respect to β_j is

$$L^*_{x_j} = \frac{\partial L}{\partial \beta_j} = \sum_{i=1}^{n} c_i (y_i - \mu_i) x_{ij}.$$

Maximum Likelihood Estimates (MLE)

The maximum likelihood estimates for $\beta_0, \ldots, \beta_k$ satisfy the following equations

$$\sum_{i=1}^{n} c_i (y_i - \mu_i) x_{ij} = 0, \text{ for } j = 0, \ldots, k,$$

where $x_{i0} = 1$ for $i = 1, \ldots, n$.

Note:

(1) A Newton-Raphson type algorithm is used to obtain the MLEs. Convergence can be based on
   (a) absolute difference for the parameter estimates between the iterations.
   (b) percent difference in the log-likelihood function between successive iterations.
   (c) maximum number of iterations specified.

(2) During the iterations, if predicted*(1-predicted) is smaller than 10^{-8} for all cases, the log-likelihood function is very close to zero. In this situation, iteration stops and the message "All predicted values are either 1 or 0" is issued.

After the maximum likelihood estimates $\hat{\beta}_0, \ldots, \hat{\beta}_k$ are obtained, the asymptotic covariance matrix is estimated by I^{-1}, the inverse of the information matrix I, where

$$I = -\left[E\left(\frac{\partial^2 L}{\partial \beta_i \partial \beta_j}\right)\right] = X'C\hat{V}X,$$

$$\hat{V} = Diag\{\hat{\mu}_1(1-\hat{\mu}_1), \ldots, \hat{\mu}_n(1-\hat{\mu}_n)\},$$

$$C = Diag\{c_1, \ldots, c_n\},$$

$$\hat{\mu}_i = \frac{exp(\hat{\eta}_i)}{1 + exp(\hat{\eta}_i)},$$

and

$$\hat{\eta}_i = \hat{\beta}_0 + \hat{\beta}_1 x_{i1} + \ldots + \hat{\beta}_k x_{ik}.$$

Stepwise Methods of Selecting Variables

Several methods are available for selecting independent variables. With the forced entry method, any variable in the variable list is entered into the model. There are two stepwise methods: forward and backward. The stepwise methods can use either the Wald statistic, the likelihood ratio, or a conditional algorithm for variable removal. For both stepwise methods, the score statistic is used to select variables for entry into the model.

Three statistics used later are defined as follows:

Score Statistic

The score statistic is calculated for each variable not in the model to determine whether the variable should enter the model. Assume that there are r_1 variables, namely, $u_1, \ldots, u_{r_1}$ in the model and r_2 variables, $w_1, \ldots, w_{r_2}$, not in the model. Based on the MLEs for the parameters in the model, V is estimated by $\hat{V} = Diag\{\hat{\mu}_1(1-\hat{\mu}_1), \ldots, \hat{\mu}_n(1-\hat{\mu}_n)\}$. The score statistic for w_i is defined as

$$S_i = (L^*_{w_i})^2 B_{22,i}$$

if w_i is not a categorical variable. If w_i is a categorical variable with m categories, it is converted to a (m-1)-dimension dummy vector. Denote these new m-1 variables as $\tilde{w}_i, \ldots, \tilde{w}_{i+m-2}$. The score statistic for w_i is

$$S_i = (L^*_{\tilde{w}})' B_{22,i} L^*_{\tilde{w}},$$

where $L^{*\prime}_{\tilde{w}} = (L^*_{\tilde{w}_i}, \ldots, L^*_{\tilde{w}_{i+m-2}})$ and the $(m-1)\times(m-1)$ matrix $B_{22,i}$ is

$$B_{22,i} = (A_{22,i} - A_{21,i}A_{11}^{-1}A_{12,i})^{-1}$$

with

$$A_{11} = \underset{\sim}{u}'\hat{V}\underset{\sim}{u},$$

$$A_{12,i} = \underset{\sim}{u}'\hat{V}\underset{\sim}{w}_i,$$

$$A_{22,i} = \underset{\sim}{w}_i'\hat{V}\underset{\sim}{w}_i$$

in which $\underset{\sim}{u}$ is the design matrix for variables $u_1, \ldots, u_{r_1}$ and $\underset{\sim}{w}_i$ is the design matrix for dummy variables $\tilde{w}_i, \ldots, \tilde{w}_{i+m-2}$. Note that $\underset{\sim}{u}$ contains a column of ones unless the constant term is excluded from η. The asymptotic distribution of the score statistic is a chi-square with degrees of freedom equal to the number of variables involved.

Note:

(1) If the model is through the origin and there are no variables in the model, $B_{22,i}$ is defined by $A_{22,i}^{-1}$ and $\hat{V}$ is equal to $\frac{1}{4}I_n$.

(2) If $B_{22,i}$ is not positive definite, the score statistic and residual chi-square statistic are set to be zero.

Wald Statistic

The Wald statistic is calculated for the variables in the model to determine whether a variable should be removed. If variable X_i is not categorical, the Wald statistic is defined by

$$Wald_i = \frac{\hat{\beta}_i^2}{\hat{\sigma}_{\hat{\beta}_i}^2}$$

If X_i is a categorical variable, the Wald statistic is computed as follows:

Let $\hat{\beta}_i$ be the vector of maximum likelihood estimates associated with the m-1 dummy variables, and ACOV the asymptotic covariance matrix for $\hat{\beta}_i$. The Wald statistic for X_i is

$$Wald_i = \hat{\beta}_i'(ACOV)^{-1}\hat{\beta}_i$$

The asymptotic distribution of the Wald statistic is Chi-Square with degrees of freedom equal to the number of parameters estimated.

Likelihood Ratio (LR) Statistic

The LR statistic is defined as two times the log of the ratio of the likelihood functions of two models evaluated at their MLEs. The LR statistic is used to determine if a variable should be removed from the model. Assume that there are r_1 variables in the current model, which is referred to as a full model. Based on the MLEs of the full model, $l\,(full)$ is calculated. For each of the variables removed from the full model one at a time, MLEs are computed and the likelihood function $l\,(reduced)$ is calculated. The LR statistic is then defined as

$$LR = -2ln\left(\frac{l\,(reduced)}{l\,(full)}\right) = -2\,(L\,(reduced) - L\,(full))$$

LR is asymptotically Chi-square distributed with degrees of freedom equal to the difference between the numbers of parameters estimated in the two models.

Conditional Statistic

The conditional statistic is also computed for every variable in the model. The formula for the conditional statistic is the same as the LR statistic except that the parameter estimates for each reduced model are conditional estimates, not MLEs. The conditional estimates are defined as follows. Let $\hat{\beta} = (\hat{\beta}_1, \ldots, \hat{\beta}_{r_1})'$ be the MLE for the r_1 variables in the model and C be the asymptotic covariance matrix for $\hat{\beta}$. If variable x_i is removed from the model, the conditional estimate for the parameters left in the model given $\hat{\beta}_i$ is

$$\tilde{\beta}_{(i)} = \hat{\beta}_{(i)} - c_{12}^{(i)}\,(c_{22}^{(i)})^{-1}\hat{\beta}_i,$$

where $\hat{\beta}_i$ is the MLE for the parameter(s) associated with x_i and $\hat{\beta}_{(i)}$ is $\hat{\beta}$ with $\hat{\beta}_i$ removed, $c_{12}^{(i)}$ is the covariance between $\hat{\beta}_{(i)}$ and $\hat{\beta}_i$, and $c_{22}^{(i)}$ is the covariance of $\hat{\beta}_i$. Then the conditional statistic is computed by

$$-2\,(L\,(\tilde{\beta}_{(i)}) - L\,(full))$$

where $L\,(\tilde{\beta}_{(i)})$ is the log likelihood function evaluated at $\tilde{\beta}_{(i)}$.

Stepwise Algorithms

- Forward stepwise (FSTEP)

(1) If FSTEP is the first method requested, estimate the parameter and likelihood function for the initial model. Otherwise, the final model from the previous method is the initial model for FSTEP. Obtain the necessary information: MLEs of the parameters for the current model, predicted probability μ_i, likelihood function for the current model, etc.

(2) Based on the MLEs of the current model, calculate the score statistic for every variable eligible for inclusion and find its significance.

(3) Choose the variable with the smallest significance. If that significance is less than the probability for a variable to enter, then go to (4); otherwise, stop FSTEP.

(4) Update the current model by adding a new variable. If this results in a model which has already been evaluated, stop FSTEP.

(5) Calculate LR or Wald statistic or conditional statistic for each variable in the current model. Then calculate its corresponding significance.

(6) Choose the variable with the largest significance. If that significance is less than the probability for variable removal, then go to (2); otherwise, if the current model with the variable deleted is the same as a previous model, stop FSTEP; otherwise, go to next step.

(7) Modify the current model by removing the variable with the largest significance from the previous model. Estimate the parameters for the modified model and go to step (5).

- Backward stepwise (BSTEP)

(1) Estimate the parameters for the full model which includes the final model from previous method and all eligible variables. Only variables listed on the BSTEP variable list are eligible for entry and removal. Let the current model be the full model.

(2) Based on the MLEs of the current model, calculate the LR or Wald statistic or conditional statistic for every variable in the model and find its significance.

(3) Choose the variable with the largest significance. If that significance is less than the probability for variable removal, then go to (5); otherwise, if the current model without the variable with the largest significance is the same as the previous model, stop BSTEP; otherwise, go to next step.

(4) Modify the current model by removing the variable with the largest significance from the model. Estimate the parameters for the modified model and go to step (2).

(5) Check to see any eligible variable is not in the model. If there is none, stop BSTEP; otherwise, go to next step.

(6) Based on the MLEs of the current model, calculate the score statistic for every variable not in the model and find its significance.

(7) Choose the variable with the smallest significance. If that significance is less than the probability for variable entry, then go to next step; otherwise, stop BSTEP.

(8) Add the variable with the smallest significance to the current model. If the model is not the same as any previous models, estimate the parameters for the new model and go to step (2); otherwise, stop BSTEP.

Statistics

- Initial Model Information

If β_0 is not included in the model, the predicted probability is estimated to be 0.5 for all cases and the log likelihood function $l(0)$ is

$$l(0) = W\ln(0.5) = -0.6931472W$$

with $W = \sum_{i=1}^{n} c_i$. If β_0 is included in the model, the predicted probability is estimated as

$$\hat{\mu}_0 = \frac{\sum_{i=1}^{n} c_i y_i}{W}$$

and β_0 is estimated by

$$\hat{\beta}_0 = ln\left(\frac{\hat{\mu}_0}{1-\hat{\mu}_0}\right)$$

with asymptotic standard error estimated by

$$\hat{\sigma}_{\hat{\beta}_0} = \frac{1}{\sqrt{W\hat{\mu}_0(1-\hat{\mu}_0)}}$$

The log likelihood function is

$$l(0) = W\left[\hat{\mu}_0 ln\left(\frac{\hat{\mu}_0}{1-\hat{\mu}_0}\right) + ln(1-\hat{\mu}_0).\right]$$

- Model Information

The following statistics are computed if a stepwise method is specified.

(a) -2 log likelihood

$$-2\sum_{i=1}^{n}(c_i y_i ln(\hat{\mu}_i) + c_i(1-y_i) ln(1-\hat{\mu}_i))$$

where

$$\hat{\mu}_i = \frac{exp(\hat{\eta}_i)}{1+exp(\hat{\eta}_i)}$$

and

$$\hat{\eta}_i = \begin{cases} \hat{\beta}_0 + \hat{\beta}_1 x_{i1} + \ldots + \hat{\beta}_k x_{ik} & \text{if } \beta_0 \text{ is include} \\ \hat{\beta}_1 x_{i1} + \ldots + \hat{\beta}_k x_{ik} & \text{otherwise} \end{cases}$$

(b) Model Chi-Square

2 (log likelihood function for current model -

log likelihood function for initial model)

where the initial model is the final model from the previous method. If this stepwise method is the first method, then the initial model contains a constant if it is in the model; otherwise the model has no terms. The degrees of freedom for model Chi-Square are equal to the difference between the number of parameters estimated in the two models. If the degrees of freedom is zero, the model Chi-Square is not computed.

(c) Improvement Chi-Square

2 (log likelihood function for current model -

log likelihood function for previous model)

where the previous model is the model from the last step. The degrees of freedom for improvement Chi-Square are equal to the difference between the numbers of parameters estimated in the two models.

(d) Goodness of Fit

$$\sum_{i=1}^{n}\frac{c_i(y_i-\hat{\mu}_i)^2}{\hat{\mu}_i(1-\hat{\mu}_i)}$$

where $\hat{\mu}_i$ is the predicted probability for case i from the current model.

- Information for the variables not in the equation

For each of the variables not in the equation, the score statistic is calculated along with the associated degrees of freedom, significance and partial R. Let X_i be a variable not currently in the model and S_i the score statistic. The partial R is defined by

$$Partial\_R = \begin{cases} \sqrt{\dfrac{S_i - 2 \times df}{-2L(initial)}} & \text{if } S_i > 2 \times df \\ 0 & \text{otherwise} \end{cases}$$

where df is the degrees of freedom associated with S_i, and $L(initial)$ is the log likelihood function for the initial model.

The residual Chi-Square printed for the variables not in the equation is defined as $R_{CS} = (L^*_w)' B_{22} L^*_w$

where $L^*_w = (L^*_{w_1}, \ldots, L^*_{w_{r_2}})'$.

- Information for the Variables in the equation

For each of the variables in the equation, the MLE of the Beta coefficients is calculated along with the standard errors, Wald statistics, degrees of freedom, significances, and partial R. If X_i is not a categorical variable currently in the equation, the partial R is computed as

$$Partial\_R = \begin{cases} sign(\hat{\beta}_i) \sqrt{\dfrac{Wald_i - 2}{-2L(initial)}} & \text{if } Wald_i > 2 \\ 0 & \text{otherwise} \end{cases}$$

If X_i is a categorical variable with m categories, the partial R is then

$$Partial\_R = \begin{cases} \sqrt{\dfrac{Wald_i - 2(m-1)}{-2L(initial)}} & \text{if } Wald_i > 2(m-1) \\ 0 & \text{otherwise} \end{cases}$$

- Casewise Statistics

(a) Individual Deviance

$$G_i = \begin{cases} \sqrt{2(y_i ln(\hat{\mu}_i) + (1-y_i) ln(1-\hat{\mu}_i))} & \text{if } y_i > \hat{\mu}_i \\ -\sqrt{2(y_i ln(\hat{\mu}_i) + (1-y_i) ln(1-\hat{\mu}_i))} & \text{otherwise} \end{cases}$$

(b) Leverage (h_i)

h_i is the ith diagonal element of the matrix

$$\hat{V}^{\frac{1}{2}} X (X' C \hat{V} X)^{-1} X' \hat{V}^{\frac{1}{2}}$$

where

$$\hat{V} = Diag\{\hat{\mu}_1(1-\hat{\mu}_1), \ldots, \hat{\mu}_n(1-\hat{\mu}_n)\}$$

(c) Studentized Residual

$$\tilde{G}_i^* = \frac{G_i}{\sqrt{1-h_i}}$$

(d) Logit Residual ($\tilde{e}_i$)

$$\tilde{e}_i = \frac{e_i}{\hat{\mu}_i(1-\hat{\mu}_i)}$$

where $e_i = y_i - \hat{\mu}_i$.

(e) Standardized Residual

$$z_i = \frac{e_i}{\sqrt{\hat{\mu}_i(1-\hat{\mu}_i)}}$$

(f) Cook's Distance (D_i)

$$D_i = \frac{z_i^2 h_i}{1-h_i}$$

(g) DFBETA

Let $\Delta\beta$ be the change of the coefficient estimates from the deletion of case i. It is computed as

$$\Delta\beta = \frac{(X'C\hat{V}X)^{-1}X'_i e_i}{1-h_i}$$

(h) Predicted Group

If $\hat{\mu}_i \geq 0.5$, predicted group = group in which $y = 1$.

Note:

For the unselected cases with nonmissing values for the independent variables in the analysis, the leverage ($\tilde{h}_i$) is computed as

$$\tilde{h}_i = h_i - \frac{\hat{V}_i h_i^2}{1+\hat{V}_i h_i}$$

where

$$h_i = \hat{V}_i X'_i (X'C\hat{V}X)^{-1} X_i$$

For the unselected cases, the Cook's distance and DFBETA are calculated based on $\tilde{h}_i$.

MANOVA

General

The program performs univariate and multivariate analysis of variance and covariance for any crossed and/or nested design.

ANALYSIS OF VARIANCE

Notation

The experimental design model (the model with covariates will be discussed later) can be expressed as

$$\underset{N\times p}{Y} = \underset{N\times m}{W}\ \underset{m\times p}{\beta} + \underset{N\times p}{E}$$

where

Y	is the observed matrix
W	is the design matrix
β	is the matrix of parameters
E	is the matrix of random errors
N	is the total number of observations
p	is the number of dependent variables
m	is the number of parameters

Since the rows of W will be identical for all observations in the same cell, the model is rewritten in terms of cell means as

$$\underset{g\times p}{Y_{\bullet}} = \underset{g\times m}{A}\ \underset{m\times p}{\beta} + \underset{g\times p}{E_{\bullet}}$$

where g is the number of cells and $Y_{\bullet}$ and $E_{\bullet}$ denote matrices of means.

Reparameterization

The reparameterization of the model (Bock, 1975, Finn, 1977) is done by factoring A into

$$\underset{g\times m}{A} = \underset{g\times r}{K}\ \underset{r\times m}{L}$$

K forms a column basis for the model and has rank r. L contains the coefficients of linear combinations of parameters and has rank r. The contrast matrix L can be specified by the user. Given L, K can be obtained from $AL'(LL')^{-1}$. For designs with more than one factor,

L, and hence K, can be constructed from Kronecker products of contrast matrices of each factor. After reparameterization, the model can be expressed as

$$\underset{g \times p}{Y} = A\beta + E$$

$$= K(L\beta) + E$$

$$= \underset{g \times r}{K} \; \underset{r \times p}{\theta} + \underset{g \times p}{E}$$

Parameter Estimation

An orthogonal decomposition (Golub, 1969) is performed on K. That is, K is represented as

$$K = QR$$

where Q is an orthonormal matrix such that $Q'DQ = I$; D is the diagonal matrix of cell frequencies; and R is an upper-triangular matrix.

The normal equation of the model is

$$(K'DK)\hat{\theta} = K'DY$$

or

$$R\hat{\theta} = Q'DY = U$$

This triangular system can therefore be solved for $\hat{\theta}$ without forming the cross-product matrix.

Significance Tests

The sum of squares and cross-products (SSCP) matrix due to the model is

$$\hat{\theta}'R'R\hat{\theta} = U'U$$

and since $\mathrm{Var}(U) = R\,\mathrm{Var}(\theta)R' = I \otimes \Sigma$ the SSCP matrix of each individual effect can be obtained from the components of

$$U'U = (U_1, \ldots, U_k)\begin{pmatrix} U_1' \\ \vdots \\ U_k' \end{pmatrix} = U_1U_1' + \ldots + U_kU_k'$$

Therefore the hypothesis SSCP matrix for testing $H_O : \theta_h = 0$ is

$$\underset{p \times p}{S_H} = \underset{p \times n_h}{U_h} \; \underset{n_h \times p}{U_h'}$$

The default error SSCP matrix is the pooled within-groups SSCP:

$$S_E = Y'Y - Y'DY$$

If the pooled within-groups SSCP matrix does not exist, the residual SSCP matrix is used:

$$S_E = Y'Y - U'U$$

Four test criteria are available. Each of these statistics is a function of the nonzero eigenvalues λ_i of the matrix $S_H S_E^{-1}$. The number of nonzero eigenvalues, s, is equal to $\min(p, n_h)$.

- Pillai's Criterion (Pillai, 1967)

$$T = \sum_{i=1}^{s} \lambda_i / (1 + \lambda_i)$$

Approximate $F = (n_e - p - s) T / (b(s - T))$ with b_s and $s(n_e - p + s)$ degrees of freedom, where

n_e = degrees of freedom for S_E

$b = \max (p, n_h)$

- Hotelling's Trace

$$T = \sum_{i=1}^{s} \lambda_i$$

Approximate $F = 2(sn+1) T / (s^2 (2m+s+1))$ with $s(2m+s+1)$ and $2(sn+1)$ degrees of freedom where

$$m = (|n_h - p| - 1) / 2$$

$$n = (|n_e - p| - 1) / 2$$

- Wilks' Lambda (Rao, 1973)

$$T = \prod_{i=1}^{s} 1/(1+\lambda_i)$$

Approximate $F = (1 - T^{1/l}) (Ml + 1 - n_h p/2) / (T^{1/l} n_h p)$ with $n_h p$ and $(Ml + 1 - n_h p/2)$ degrees of freedom, where

$$l^2 = (p^2 n_h^2 - 4) / (p^2 + n_h^2 - 5)$$

$$M = n_e - (p + 1 - n_h) / 2$$

- Roy's Largest Root

$$T = \lambda_1 / (1 + \lambda_1)$$

Stepdown *F* Tests

The stepdown *F* statistics are

$$F_i = \frac{(t^2 - t_e^2) / n_h}{t_e^2 / (n_e - i + 1)}$$

with n_h and $n_e - i + 1$ degrees of freedom, where t_e and t are the ith diagonal element of T_E and T respectively, and where

$$S_E = T'_E T_E$$

$$S_E + S_H = T'T$$

Design Matrix

K

Estimated Cell Means

$$\hat{Y}. = K\hat{\theta}$$

ANALYSIS OF COVARIANCE

Model

$$\underset{g \times p}{Y_{\bullet}} = \underset{g \times r}{K} \; \underset{r \times p}{\theta} + \underset{g \times q}{X_{\bullet}} \; \underset{q \times p}{B} + \underset{g \times p}{E_{\bullet}}$$

where g, p, and r are as before and q is the number of covariates, and $X_{\bullet}$ is the mean of X, the matrix of covariates.

Parameter Estimation and Significance Tests

For purposes of parameter estimation, no initial distinction is made between dependent variables and covariates.

Let

$$V = (Y\ X)$$

$$V_{\bullet} = (Y_{\bullet}\ X_{\bullet})$$

The normal equation of the model

$$\underset{g \times (p+q)}{V_{\bullet}} = \underset{g \times r}{K} \; \underset{r \times (p+q)}{\theta} + \underset{g \times (p+q)}{E_{\bullet}}$$

is

$$(K'DK)\hat{\theta} = K'DY_{\bullet}$$

or

$$R\hat{\theta} = Q'DV_{\bullet} = U$$

or

$$\underset{r \times (p+q)}{\hat{\theta}} = (\underset{r \times p}{\hat{\theta}_y} \quad \underset{r \times q}{\hat{\theta}_x})$$

If S_E and S_T are partitioned as

$$S_E = \begin{pmatrix} S_E^{(Y)} & S_E^{(YX)} \\ S_E^{(XY)} & S_E^{(X)} \end{pmatrix}$$

$$S_T = \begin{pmatrix} S_T^{(Y)} & S_T^{(YX)} \\ S_T^{(XY)} & S_T^{(X)} \end{pmatrix}$$

then the adjusted error SSCP matrix is

$$S_E^* = S_E^{(Y)} - S_E^{(YX)} \left(S_E^{(X)}\right)^{-1} S_E^{(XY)}$$

and the adjusted total SSCP matrix is

$$S_T^* = S_T^{(Y)} - S_T^{(YX)} \left(S_T^{(X)}\right)^{-1} S_T^{(XY)}$$

The adjusted hypothesis SSCP matrix is then

$$S_H^* = S_T^* - S_E^*$$

The estimate of B is

$$\hat{B} = \left(S_T^{(X)}\right)^{-1} S_T^{(XY)}$$

The adjusted parameter estimates are

$$\hat{\theta}^* = \hat{\theta}_Y - \hat{\theta}_X \hat{B}$$

The adjusted cell means are

$$\hat{Y}^* = K\hat{\theta}^*$$

Repeated Measures

Notation

k	degrees of freedom for the within-subject factor
SSE^*	orthonormal transformed error matrix
N	total number of observations
$ndfb$	degrees of freedom for all between-subject factors (including the constant)

Statistics

- Greenhouse-Geisser epsilon

$$\text{ggeps} = \frac{(\text{tr}(\text{SSE}^*))^2}{k \times \text{tr}((\text{SSE}^*)^2)}$$

- Huynh-Feldt epsilon

$$\text{hfeps} = \frac{N \times k \times \text{ggeps} - 2}{k \times (N - \text{ndfb}) - k^2 \times \text{ggeps}}$$

if hfeps > 1, set hfeps = 1

- Lower bound epsilon

$$\text{lbeps} = \frac{1}{k}$$

Effect Size

Notation

dfh	hypothesis degrees of freedom
dfe	error degrees of freedom
F	F test
W	Wilks' Lambda
s	number of non-zero eigenvalues of HE^{-1}
T	Hotelling's Trace
V	Pillai's Trace

Statistics

- Partial eta-squared = $\dfrac{\text{dfh} \times F}{\text{dfh} \times F + \text{dfe}}$

- Eta-squared (Wilks') = $1 - W^{1/s}$

- Eta-squared (Hotelling's) = $\dfrac{T/s}{T/s + 1}$

- Total eta-squared = $\dfrac{\text{sum of squares for effect}}{\text{total (corrected) sum of squares}}$

- Hay's omega-squared = $\dfrac{\text{SS for effect - df(effect)} \times \text{MSE}}{\text{corrected total SS} + \text{MSE}}$

- Pillai = V/S

Power

- Univariate non-centrality

  $$\lambda = \frac{\text{SS hyp}}{\text{SS error}} \times dfe$$

- Multivariate non-centrality

  For a single degree of freedom hypothesis

  $$\lambda = T \times dfe$$

  where *T* is Hotelling's Trace and *dfe* is the error degrees of freedom. Approximate power non-centrality based on Wilks' Lambda is

  $$\lambda = \frac{\text{Wilks' eta square}}{1 - \text{Wilks' eta square}} \times dfe\,(W)$$

  where *dfe(W)* is the error *df* from Rao's F-approximation to the distribution of Wilks' Lambda.

- Hotelling's Trace

  $$\lambda = \frac{\text{Hotelling's eta square}}{1 - \text{Hotelling's eta square}} \times dfe\,(H)$$

  where *dfe(H)* is the error *df* from the F-approximation to the distribution of Hotelling's Trace.

- Pillai's Trace

  $$\lambda = \frac{\text{Pillai's eta square}}{1 - \text{Pillai's eta square}} \times dfe\,(P)$$

  where *dfe(P)* is the error *df* from Pillai's F-approximation to the distribution of Pillai's Trace.

- Approximate power

Approximate power is computed using an Edgeworth Series Expansion (Mudholkar, Chaubey, & Lin, 1976).

$$r = \upsilon_1 + \lambda$$

$$b = \lambda / r$$

$$K_1 = \{ \left(\frac{r}{\upsilon_1}\right)^{1/3} \left(1 - \frac{2(b+1)}{9r} - \frac{40b^2}{3^4 r^2} + \frac{80(1+3b+33b^2-77b^3)}{3^7 r^3}\right.$$

$$\left. + \frac{176(1+4b-210b^2+2380b^3-2975b^4)}{3^9 r^4}\right) \}$$

$$- c^{1/3} \{ \left(1 - \frac{2}{9\upsilon_2} + \frac{80}{3^7 \upsilon_2^3} + \frac{176}{3^9 \upsilon_2^4}\right) \}$$

$$K_2 = \{ \left(\frac{r}{\upsilon_1}\right)^{2/3} \left(\frac{2(b+1)}{9r} + \frac{16b^2}{3^3 r^2} - \frac{8(13+39b+405b^2-1025b^3)}{3^7 r^3}\right.$$

$$\left. - \frac{160(1+4b-87b^2+1168b^3-1544b^4)}{3^8 r^4}\right) \}$$

$$+ c^{2/3} \left(\frac{2}{9\upsilon_2} - \frac{104}{3^7 \upsilon_2^3} - \frac{160}{3^8 \upsilon_2^4}\right)$$

$$K_3 = \{ \left(\frac{-r}{\upsilon_1}\right) \left(\frac{8b^2}{27r^2} - \frac{32(1+3b+21b^2-62b^3)}{3^6 r^3}\right.$$

$$\left. - \frac{32(8+32b-177b^2+4550b^3-6625b^4)}{3^8 r^4}\right) \}$$

$$- c \left(\frac{32}{3^6 \upsilon_2^3} + \frac{256}{3^8 \upsilon_2^4}\right)$$

$$K_4 = - \{ \left(\frac{r}{\upsilon_1}\right)^{4/3} \left(\frac{16(1+3b+12b^2-44b^3)}{3^6 r^3}\right.$$

$$\left. + \frac{256(1+4b+6b^2+274b^3-458b^4)}{3^8 r^4}\right)$$

$$- c^{4/3} \left(\frac{16}{3^6 \upsilon_2^3} + \frac{256}{3^8 \upsilon_2^4}\right)$$

$$Y = \frac{K_1}{\sqrt{K_2}}$$

$$\text{Power} = 1 - \Phi(Y) - \frac{1}{\sqrt{2\pi}} e^{-Y^2/2} \{ \frac{K_3}{6}(Y^2 - 1) + \frac{K_4}{24}(Y^3 - 3Y) \frac{K_1^2}{72}(Y^5 - 10Y^3 + 15Y) \}$$

Joint and Individual Confidence Intervals

The intervals are calculated as follows:

Lower bound = parameter estimate - k* stderr

Upper bound = parameter estimate + k* stderr

where *stderr* is the standard error of the parameter estimate, and k is the critical constant whose value depends upon the type of confidence interval requested.

Univariate Intervals

- Individual Confidence Intervals

$$k = \sqrt{(F(a;1,ne))}$$

where

$ne$is the error degrees of freedom

$a$is the confidence level desired

F is the percentage point of the F distribution

- Joint Confidence Intervals

For Scheffé intervals:

$$k = \sqrt{(nh * F(a;nh,ne))}$$

where

$ne$is the error degrees of freedom

$nh$is the hypothesis degrees of freedom

$a$is the confidence level desired

$F$is the percentage point of the F distribution

For Bonferroni intervals:

$$k = t(a/(2 * nh), ne)$$

where

$ne$is the error degrees of freedom

$nh$is the hypothesis degrees of freedom

$a$is 100 minus the confidence level desired

$t$is the percentage point of Student's t distribution

Multivariate Intervals

The value of the multipliers $\underline{k}$ for the multivariate case is computed as follows:

Let

p= the number of dependent variables

nh= the hypothesis degrees of freedom

ne= the error degrees of freedom

a= the desired confidence level

s= min (p, nh)

m= $(|nh - p| - 1)/2$

n= $(ne - p - 1)/2$

For Roy's largest root define:

$$c = G/(1-G)$$

where

$G = \text{GCR}\,(a; s, m, n)$, the percentage point of the largest root distribution

For Wilks' Lambda define:

$t = (p*nh)^2 - 4$

$b = p*p + nh*nh - 5$

$r = \sqrt{(t/b)}$ if $b \neq 0$, else $r = 1$

$u = (p*nh - 2)/4$

$t = p*nh$

$b = (nh + ne - (p + nh + 1)/2)*r - 2*u$

$f = (t*F(a; t, b))/b$

$W = (1/(1+c))^r$

$c = (1 - W)/W$

For Hotelling's Trace define:

$t = s(2m + s + 1)$

$b = 2(sn + 1)$

$T = (stF(a; t, b))/b$

$c = T$

For Pillai's Trace define:

$t = s(\max(p, nh))$

$b = s(ne - p + s)$

$D = (F(a; t, b)t)/b$

$V = (sc)/(c + 1)$

$c = V/(1 - V)$

Now for each of the above criteria, the critical value is:

$K = \sqrt{(ne*c)}$

For Bonferroni intervals:

$K = t(a/(2p(nh)); ne)$

where t is the percentage point of the Student's t distribution

Regression Statistics

Correlation between independent variables and predicted dependent variables

$$r(X_i, \hat{Y}_j) = \frac{r_{ij}}{R_j}$$

where

$X_i = i^{th}$ predictor (covariate)

$\hat{Y}_j = j^{th}$ predicted dependent variable

$r_{ij} =$ error correlation between i^{th} predictor and j^{th} dependent variable

$R_j =$ multiple R for j^{th} dependent variable across all predictors

References

Bock (1975)

Finn (1977)

Golub (1969)

Green (1977)

Mudholkar, Chaubey, & Lin (1976)

Muller and Peterson (1984)

Pillai (1967)

Timm (1975)

MEANS

General

Cases are crossclassified on the basis of multiple independent variables, and for each cell of the resulting crossclassification, basic statistics are calculated for a dependent variable.

Notation

X_{ij}	value for the *i*th independent variable for case *j*
Y_j	value for the dependent variable for case *j*
w_j	weight for case *j*
k	number of independent variables
N	number of cases

Statistics

For each value of the first independent variable (X_1), for each value of the pair (X_1, X_2), for the triple (X_1, X_2, X_3), and similarly for the *k*-tuple $(X_1, X_2, ..., X_k)$, the following are computed:

- Sum of Caseweights for the Cell

$$W = \sum_{i=1}^{N} w_i l_i$$

where $l_i = 1$ if the *i*th case is in the cell, $l_i = 0$ otherwise.

- The Sum and Corrected Sum of Squares

$$SMY = \sum_{i=1}^{N} w_i l_i Y_i$$

$$SSY = \sum_{i=1}^{N} w_i l_i Y_i^2$$

$$CSS = SSY - SMY^2 / W$$

- The Mean

$$\bar{Y} = \frac{\sum_{i=1}^{N} w_i l_i Y_i}{W}$$

- Variance

$$S^2 = \frac{CSS}{W-1}$$

ANOVA and Test for Linearity

If the analysis of variance table or test for linearity are requested, only the first independent variable is used. Assume it takes on J distinct values (groups). The previously described statistics are calculated and printed for each group separately, as well as for all cases pooled. Symbols subscripted from 1 to J will denote group statistics, unsubscripted the total. Thus for group j, SMY_j is the sum of the dependent variable, and X_j the value of the independent variable. Note that the standard deviation and sum of squares printed in the last row of the summary table are pooled within group values.

- Analysis of Variance

Source	Sum of Squares	df
Between Groups	Total-Within Groups	J-1
Regression	$\dfrac{\left(\sum_{j=1}^{J} X_j SMY_j - \left(\sum_{j=1}^{J} w_j X_j\right)\left(\sum_{j=1}^{J} SMY_j\right)/W\right)^2}{\sum_{j=1}^{J} w_j X_j^2 - \left(\sum_{j=1}^{J} w_j X_j\right)^2/W}$	1
Deviation from Regression	Between-Regression	J-2
Within Groups	$\sum_{j=1}^{J} CSS_j$	W-J
Total	$\sum_{j=1}^{J} SSY_j - \left(\sum_{j=1}^{J} SMY_j\right)^2/W$	W-1

The mean squares are calculated by dividing each sum of squares by its degrees of freedom. The F ratios are the mean squares for each source divided by the within groups mean square. The significance level for the F is from the F distribution with the degrees of freedom for the numerator and denominator mean squares. If there is only one group the ANOVA is not done; if there are fewer than three groups or the independent variable is a string variable, the test for linearity is not done.

- Correlation Coefficient

$$r = \frac{\sum_{j=1}^{J} X_j SMY_j - \left(\sum_{j=1}^{J} W_j X_j\right) SMY / W}{\sqrt{\left(\sum_{j=1}^{J} W_j X_j^2 - \left(\sum_{j=1}^{J} W_j X_j\right)^2 / W\right)(SSY - SMY^2 / W)}}$$

- Eta

$$(eta)^2 = \frac{\text{Sum of Squares Between Groups}}{\text{Total Sum of Squares}}$$

References

Hays (1973)

NLR

General

NLR produces the least square estimates of the parameters for models that are not linear in their parameters. Unlike in other procedures, the weight function is not treated as a case replicate in NLR.

Model

Consider the model

$$f = f(\underset{\sim}{x}, \underset{\sim}{\Theta})$$

where $\underset{\sim}{\Theta}$ is a $p \times 1$ parameter vector, $\underset{\sim}{x}$ is a vector of independent variables, and f is a function of $\underset{\sim}{x}$ and $\underset{\sim}{\Theta}$.

Goal

Find the least square estimate $\underset{\sim}{\Theta}^*$ of $\underset{\sim}{\Theta}$ such that $\underset{\sim}{\Theta}^*$ minimizes the objective function

$$F(\underset{\sim}{\Theta}) = R'WR \qquad (1)$$

where

$$R' = (R_1, \ldots, R_n)$$
$$R_i = y_i - f_i$$
$$f_i = f(x_i, \underset{\sim}{\Theta}^*) \qquad , i = 1, \ldots, n$$
$$W = \text{Diag}\,(W_1, \ldots, W_n)$$

and n is the number of cases. For case i, y_i is the observed dependent variable, x_i is the vector of observed independent variables, W_i is the weight function which can be a function of $\underset{\sim}{\Theta}$.

The gradient of F at $\underset{\sim}{\Theta}$ is defined as

$$\nabla F = 2J._j{}'WR$$

where $J._j$ is the jth column of the $n \times p$ Jacobian matrix J whose (i,j)th element J_{ij} is defined by

$$J_{ij} = \frac{R_i}{2W_i}\frac{\partial W_i}{\partial \underset{\sim}{\Theta}} - \frac{\partial f_i}{\partial \underset{\sim}{\Theta}} \,.$$

Estimation

The modified Levenberg-Marquardt algorithm that was proposed by Moré (1977) and is contained in MINPACK is used in NLR to solve (1).

Given an initial value $\underset{\sim}{\Theta}^{(0)}$ for $\underset{\sim}{\Theta}$, the algorithm is as follows:

At stage $k+1$, $k = 0, 1, 2, \ldots$

- Compute

$$f_i^{(k)} = f_i(\underset{\sim}{\Theta}^{(F)}),\ R_i^{(k)} = y_i - f_i^{(k)},\ F_k = F(\underset{\sim}{\Theta}^{(k)}),\ \text{and}\ J^{(k)} = J(\underset{\sim}{\Theta}^{(k)})$$

- Choose an appropriate non-negative scalar such that

$$F(\underset{\sim}{\Theta}^k + h_k) < F_k$$

where

$$h_k = -(J^{(k)\prime} J^{(k)} + \alpha_k I)^{-1} J^{(k)\prime} R^{(k)}$$

- Set

$$\Theta^{(k+1)} = \Theta^{(k)} + h_k$$

and compute $J^{(k+1)}$, $R^{(k+1)}$, $W^{(k+1)}$, and F_{k+1}.

- Check the following conditions:

(1) $1 - (F_{k-1}/F_k) < \varepsilon_1$ $(SSCON)$

(2) For every element of h_k,

$$\left|h_{ki}/\Theta_i^{(k)}\right| < \varepsilon_2 (PCON)$$

(3) $k+1 \geq ITER$ (maximum number of iterations)

(4) For every parameter Θ_j, the gradient of F at Θ_j, ∇F_j, is evaluated at $\underset{\sim}{\Theta}^{(k+1)}$ by checking

$$\left|r_j^{(k+1)}\right| < \varepsilon_2 (RCON)$$

where $r_j^{(k+1)}$ is the correlation between the jth column $J_j^{(k+1)}$ of $J^{(k+1)}$ and $W^{(k+1)} R^{(k+1)}$.

If any of these four conditions is satisfied, the algorithm will stop. Then the final parameter estimate Θ^*

$$\underset{\sim}{\Theta}^* = \Theta^{(k+1)}$$

and the termination reason is reported. Otherwise, iteration continues.

Statistics

When iteration terminates, the following statistics are printed.

- Parameter Estimates and Standard Errors

The asymptotic standard error of Θ_j^* is estimated by the square root of the jth diagonal element a_{jj} of A, where

$$A = \frac{F(\underset{\sim}{\Theta}^*)}{n-p} (J^{*\prime} W^* J^*)^{-1}$$

and J^* and W^* are the Jacobian matrix J and weight function W evaluated at $\underset{\sim}{\Theta}^*$, respectively.

- Asymptotic 95% confidence interval for Θ

$$\Theta_j^* \pm t(0.975, n-p)\, a_{ii}$$

- Asymptotic correlation matrix of the parameter estimates

$$C = D^{-1/2} A D^{-1/2}$$

where

$$D = \text{Diag}\,(a_{11}, \ldots, a_{pp})$$

and a_{ii} is the ith diagonal element of A.

- Analysis of Variance Table

Source	df	Sum of Squares
Residual	$n\text{-}p$	$F(\underset{\sim}{\Theta}^*)$
Regression	p	$SS_{\text{uncorrected}} - F(\underset{\sim}{\Theta}^*)$
Uncorrected Total	n	$SS_{\text{uncorrected}}$
Corrected Total	$n\text{-}1$	$SS_{\text{uncorrected}} - \bar{y}^2 \sum_{i=1}^{n} W_i(\Theta^*)$

where

$$SS_{\text{uncorrected}} = \sum_{i=1}^{n} W_i\,(\underset{\sim}{\Theta}^*)\, y_i^2$$

$$\bar{y} = \left(\sum_{i=1}^{n} W_i\,(\underset{\sim}{\Theta}^*)\, y_i\right) \Big/ \left(\sum_{i=1}^{n} W_i(\underset{\sim}{\Theta}^*)\right)$$

References

Moré (1977)

NONPAR CORR

General

If a WEIGHT variable is specified, it is used to replicate a case as many times as indicated by the integer portion of the weight value. The case then has a probability of additional inclusion equal to the fractional portion of the weight value. If the workspace requirements are exceeded and sampling has been selected, a random sample of cases is chosen for analysis using the algorithm described in SAMPLE.

Spearman Correlation Coefficient

For each of the variables X and Y separately, the observations are sorted into ascending order and replaced by their ranks. In situations where t observations are tied, the average rank is assigned. Each time $t > 1$ the quantity $t^3 - t$ is calculated and summed separately for each variable. These sums will be designated ST_x and ST_y.

For each of the N observations, the difference between the rank of X and rank of Y is computed as:

$$d_i = R(X_i) - R(Y_i)$$

Spearman's rho is calculated as (Siegel (1956)):

$$r_s = \frac{T_x + T_y - \sum_{i=1}^{N} d_i^2}{2\sqrt{T_x T_y}}$$

where

$$T_x = \frac{N^3 - N - ST_x}{12} \quad \text{and} \quad T_y = \frac{N^3 - N - ST_y}{12}$$

If T_x or T_y is zero, the statistic is not computed.

The significance level is calculated assuming that, under the null hypothesis,

$$t = r_s \sqrt{\frac{N-2}{1-r_s^2}}$$

is distributed as a t with N-2 degrees of freedom. A one- or two-tailed significance level is printed depending on the user-selected option.

Kendall's Tau

For each of the variables X and Y separately, the observations are sorted into ascending order and replaced by their ranks. In situations where t observations are tied, the average rank is assigned.

Each time $t > 1$ the following quantities are computed and summed over all groups of ties for each variable separately.

$$T_v = \sum t^2 - t$$
$$T_v' = \sum (t^2 - t)\ (t - 2)$$
$$T_v'' = \sum (t^2 - t)\ (2t + 5)\ \text{, and } v = x \text{ or } y$$

Each of the N cases is compared to the others to determine with how many cases its ranking of X and Y is concordant or discordant. The following procedure is used. For each distinct pair of cases (i, j), $i < j$ the quantity

$$d_{ij} = [R(X_j) - R(X_i)]\ [R(Y_j) - R(Y_i)]$$

is computed. If the sign of this product is positive the pair of observations (i, j) is concordant, since both members of observation i are either less than or greater than their respective measurement in observation j. If the sign is negative, the pair is discordant.

The number of concordant pairs minus the number of discordant pairs is

$$S = \sum_{i=1}^{N-1} \sum_{j=i+1}^{N} \text{sign}\,(d_{ij})\ 1$$

where sign $(d_{ij})1$ is defined as +1 or -1 depending on the sign of d_{ij}. Pairs in which $d_{ij} = 0$ are ignored in the computation of S.

Kendall's Tau is computed as

$$T = \frac{S}{\sqrt{\dfrac{N^2 - N - T_x}{2}}\sqrt{\dfrac{N^2 - N - T_y}{2}}}$$

If the denominator is zero, the statistic is not computed.

The variance of S is estimated by (Kendall (1955)):

$$d = \frac{1}{18}\{K(2N+5) - T_x'' - T_y''\} + \frac{T_x'\,T_y'}{9K(N-2)} + \frac{T_xT_y}{2K}$$

where

$$K = N^2 - N$$

The significance level is obtained using

$$Z = \frac{S}{\sqrt{d}}$$

which, under the null hypothesis, is approximately normally distributed. The significance level is either one- or two-sided, depending on the user specification.

References

Kendall (1955)

Siegel (1956)

NPAR TESTS

General

If a WEIGHT variable is specified, it is used to replicate a case as many times as indicated by the integer portion of the weight value. The case then has a probability of additional inclusion equal to the fractional portion of the weight value. If the workspace requirements are exceeded and sampling has been selected, a random sample of cases is chosen for analysis using the algorithm described in SAMPLE. For the RUNS test, if sampling is specified, it is ignored. The tests are described in Siegel (1956).

One-Sample Chi-Square Test

Cell Specification

If the (lo, hi) specification is used, each integer value in the lo to hi range is designated a cell. Otherwise, each distinct value encountered is considered a cell.

Observed Frequencies (O_i)

If (lo, hi) has been selected, every observed value is truncated to an integer and, if it is in the lo to hi range, it is included in the frequency count for the corresponding cell. Otherwise, a count of the frequency of occurrence of the distinct values is obtained.

Expected Frequencies (EXP_i)

If none or EQUAL is specified,

$$EXP_i = \frac{\text{number of observations (N) [in range]}}{\text{number of cells (k)}}$$

When the expected values (E_i) are specified either as counts, percentages, or proportions,

$$EXP_i = \left(\frac{E_i}{\sum_{i=1}^{k} E_i} \right) N$$

If there are cells with expected values less than 5, the number of such cells and the minimum expected value are printed.

If the number of user-supplied expected frequencies is not equal to the number of cells generated, or if an expected value is less than or equal to zero, the test terminates with an error message.

Chi-Square and Its Degrees of Freedom

$$\chi^2 = \sum_{i=1}^{k} \frac{(O_i - \mathrm{Exp}_i)^2}{\mathrm{Exp}_i}$$

$$df = k - 1$$

The significance level is from the chi-square distribution with k-1 degrees of freedom.

Kolmogorov-Smirnov One-Sample Test

Calculation of Empirical Cumulative Distribution Function

The observations are sorted into ascending order $X_{(1)}$ to $X_{(N)}$. The empirical cdf, $\hat{F}(X)$, is

$$\hat{F}(X) = \begin{cases} 0 & -\infty < X < X_{(1)} \\ i/N & X_{(i)} \le X < X_{(i+1)} \qquad i = 1,\ldots,N-1 \\ 1 & X_{(N)} \le X < \infty \end{cases}$$

Estimation of Parameters for Theoretical Distribution

It is possible to test that the underlying distribution is either uniform, normal, or Poisson. If the parameters are not specified, they are estimated from the data.

- Uniform
  minimum = $X_{(1)}$
  maximum = $X_{(N)}$

- Normal

$$\text{mean } (\bar{X}) = \sum_{i=1}^{N} X_i/N$$

$$\text{standard deviation (S)} = \sqrt{\left(\sum_{i=1}^{N} X_i^2 - \left(\sum_{i=1}^{N} X_i/N\right)\left(\sum_{i=1}^{N} X_i\right)\right)/(N-1)}$$

- Poisson

$$\text{mean } (\lambda) = \sum_{i=1}^{N} X_i/N$$

The test is not done if, for the uniform, all data are not within the user-specified range or, for the Poisson, the data are not non-negative integers. If the variance of the normal or the mean of the Poisson is zero, the test is also not done.

Calculation of Theoretical Cumulative Distribution Functions

- For Uniform

$$F_0(X_i) = \frac{X_i - \min}{\max - \min}$$

- For Poisson

$$F_0(X_i) = \sum_{l=0}^{X_i} \frac{e^{-\lambda}\lambda^l}{l!}$$

If $\lambda \ge 100,000$, the normal approximation is used.

- For Normal

$$F_0(X_i) = F_{0,1}\left(\frac{X_i - \bar{X}}{S}\right)$$

where the algorithm for the generation of $F_{0,1}(Z)$ is described in Appendix 1.

Calculation of Differences

For the Uniform and Normal, two differences are computed:

$$D_i = \hat{F}(X_{i-1}) - F_0(X_i)$$
$$\tilde{D}_i = \hat{F}(X_i) - F_0(X_i) \qquad i = 1, \ldots, N$$

For the Poisson only the $\tilde{D}_i$ are computed. The maximum positive, negative, and absolute differences are printed.

Test Statistic and Significance

The test statistic is

$$Z = \sqrt{N}\ max_i(|D_i|, |\tilde{D}_i|)$$

The two-tailed probability level is estimated using the first three terms of the Smirnov (1948) formula.

If $0 \le Z < 0.27$, $p = 1$

If $0.27 \le Z < 1$, $p = 1 - \frac{2.506628}{Z}(Q + Q^9 + Q^{25})$

where $Q = e^{-1.233701Z^{-2}}$.

If $1 \le Z < 3.1$, $p = 2(Q - Q^4 + Q^9 - Q^{16})$

where $Q = e^{-2Z^2}$.

If $Z \ge 3.1$, $p = 0$.

Runs Test

Computation of Cutting Point

The cutting point which is used to dichotomize the data can be specified as a particular number, or the value of a statistic which is to be calculated. The possible statistics are:

$$\text{Mean} = \frac{\sum_{i=1}^{N} X_i}{N}$$

$$\text{Median} = \begin{cases} (X_{(N/2+1)} + X_{(N/2)})/2 & \text{if } N \text{ is even} \\ X_{((N+1)/2)} & \text{if } N \text{ is odd} \end{cases}$$

where the data are sorted in ascending order from $X_{(1)}$, the smallest, to $X_{(N)}$, the largest.

Mode = most frequently occurring value

If there are multiple modes, the one largest in value is selected and a warning printed.

Number of Runs

For each of the data points, in the sequence in the file, the difference

$$D_i = X_i - \text{CUTPOINT}$$

is computed. If $D_i \geq 0$, the difference is considered positive, otherwise negative. The number of times the sign changes, that is, $D_i \geq 0$ and $D_{i+1} < 0$, or $D_i < 0$ and $D_{i+1} \geq 0$, as well as the number of positive (n_p) and negative (n_a) signs, are determined. The number of runs (R) is the number of sign changes plus one.

Significance Level

The sampling distribution of the number of runs (R) is approximately normal with

$$\mu_r = \frac{2n_p n_a}{n_p + n_a} + 1$$

$$\sigma_r = \sqrt{\frac{2n_p n_a (2n_p n_a - n_a - n_p)}{(n_p + n_a)^2 (n_p + n_a - 1)}}$$

The two-sided significance level is based on

$$Z = \frac{R - \mu_r}{\sigma_r}$$

unless $n < 50$; then

$$Z_c = \begin{cases} (R - \mu_r + 0.5) / \sigma_r & \text{if } R - \mu_r < 0 \\ (R - \mu_r - 0.5) / \sigma_r & \text{if } R - \mu_r > 0 \end{cases}$$

Binomial Test

n_1	number of observations in category 1
n_2	number of observations in category 2
p	test probability
m	$\min(n_1, n_2)$
N	$n_1 + n_2$
p^*	p if $m = n_1$, $1 - p$ if $m = n_2$

2-tailed exact probability =

$$2\left(\sum_{i=0}^{m} \binom{N}{i} p^{*i} (1 - p^*)^{N-i}\right) - \binom{N}{m} p^{*m} (1 - p^*)^{N-m}$$

If an approximate probability is reported, the following algorithm is used:

$$Z_1 = \frac{n_1 + 0.5 - Np}{Np(1-p)} \qquad Z_2 = \frac{n_1 - 0.5 - Np}{Np(1-p)}$$

$P(Z_i)$ = probability from standard normal distribution

Then

$$P(X = n_1) = P(Z_2) - P(Z_1)$$

$$P(X \leq n_1) = P(Z_1)$$

and the 2-tailed approximate probability is

$$2P(X \le n_1) - P(X = n_1)$$

McNemar's Test

Table Construction

The data values are searched to determine the two unique response categories. If the variables X and Y take on more than 2 values, or only one value, a message is printed and the test is not done. The number of cases that have $X_i < Y_i\,(n_1)$ or $X_i > Y_i\,(n_2)$ are counted.

Test Statistic and Significance Level

If $n_1 + n_2 \le 25$, the exact probability of r or fewer "successes" occurring in $n_1 + n_2$ trials when $p = 0.5$ and $r = min\,(n_1, n_2)$ is calculated recursively from the binomial.

$$p(X \le r) = \sum_{i=0}^{r} \binom{n_1 + n_2}{i} (0.5)^{n_1 + n_2}$$

The two-tailed probability level is obtained by doubling the computed value. If $n_1 + n_2 > 25$, a χ^2 approximation with a correction for continuity is used.

$$\chi_c^2 = \frac{(|n_1 - n_2| - 1)^2}{n_1 + n_2}, \text{df} = 1.$$

Sign Test

Count of Signs

For each case, the difference

$$D_i = X_i - Y_i$$

is computed and the number of positive (n_p) and negative (n_n) differences counted. Cases in which $X_i = Y_i$ are ignored.

Test Statistic and Significance Level

If $n_p + n_n \le 25$, the exact probability of r or fewer "successes" occurring in $n_p + n_n$ trials, when $p = 0.5$ and $r = \min\,(n_p, n_n)$, is calculated recursively from the binomial

$$p(X \le r) = \sum_{i=0}^{r} \binom{n_p + n_n}{i} (0.5)^{n_p + n_n}$$

If $n_p + n_n > 25$, the significance level is based on the normal approximation

$$Z_c = \frac{\text{Max}\,(n_p, n_n) - 0.5\,(n_p + n_n) - 0.5}{0.5\sqrt{n_p + n_n}}$$

A two-tailed significance level is printed.

Wilcoxon Matched-Pairs Signed-Rank Test

Computation of Ranked Differences

For each case the difference

$$D_i = X_i - Y_i$$

is computed, as well as the absolute value of D_i. All nonzero absolute differences are then sorted into ascending order, and ranks assigned. In the case of ties, the average rank is used. The sums of the ranks corresponding to positive differences (S_p) and negative differences (S_n) are calculated. The average positive rank is

$$\bar{X}_p = S_p / n_p$$

and the average negative rank is

$$\bar{X}_n = S_n / n_n$$

where n_p is the number of cases with positive differences and n_n the number with negative differences.

Test Statistic and Significance Level

The test statistic is

$$Z = \frac{\min(S_p, S_n) - (n(n+1)/4)}{\sqrt{n(n+1)(2n+1)/24}}$$

where

n = number of cases with nonzero differences

For large sample sizes the distribution of Z is approximately standard normal. A two-tailed probability level is printed.

Cochran's *Q* Test

Computation of Basic Statistics

For each of the N cases the k variables specified may take on only one of two possible values. If more than two values, or only one, are encountered, a message is printed and the test is not done. The first value encountered is designated a "success," and for each case the number of variables that are "successes" are counted. The number of "successes" for case i will be designated R_i and the total number of "successes" for variable l will be designated C_l.

Test Statistic and Level of Significance

Cochran's Q is calculated as

$$Q = \frac{(k-1)\left[k\sum_{l=1}^{k} C_l^2 - \left(\sum_{l=1}^{k} C_l\right)^2\right]}{k\sum_{l=1}^{k} C_l - \sum_{i=1}^{N} R_i^2}$$

The significance level of Q is from the χ^2 distribution with $k-1$ degrees of freedom.

Friedman's Two-Way Analysis of Variance by Ranks

Sum of Ranks

For each of the N cases, the k variables are sorted and ranked, with average rank being assigned in the case of ties. For each of the k variables, the sum of ranks over the cases is calculated. This will be denoted as C_l. The average rank for each variable is

$$\bar{R}_l = C_l / N$$

Test Statistic and Significance Level

The test statistic is

$$\chi^2 = \frac{12}{Nk(k+1)} \sum_{l=1}^{k} C_l^2 - 3N(k+1)$$

The significance level is from the χ^2 distribution with $k-1$ degrees of freedom.

Kendall's Coefficient of Concordance

N, k, and l are the same as in Friedman, above.

Coefficient of Concordance (*W*)

$$W = \left(\frac{F}{N(k-1)}\right)\left(\frac{N^2k(k^2-1)/12}{N^2k(k^2-1)/12 - N\Sigma T}\right)$$

where F = Friedman χ^2 statistic.

$$\Sigma T = \sum_{i=1}^{N} \sum_{l=1}^{k} (t^3 - t)$$

with t = number of variables tied at each tied rank for each case.

Test Statistic and Significance Level

$$\chi^2 = N(k-1)W$$

The significaance level is from the χ^2 distribution with k-1 degrees of freedom.

The Two-Sample Median Test

Table Construction

If the median value is not specified by the user, the combined data from both samples are sorted and the median calculated.

$$Md = \begin{cases} (X_{[N/2]} + X_{[N/2+1]})/2 & \text{if } N \text{ is even} \\ X_{[(N+1)/2]} & \text{otherwise} \end{cases}$$

where $X_{[N]}$ is the largest value and $X_{[1]}$ the smallest. The number of cases in each of the two groups which exceed the median are counted. These will be denoted as g_1 and g_2, and the corresponding sample sizes as n_1 and n_2.

Test Statistic and Significance Level

- If $N \leq 30$, the significance level is from Fisher's exact test. (See Appendix 5.)

- If $N > 30$, the test statistic is

$$\chi_c^2 = \frac{[|g_1(n_2 - g_2) - g_2(n_1 - g_1)| - N/2]^2 N}{(g_1 + g_2)(n_1 + n_2 - g_1 - g_2) n_1 n_2}$$

which is distributed as a χ^2 with 1 degree of freedom.

Mann-Whitney *U* Test

Calculation of Sums of Ranks

The combined data from both groups are sorted and ranks assigned to all cases, with average rank being used in the case of ties. The sum of ranks for each of the groups (S_1 and S_2) is calculated, as well as, for tied observations, $T_i = \frac{t^3 - t}{12}$, where t is the number of observations tied for rank i.

The average rank for each group is

$$\bar{S}_i = S_i / n_i$$

where n_i is the sample size in group i.

Test Statistic and Significance Level

The U statistic for group 1 is

$$U = n_1 n_2 + \frac{n_1(n_1 + 1)}{2} - S_1$$

- If $U > n_1 n_2 / 2$, the statistic used is

$$U' = n_1 n_2 - U$$

- If $n_1 + n_2 \leq 30$ the exact significance level is based on an algorithm of Dineen and Blakesley (1973).

- The test statistic corrected for ties is

$$Z = \frac{(U - n_1 n_2 / 2)}{\sqrt{\frac{n_1 n_2}{N(N-1)} \left(\frac{N^3 - N}{12} - \Sigma_i T_i\right)}}$$

which is distributed approximately as a standard normal. A two-tailed significance level is printed.

Kolmogorov-Smirnov Two-Sample Test

Calculation of the Empirical Cumulative Distribution Functions and Differences

For each of the two groups separately the data are sorted into ascending order, from $X_{[1]}$ to $X_{[n_i]}$, and the empirical cdf for group i is computed as

$$\hat{F}_i(X) = \begin{cases} 0 & -\infty < X < X_{[1]} \\ j/n_i & X_{[j]} \le X < X_{[j+1]} \\ 1 & X_{[n_i]} \le X < \infty \end{cases}$$

For all of the X_j values in the two groups, the difference between the two groups is

$$D_j = \hat{F}_1(X_j) - \hat{F}_2(X_j)$$

where $\hat{F}_1(X_j)$ is the cdf for the group with the larger sample size. The maximum positive, negative, and absolute differences are also computed.

Test Statistic and Level of Significance

The test statistic (Smirnov (1948)) is

$$Z = \max_j |D_j| \sqrt{\frac{n_1 n_2}{n_1 + n_2}}$$

and the significance level is calculated using the Smirnov approximation described in the K-S one-sample test.

Wald-Wolfowitz Runs Test

Calculation of Number of Runs

All observations from the two samples are pooled and sorted into ascending order. The number of changes in the group numbers corresponding to the ordered data are counted. The number of runs (R) is the number of group changes plus one.

If there are ties involving observations from the two groups, both the minimum and maximum number of runs possible are calculated.

Significance Level

If $n_1 + n_2$, the total sample size, is less than or equal to 30, the one-sided significance level is exactly calculated from

$$P(r \le R) = \frac{1}{\binom{n_1 + n_2}{n_1}} \sum_{r=2}^{R} 2 \binom{n_1 - 1}{\frac{r}{2} - 1} \binom{n_2 - 1}{\frac{r}{2} - 1}$$

when r is even. When r is odd

$$P(r \le R) = \frac{1}{\binom{n_1 + n_2}{n_1}} \sum_{r=2}^{R} \left[\binom{n_1 - 1}{k - 1} \binom{n_2 - 1}{k - 2} + \binom{n_1 - 1}{k - 2} \binom{n_2 - 1}{k - 1} \right]$$

where

$$r = 2k - 1$$

For sample sizes greater than 30, the normal approximation is used (see the RUNS test described previously).

Moses Test of Extreme Reaction

Span Computation

Observations from both groups are jointly sorted and ranked, with the average rank being assigned in the case of ties. The ranks corresponding to the smallest and largest control group (first group) members are determined, and the span is computed as

SPAN = Rank (Largest Control Value) - Rank (Smallest Control Value) + 1

rounded to the nearest integer.

Significance Level

The exact one-tailed probability level is computed from

$$P(\text{SPAN} \le n_c - 2h + g) = \frac{\sum_{i=0}^{g} \binom{i + n_c - 2h - 2}{i} \binom{n_e + 2h + 1 - i}{n_e - i}}{\binom{n_c + n_e}{n_c}}$$

where $h = 0$, n_c is the number of cases in the control group, and n_e is the number of cases in the experimental group.

Censoring of Range

The test is repeated, dropping the h lowest and h highest ranks from the control group. If not specified by the user, h is taken to be the integer part of 0.05 n_c or 1, whichever is greater. If h is user specified, the integer value is used unless it is less than one. The significance level is determined as above.

K-Sample Median Test

Table Construction

If the median value is not specified by the user, the combined data from all groups are sorted and the median calculated.

$$Md = \begin{cases} (X_{[N/2]} + X_{[N/2+1]})/2 & \text{if } N \text{ is even} \\ X_{[(N+1)/2]} & \text{if } N \text{ is odd} \end{cases}$$

where $X_{[N]}$ is the largest value and $X_{[1]}$ the smallest.

The number of cases in each of the groups that exceed the median are counted and the following table formed.

	Group				
	1	2	3 ...	k	
LE Md	0_{11}	0_{12}	0_{13} ...	0_{1k}	R_1
GT Md	0_{21}	0_{22}	0_{23} ...	0_{2k}	R_2
	n_1	n_2	n_3	n_k	N

Test Statistic and Level of Significance

The χ^2 statistic for all nonempty groups is calculated as

$$\chi^2 = \sum_{j=1}^{k} \sum_{i=1}^{2} (O_{ij} - E_{ij})^2 / E_{ij}$$

where

$$E_{ij} = \frac{R_i n_j}{N}$$

The significance level is from the χ^2 distribution with k-1 degrees of freedom, where k is the number of nonempty groups. A message is printed if any cell has an expected value less than one, or more than 20% of the cells have expected values less than five.

Kruskal-Wallis One-Way Analysis of Variance

Computation of Sums of Ranks

Observations from all k nonempty groups are jointly sorted and ranked, with the average rank being assigned in the case of ties. The number of tied scores in a set of ties, t_i, is also found, and the sum of $T_i = t_i^3 - t_i$ accumulated. For each group the sum of ranks, R_i, as well as the number of observations, n_i, is obtained.

Test Statistic and Level of Significance

The test statistic unadjusted for ties is

$$H = \frac{12}{N(N+1)} \sum_{i=1}^{k} R_i^2 / n_i - 3(N+1)$$

where N is the total number of observations.

Adjusted for ties, the statistic is

$$H' = \frac{H}{1 - \sum_{i=1}^{m} T_i / (N^3 - N)}$$

where m is the total number of tied sets.

The significance level is based on the χ^2 distribution, with k-1 degrees of freedom.

References

Dineen & Blakesley (1973)

Siegel (1956)

Smirnov (1948)

Normal Probability Plot (NPPLOT)

General

NPPLOT produces a normal probability plot for a given series. The purpose of NPPLOT is to investigate whether the data are from a normal distribution.

Notation

X_i	value of the *i*th observation
$X_{(i)}$	the *i*th smallest observation
R_i	corresponding rank for X_i
n	the length of the series
f_i	fractional rank for X_i
a_i	normal score

Fractional Ranks

Based on the rank R_i for the observation X_i, the fractional rank f_i is computed and used to estimate the expected cumulative distribution function of *X*. There are four methods to calculate the fractional rank f_i:

$$f_i = \begin{cases} (R_i - \frac{3}{8}) / (n + \frac{1}{4}) & \text{Blom} \\ (R_i - \frac{1}{2}) / n & \text{Rankit} \\ (R_i - \frac{1}{3}) / (n + \frac{1}{3}) & \text{Tukey} \\ R_i / (n + 1) & \text{Van der Waerden} \end{cases}$$

Normal Scores

The normal score for case *i* is defined as

$$a_i = \psi(f_i) \qquad , \ i = 1, \ldots, n ,$$

where ψ is the inverse cumulative standard normal (PROBIT) function. The resulting normal scores $a_1, \ldots, a_n$ follow a standard normal distribution. If $X_1, \ldots, X_n$ are from a normal distribution, the normal scores should be a linear function of the original values and a plot of the scores versus original values should be close to a straight line.

Deviations

$$D_i = \frac{X_i - \bar{X}}{S} - a_i \qquad , i = 1, \ldots, n$$

where S is the standard deviation.

References

Blom (1958)

Chambers, Cleveland, Kleiner & Tukey (1983)

Lehmann (1975)

Tukey (1962)

ONEWAY

Notation

X_{lj}	value of the *j*th observation in group *l*
w_{lj}	weight for the *j*th observation in group *l*
$W_{l,j}$	sum of weights of the first *j* cases in group *l*
W_l	sum of weights of all cases in group *l*
k	number of groups, determined as maximum group values minus minimum plus one
k'	number of nonempty groups
n_l	number of cases in group *l*
W	sum of weights of cases in all groups

Group Statistics

- Computation of Group Statistics

A weighted version of the Young-Cramer (1971) algorithm is used to compute recursively the corrected sum of squares for each group.

$$SSQ_{l,i} = SSQ_{l,i-1} + \frac{w_{li}\left(X_{li}W_{l,i-1} - \sum_{j=1}^{i-1} w_{lj}X_{lj}\right)^2}{W_{l,i-1}W_{li}}$$

The initial value is zero, the value for each group after the last observation has been processed is the corrected sum of squares.

$$SS_l = SSQ_{l,n_l}$$

The sum and mean for each group are

$$T_l = \sum_{i=1}^{n_l} X_{li}w_{li}$$

$$\bar{T}_l = T_l / W_l$$

The variance is

$$S_l^2 = SS_l \,/\, (W_l - 1)$$

The grand sum is

$$G = \sum_{i=1}^{k} T_i$$

- Group Statistics from Summary Statistics

With matrix data input, the user supplies sum of weights in each group (W_l), means ($\bar{T}_l$) and standard deviations (S_l). From these,

$$T_l = W_l \bar{T}_l$$
$$SS_l = (W_l - 1) S_l^2$$
$$G = \sum_{i=1}^{k} T_i$$

If the user supplies the pooled variance S_p^2 and its degrees of freedom (D) instead of the individual S_l, and $D < 1$, the program will reset it to

$$D = \sum_{l=1}^{k} W_l - k'$$

The within-group sum of squares is

$$WSS = S_p^2 D$$

The ANOVA Table

Source of Variation	SS	df
Between (BSS)	$\sum_{l=1}^{k} T_l^2 / n_l - G^2 / W$	$k' - 1$
Within (WSS)	$\sum_{l=1}^{k} SS_l$	$W - k'$
	($s_p^2 D$ for matrix input)	(D)
Total (TSS)	$BSS + WSS$	$W - 1$

Mean squares are calculated by dividing each sum of squares by its degree of freedom. The F ratio for testing equality of group means is

$$F = \frac{\text{Mean Square Between}}{\text{Mean Square Within}} = \frac{BSSM}{WSSM}$$

The significance level is obtained from the F distribution with numerator and denominator degrees of freedom.

Basic Statistics

- Descriptive Statistics

Sample size = W_q

Mean = $\bar{T}_q$

Standard deviation = S_q

Standard error = $S_q / \sqrt{W_q}$

- 95% Confidence Interval for the Mean

  $\bar{T}_q \pm t_{W_q - 1} S_q / \sqrt{W_q}$

  where $t_{W_q - 1}$ is the upper 2.5% critical value for the t distribution with $W_q - 1$ degrees of freedom.

Variance Estimates and Confidence Interval for Mean

Fixed-Effects Model

- Pooled Standard Deviation

  $S_p = \sqrt{WSSM}$

- Standard Error

  Standard error = $\sqrt{WSSM / W}$

- 95% Confidence Interval for the Mean

  $\bar{G} \pm t_{W-k'} \sqrt{WSSM / W}$

  where $t_{W-k'}$ is the upper 2.5% critical value for the t distribution with $W - k'$ degrees of freedom.

Random-Effects Model

- Between-Groups Component of Variance (Snedecor and Cochran (1967))

$$\omega^2 = \frac{(BSSM - WSSM)\ (W(k' - 1))}{\left(W^2 - \sum_{i=1}^{k} W_i^2\right)}$$

- Standard Error of the Mean = $\sqrt{V(\bar{G})}$ (Brownlee (1965))

  where

$$V(\bar{G}) = \frac{\left(\sum_{i=1}^{k} W_i^2\right)(k' - 1)\ (BSSM - WSSM)}{W\left(W^2 - \sum_{i=1}^{k} W_i^2\right)} + \frac{WSSM}{W}$$

If $BSSM < WSSM$, $V(\bar{G}) = \frac{WSSM}{W}$ and a warning is printed that the variance component estimate is negative.

- 95% Confidence Interval for the Mean

$$\bar{G} \pm t_{k'-1} \sqrt{V(\bar{G})}$$

where $t_{k'-1}$ is the upper 2.5% critical value for the t distribution with $k' - 1$ degrees of freedom.

Tests for Homogeneity of Variances

- Cochran's C

$$C = \frac{\max_i S_i^2}{\sum_{i=1}^{k} S_i^2}$$

The significance level is based on (Eisenhart (1947)):

$$\Pr\{C > C_{\text{observed}}\} \cong k' \Pr\{F(\bar{n}-1, (\bar{n}-1)(k'-1)) > F_{\text{observed}}\}$$

where

$$F = \frac{(k'-1)C}{1-C}$$
$$\bar{n} = W/k'$$

- Bartlett-Box Test

Computed using only groups which have nonzero variances.

$$M = (W' - g)\log\left[\sum_{j=1}^{k} (W_j - 1) S_j^2 / (W' - g)\right] - \sum_{j=1}^{k} (W_j - 1)\log S_j^2$$

where

g = the number of groups with nonzero variances
W' = sum of weights in groups with nonzero variances

The significance level is based on

$$F = \frac{f_2 M}{(g-1)(f_2/f_1 - M)}$$

where

$$f_1 = 1 - A + 2/f_2$$
$$f_2 = (g+1)/A^2$$
$$A = \frac{1}{3(g-1)}\left[\sum_{i=1}^{k} \frac{1}{W_i - 1} - \frac{1}{W' - g}\right].$$

The computed F is compared to the F distribution with $g - 1$ and f_2 degrees of freedom.

- Hartley's F-Max

$$F = \frac{\max_i S_i^2}{\min_i S_i^2}$$

- Levene Test

$$L = \frac{(W-k')}{(k'-1)} \frac{\sum_{i=1}^{k'} W_i (\bar{Z}_i - \bar{Z})^2}{\sum_{i=1}^{k'} \sum_{l=1}^{n_i} w_{il} (Z_{il} - \bar{Z}_i)^2}$$

where

$$Z_{il} = \left| X_{il} - \bar{T}_i \right|$$

$$\bar{Z}_i = \frac{\sum_{l=1}^{n_i} w_{il} Z_{il}}{W_i}$$

$$\bar{Z} = \frac{\sum_{i=1}^{k'} W_i \bar{Z}_i}{W}$$

User-Supplied Contrasts

Let C_1 through C_k be the coefficients for a particular contrast. If the sum of the coefficients is not zero, a warning is printed and the contrast number starred. For each contrast the following are printed.

Value of the Contrast

$$V = \sum_{i=1}^{k} \bar{T}_i C_i$$

Pooled Variance Statistics

- Standard Error

$$SE = \sqrt{S_p^2 \sum_{i=1}^{k} C_i^2 / W_i}$$

- t Value

$$t = V / SE$$

- Degrees of Freedom

$$W - k'$$

- Two-tailed significance level based on the t distribution with $W - k'$ degrees of freedom.

Separate Variance Statistics

- Standard Error

$$SE = \sqrt{\sum_{i=1}^{k} C_i^2 (S_i^2 / W_i)}$$

- t Value

$$t = V / SE$$

- Degrees of Freedom (Brownlee (1965))

$$df = \frac{\left(\sum_{i=1}^{k} C_i^2 S_i^2 / W_i\right)^2}{\sum_{i=1}^{k} (C_i^2 S_i^2 / W_i)^2 / (W_i - 1)}$$

The two-tailed significance level based on the t distribution with df degrees of freedom.

Polynomial Contrasts (Speed (1976))

If the specified degree of the polynomial (NP) is less than or equal to zero, or greater than five, a message is printed and the procedure terminated. If the degree of the polynomial specified is greater than the number of nonempty groups, it is set to $k' - 1$. If the sums of the weights in each group are equal, only the WEIGHTED contrasts will be generated. For unequal sample sizes with equal spacing between groups, both WEIGHTED and UNWEIGHTED contrasts are computed. For unequal sample sizes and unequal spacing, only WEGHTED contrasts are computed. The metric for the polynomial is the group code.

UNWEIGHTED Contrasts and Statistics

The coefficients for the orthogonal polynomial are calculated recursively from the following relations:

$$c_{i,q} = (i - A_q) c_{i,q-1} - C_q c_{i,q-2}$$

for

$$q = 1, 2, \ldots, \text{NP}.$$
$$i = 1, 2, \ldots, \text{k}.$$

with the initial values

$$c_{i,-1} = 0, c_{i,0} = 1$$

and

$$A_q = \frac{\sum_{i=1}^{k} i\,c_{i,q-1}^2}{\sum_{i=1}^{k} c_{i,q-1}^2}$$

$$C_q = \frac{\sum_{i=1}^{k} c_{i,q-1}^2}{\sum_{i=1}^{k} c_{i,q-2}^2} \qquad \text{for } q \ge 2$$

$$C_q = 0 \qquad \text{for } q = 1$$

The F statistic for the qth degree contrast is computed as

$$F = \frac{\left[\sum_{i=1}^{k} (\bar{T}_i - \bar{G})\,c_{i,q}\right]^2}{\sum_{i=1}^{k} c_{i,q}^2 / W_i} / WSSM$$

where $WSSM$ is the mean square within. The significance level is obtained from the F distribution with 1 and $W - k'$ degrees of freedom.

WEIGHTED Contrasts and Statistics (Emerson (1968), Robson (1959))

The contrast for the qth degree polynomial component is computed from the following recursive relations:

$$d_{i,q} = (i - A'_q)\,d_{i,q-1} - C'_q d_{i,q-2}$$

for

$$q = 1, 2, \ldots, \text{NP}.$$
$$i = 1, \ldots, \text{k}.$$

with initial values

$$d_{i,0} = 1,\ d_{i,-1} = 0$$

$$A'_q = \frac{\sum_{i=1}^{k} i\,W_i d_{i,q-1}^2}{\sum_{i=1}^{k} W_i d_{i,q-1}^2}$$

$$C'_q = \frac{\sum_{i=1}^{k} i W_i d_{i,q-1} d_{i,q-2}}{\sum_{i=1}^{k} W_i d_{i,q-2}^2} \qquad \text{for } q \ge 2$$

$$C'_q = 0 \qquad \text{for } q = 1$$

The test for the contribution of the qth degree orthogonal polynomial component is based on

$$F = D_q / WSSM$$

where

$$D_q = \frac{\left(\sum_{i=1}^{k} W_i \bar{T}_i d_{i,q}\right)^2}{\sum_{i=1}^{k} W_i d_{i,q}^2}$$

The significance level is computed from the F distribution with degrees of freedom 1 and $W - k'$.

The test for deviation from the qth degree polynomial is based on

$F = DD_q / WSSM$

where

$$DD_q = \left(BSS - \sum_{j=1}^{q} D_j\right) / (k' - q - 1)$$

The significance level is computed from the F distribution with degrees of freedom $k' - q - 1$ and $W - k'$. The highest degree printed will be the minimum of $(k' - 2)$ and 5.

Multiple Comparisons (Winer (1971))

Generation of Ranges (R_r)

The Student-Newman-Keuls (SNK), TUKEY, and TUKEYB procedures are all based on the studentized range, $S_{r,f}$, where r is the number of steps between means and f is the degrees of freedom for the within-groups mean square. For the above tests, only $\alpha = 0.05$ can be used.

The appropriate range of values for the tests are

SNK $\quad R_r = S_{r,f} \qquad r = 2, \ldots, k'$

TUKEY $\quad R_r = S_{k',f}$

TUKEYB $\quad R_r = \frac{(S_{r,f} + S_{k',f})}{2}$

For the DUNCAN procedure, alphas of 0.01, 0.05, and 0.10 can be used. The ranges $(D_{r,f})$ are generated using the algorithm of Gebhardt (1966).

DUNCAN $\quad R_r = D_{r,f} \qquad r = 2, \ldots, k'$

The Scheffé, LSD, and modified LSD procedures all use critical points from the F distribution. Any $\alpha \le 0.5$ can be used.

SCHEFFE $\quad R_r = \sqrt{2(k' - 1) F_{1-\alpha}(k' - 1, f)}$

LSD $\quad R_r = \sqrt{2F_{1-\alpha}(1, f)}$

MODLSD $\quad R_r = \sqrt{2F_{1-\alpha'}(1, f)}$

where

$$\alpha' = \frac{2\alpha}{k'(k' - 1)}$$

Compute multiplier of the ranges for the difference of means i and j.

$$M_{i,j} = S_p \sqrt{\frac{1}{2}\left(\frac{1}{n_i} + \frac{1}{n_j}\right)} \qquad \text{(default)}$$

$$M_{i,j} = S_p \sqrt{\frac{\sum_{l=1}^{k} 1/n_l}{k'}} \qquad \text{(harmonic mean for all groups)}$$

Establishment of Homogeneous Subsets

If the sample sizes in all groups are equal, or the harmonic mean for all groups has been selected, or the multiple comparison procedure is SNK or DUNCAN, homogeneous subsets are established as follows:

The means are sorted into ascending order from $\bar{T}_{(1)}$ to $\bar{T}_{(k')}$. Values of i and q such that

$$\left|\bar{T}_{(q)} - \bar{T}_{(i)}\right| \le R_{q-i+1} M_{q,i} \qquad (*)$$

are systematically searched for and

$$\{\bar{T}_{(i)}, \ldots, \bar{T}_{(q)}\}$$

is considered a homogeneous subset. The search procedure is as follows:

At each step t, the value of i is incremented by 1 (starting value is 1), and $q = k'$. The value of q is then decremented by one until (*) is true. Call this value q_t. If $q_t > q_{t-1}$ and (*) is true

$$\{\bar{T}_{(i)}, \ldots, \bar{T}_{q_t}\}$$

is considered homogeneous. Otherwise i is incremented and the next step done. The procedure terminates when $i = k$ or $q_t = k$.

In all other situations, all nonredundant pairs of groups are compared using the criteria of (*). A table containing all pairs of groups is printed with symbols indicating group means which are significantly different.

References

Brownlee (1965)

Duncan (1955)

Eisenhart (1947)

Emerson (1968)

Gebhardt (1966)

Kramer (1956)

Miller (1966)

Robson (1959)

Snedecor & Cochran (1967)

Speed (1976)

Winer (1971)

Young & Cramer (1971)

ORTHOPLAN

General

This procedure generates an orthogonal main-effects design. It will find the smallest orthogonal plan to fit the factors having at least as many combinations as requested.

Picking the Plan

From a library of prepared plans, select the shortest plan that can be adapted to the design and that satisfies the minimum size requirement provided by the user. If no plan exists that satisfies the minimum size requirement, pick the largest plan that can be adapted.

Adapting the Prepared Plans

- Generating multiple factors from one column

A four-level factor may be transformed into three two-level columns using the rule in Table 1.

Table 1: Converting a four-level factor to three two-level factors

Original Code	A	B	C
0	0	0	0
1	0	1	1
2	1	0	1
3	1	1	0

An eight-level factor may be transformed into seven two-level factors using the rule in Table 2.

Table 2: Converting an eight-level factor to seven two-level factors

Original Code	A	B	C	D	E	F	G
0	0	0	0	0	0	0	0
1	1	0	0	1	1	0	1
2	0	1	0	1	0	1	1
3	1	1	0	0	1	1	0
4	0	0	1	0	1	1	1
5	1	0	1	1	0	1	0
6	0	1	1	1	1	0	0
7	1	1	1	0	0	0	1

A nine-level factor may be transformed into four three-level columns using the rule in Table 3.

Table 3: Converting a nine-level factor to four three-level factors

Original Code	A	B	C	D
0	0	0	0	0
1	0	1	1	2

2	**0**	**2**	**2**	**1**
3	**1**	**0**	**1**	**1**
4	**1**	**1**	**2**	**0**
5	**1**	**2**	**0**	**2**
6	**2**	**0**	**2**	**2**
7	**2**	**1**	**0**	**1**
8	**2**	**2**	**1**	**0**

- Changing the number of levels in a column

  Any factor of *m* levels can be transformed into a factor of $n < m$ levels by many-to-one mappings without changing its orthogonality. Any mapping may be used; i mod *n* is used here.

Library of Prepared Plans

Plackett-Burman Plans

Plackett & Burman(1946) describe a series of plans which can be generated from a single column by rotation. The general algorithm for generating any of these plans is:

- Let *L* be the number of levels for which the plan is designed. No factor in the specific design may have more than *L* levels.
- Let *N* be the number of rows (combinations) finally to be generated. Note than $N = F + 1$ where *F* is defined below.
- Starting with a given column of *N*-1 level codes, rotate one position to generate each new column.
- Finally, add a row of zeroes.

$\frac{(N-1)}{(L-1)}$ orthogonal columns may be generated in this fashion.

The Plackett-Burman plans used here are designated *PB L.F*, where *L* is the maximum number of levels and *F* is the number of factors:

Label	Generating column
PB 2.7	11101 00
PB 2.11	11011 10001 0
PB 2.15	11110 10110 01000
PB 2.19	11001 11101 01000 0110
PB 2.23	11111 01011 00110 01010 000
PB 2.31	00001 01011 10110 00111 11001 10100 1
PB 2.35	01011 10001 11110 11100 10000 10101 10010
PB 2.43	11001 01001 11011 11100 01011 10000 01000 11010 110
PB 2.47	11111 01111 00101 01110 01001 10110 00101 01100 00100 00
PB 2.59	11011 10101 00100 11101 11100 11111 00000 11000 01000 11011 01010 0010

PB 3.4	01220 211
PB 3.13	00101 21120 11100 20212 21022 2
PB 3.40	01111 20121 12120 20221 10201 10012 22021 00200 02222 10212 21210 10112 20102 20021 11012 00100
PB 5.6	04112 10322 42014 43402 3313
PB 7.8	01262 21605 32335 20413 11430 65155 61024 54425 03646 634

Addelman Plans

Addelman (1961) described general methods for generating orthogonal main effects plans. That paper included a number of such designs, and using those methods, the authors generated more.

Figure 1: 18 rows, 7 columns of 3 levels each

```
0000000 0021011
0112111 0100122
0221222 0212200
1011120 1002221
1120201 1111002
1202012 1220110
2022102 2010212
2101210 2122020
2210021 2201101
```

Figure 2: 8 rows, 1 column of 4 levels plus 4 columns of 2 levels

```
0 0000
0 1111
1 0011
1 1100
2 0101
2 1010
3 0110
3 1001
```

Figure 3: 16 rows, 5 columns of 4 levels each

```
00000 02231
10111 12320
20222 22013
30333 32102
01123 03312
11032 13203
21301 23130
31210 33021
```

Figure 4: 32 rows, 9 columns of 4 levels each

000000000	002130213
011231111	013301302
022312222	020222031
033123333	031013120
101111032	103021221
110320123	112210330
123203210	121333003
132032301	130102112
202223102	200313311
213012013	211122200
220131320	222001133
231300231	233230022
303332130	301202323
312103021	310033232
321020312	323110101
330211203	332321010

Figure 5: 64 rows, 21 columns of 4 levels each

000000000000000000000	000222233331111022220
111111111111111100000	111333322220000122220
222222222222222200000	222000011113333222220
333333333333333300000	333111100002222322220
123012301230123012301	123230132101032030121
032103210321032112301	032321023010123130121
301230123012301212301	301012310323210230121
210321032103210312301	210103201232301330121
231023102310231023102	231201331021320001322
320132013201320123102	320310220130231101322
013201320132013223102	013023113203102201322
102310231023102323102	102132002312013301322
312031203120312031203	312213030211203013023
203120312031203131203	203302121300312113023
130213021302130231203	130031212033021213023
021302130213021331203	021120303122130313023
000111122223333011110	000333311112222033330
111000033332222111110	111222200003333133330
222333300001111211110	222111133330000233330
333222211110000311110	333000022221111333330
123103223013210003211	123321010322301021031
032012332102301103211	032230101233210121031
301321001231032203211	301103232100123221031
210230110320123303211	210012323011032321031
231132020133102032012	231310213202013010232
320023131022013132012	320201302313102110232
013310202311320232012	013132031020231210232
102201313200231332012	102023120131320310232
312120321303021020313	312302112032130002133
203031230212130120313	203213003123021102133
130302103121203220313	130120330210312202133
021213012030312320313	021031221301203302133

Figure 6: 16 rows, 1 column of 8 levels plus 8 columns of 2 levels

```
0 00000000  0 11111111
1 01010101  1 10101010
2 00001111  2 11110000
3 01011010  3 10100101
4 00111100  4 11000011
5 01101001  5 10010110
6 00110011  6 11001100
7 01100110  7 10011001
```

Figure 7: 32 rows, 1 column of 8 levels plus 8 columns of 4 levels

```
0 00000000  0 22222222
1 01230123  1 23012301
2 02021313  2 20203131
3 03211230  3 21033012
4 00113322  4 22331100
5 01323201  5 23101023
6 02132031  6 20310213
7 03302112  7 21120330
0 11111111  0 33333333
1 10321032  1 32103210
2 13130202  2 31312020
3 12300321  3 30122103
4 11002233  4 33220011
5 10232310  5 32010132
6 13023120  6 31201302
7 12213003  7 30031221
```

Figure 8: 64 rows, 9 columns of 8 levels each

```
000000000  202222222  404444444  606666666
011234567  213016745  415670123  617452301
022465713  220647531  426021357  624203175
033651274  231473056  437215630  635037412
044517326  246735104  440153762  642371540
055723641  257501463  451367205  653145027
066172435  264350617  462536071  660714253
077346152  275164370  473702516  671520734
101111111  303333333  505555555  707777777
110325476  312107654  514761032  716543210
123574602  321756420  527130246  725312064
132740365  330562147  536304721  734126503
145406237  347624015  541042673  743260451
154632750  356410572  550276314  752054136
167063524  365241706  563427160  761605342
176257043  374075261  572613407  770431625
```

Figure 9: 27 rows, 1 column of 9 levels plus 9 columns of 3 levels

0 000000000	3 011001111	6 022002222
0 112121212	3 120122020	6 101120101
0 221212121	3 202210202	6 210211010
1 000111122	4 011112200	7 022110011
1 112202001	4 120200112	7 101201220
1 221020210	4 202021021	7 210022102
2 000222211	5 011220022	8 022221100
2 112010120	5 120011201	8 101012012
2 221101002	5 202102110	8 210100221

Figure 10: 81 rows, 10 columns of 9 levels each

0000000000	0336258147	0663174285
1011111111	1347036258	1674285063
2022222222	2358147036	2685063174
3033333333	3360582471	3606417528
4044444444	4371360582	4617528306
5055555555	5382471360	5628306417
6066666666	6303825714	6630741852
7077777777	7314603825	7641852630
8088888888	8325714603	8652630741
0112345678	0448561723	0775426831
1120453786	1456372804	1783507642
2101534867	2437480615	2764318750
3145678012	3472804156	3718750264
4153786120	4480615237	4726831075
5134867201	5461723048	5707642183
6178012345	6415237480	6742183507
7186120453	7423048561	7750264318
8167201534	8404156372	8731075426
0221687354	0557813462	0884732516
1202768435	1538624570	1865840327
2210876543	2546705381	2873651408
3254021687	3581246705	3827165840
4235102768	4562057813	4808273651
5243210876	5570138624	5816084732
6287354021	6524570138	6851408273
7268435102	7505381246	7832516084
8276543210	8513462057	8840327165

Decision Rules

Each value of L (the maximum number of levels in the design) has a distinct decision rule. In their descriptions, the following notation is used:

M the user-supplied minimum number of rows desired in the plan.

F the number of factors in the design.

- L=2

If all factors have two levels, simply select the smallest two-level Plackett-Burman plan for which $N_{plan} \geq max\,(M, F + 1)$

- L=3

  Let P = the number of factors with more than 2 levels, and let $K = F + 2P$.

  If $M < 9$ and $F < 6$ and $P < 2$, base the plan on Figure 2.

  If $M < 10$ and $F < 5$, base the plan on PB 3.4.

  Otherwise, if $M < 17$ and $K < 15$, base it on Figure 3.

  Otherwise, if $M < 19$ and $F < 8$, base it on Figure 1.

  Otherwise, if $M < 28$ and $F < 14$, base it on PB 3.13.

  Otherwise, if $M < 65$ and $F < 22$, use the rules for L=4 plans.

  Otherwise, if $F < 41$, base the plan on PB 3.40.

  If $F > 40$, there are too many factors.

- L=4

  Let P = the number of factors with more than 2 levels, and let $K = F + 2P$.

  If $M < 9$ and $F < 6$ and $P < 2$, base the plan on Figure 2.

  Otherwise, if $M < 17$ and $K \leq 15$, base it on Figure 3.

  Otherwise, if $M < 26$ and $K < 19$, base it on PB 5.6.

  Otherwise, if $M < 33$ and $K < 28$, base it on Figure 4.

  Otherwise, if $M < 49$ and $K < 23$, use the rules for L=7.

  Otherwise, if $K < 64$, base the plan on Figure 5.

  Otherwise, there are too many factors.

  A four-level factor may be transformed into three two-level columns using the rule in Table 1.

- L=5

  Create a plan based on the L=7 rules.

  If that plan has 26 or more rows and $M < 26$ and $F < 7$, base the plan on PB 5.6.

  Otherwise, use the plan generated in step 1.

- L=6

  Treat this case as L=7.

- L=7

  Generate the best plan based on L=8.

  If that plan has more than 49 rows and $M < 50$ and $F < 9$, base the plan on PB 7.8.

  Otherwise, use the plan generated in step 1.

- L=8

  Let P be the number of factors with more than 2 levels, and $K = F + 6P$.

  If $M < 17$ and $F < 10$ and $P < 2$, then base the plan on Figure 6.

Otherwise, if $M < 28$ and $F < 11$ and only one factor has more than 3 levels, base the plan on the L=9 rules.

Otherwise, if $M < 33$ and $F < 10$ and only one factor has more than 4 levels, base the plan on Figure 7.

Otherwise, if $M < 65$ and $K < 64$, base it on Figure 8.

Otherwise, base the plan on the L=9 rules.

An eight-level factor may be transformed into seven two-level factors using the rule in Table 2.

- L=9

Let P be the number of factors with more than three levels, and $K = F+3P$.

If $M < 28$ and $F < 11$ and $P < 2$, then base the plan on Figure 9.

Otherwise, if $K < 41$, base it on Figure 10.

Otherwise, there are too many factors.

A nine-level factor may be transformed into four three-level columns using the rule in Table 3.

Randomization

After a basic plan has been selected, columns are selected at random (if possible) to fit the given design. If the basic plan is asymmetric, i.e., one column has more levels than the others, then the factor in the plan with many levels must be assigned to the factor in the design with many levels, and the remaining plan factors assigned randomly to the remaining design factors.

If factors are to be transformed into multiple factors (e.g., eight-level factors transformed into two-level factors), one may randomly assign columns from the plan to design factors with many levels first, then transform the remaining columns, then select from the transformed columns at random the columns needed.

References

Plackett & Burman (1946)

Addelman (1962)

OVERALS

General

The OVERALS algorithm was first described in Gifi (1981) and Van der Burg, De Leeuw & Verdegaal (1984); also see Verdegaal (1986), Van de Geer (1987), Van der Burg, De Leeuw & Verdegaal (1988) and Van der Burg (1988). Characteristic features of OVERALS, conceived by De Leeuw (1973), are the partitioning of the variables into K sets and the ability to specify any of a number of measurement levels for each variable separately. Analogously to the situation in multiple regression and canonical correlation analysis, OVERALS focuses on the relationships between sets; any particular variable only contributes to the results inasmuch as it provides information that is independent of the other variables in the same set.

Notation

n	number of cases (objects)
m	total number of variables
p	number of dimensions
K	number of sets

For variable j, $j = 1, ..., m$

k_j	number of categories (distinct values) of variable j
G_j	indicator matrix for variable j, of order $n \times k_j$

The elements of G_j are defined as $i = 1, ..., n; r = 1, ..., k_j$

$$g_{(j)ir} = \begin{cases} 1 & \text{when the } i^{th} \text{ object is in the } r^{th} \text{ category of variable } j \\ 0 & \text{when the } i^{th} \text{ object is not in the } r^{th} \text{ category of variable } j \end{cases}$$

D_j diagonal matrix containing the univariate marginals, i.e., the column sums of G_j.

For set k, $k = 1, ..., K$

$J(k)$ index set of the variables that belong to set k (so that we may write $j \in J(k)$)

m_k	number of variables in set k (number of elements in $J(k)$)
M_k	binary, diagonal $n \times n$ matrix, with diagonal elements defined as

$$m_{(k)ii} = \begin{cases} 1 & \text{when the } i^{th} \text{ observation is within the range } [1, k_j] \text{ for all } j \in J(k) \\ 0 & \text{when the } i^{th} \text{ observation is outside the range } [1, k_j] \text{ for all } j \in J(k) \end{cases}$$

The quantification matrices and parameter vectors are

X	object scores, of order $n \times p$
X_j	auxiliary matrix of order $n \times p$, with corrected object scores when fitting variable j
Y_j	category quantifications for multiple variables, of order $k_j \times p$: multiple category coordinates for multiple variables
y_j	category quantifications for single variables, of order k_j
a_j	variable weights for single variables, of order p
Q_k	quantified variables of the kth set, of order $n \times m_k$ with columns $q_j = G_j y_j$
$\underline{Y}$	collection of multiple and single category quantifications across variables and sets.

Note: the matrices G_j, D_j, and M_k are exclusively notational devices; they are stored in reduced form, and the program fully profits from their sparseness by replacing matrix multiplications with selective accumulation.

Objective Function Optimization

The OVERALS objective is to find object scores X and a set of $\underline{Y}_j$ (for $j = 1, ..., m$) — the underlining indicates that they may be restricted in various ways — so that the function

$$\sigma(X;\underline{Y}) = 1/K \sum_k tr\left(X - \sum_{j \in J(k)} G_j \underline{Y}_j\right)' M_k \left(X - \sum_{j \in J(k)} G_j \underline{Y}_j\right)$$

is minimal, under the normalization restriction $X'M_*X = Kn\ I$, where the matrix $M_* = \sum_k M_k$ and I is the $p \times p$ identity matrix. The inclusion of M_k in $\sigma(X;\underline{Y})$ provides the following mechanism for weighting the loss: whenever any of the data values for object i in set k falls outside its particular range $[1, k_j]$, a circumstance which may indicate either genuine missing values or simulated missing values for the sake of analysis, all other data values for object i in set k are disregarded (listwise deletion *per set*). The diagonal of M_* contains the number of "active" sets for each object. The object scores are also centered, i.e., they satisfy $u'M_*X = 0$ with u denoting an n-vector with ones.

The following measurement levels are distinguished in OVERALS:

- Multiple nominal
  $\underline{Y}_j = Y_j$ (unrestricted)

- Single nominal
  $\underline{Y}_j = y_j q_j'$ (rank-one and equality restrictions)

- (Single) ordinal
  $\underline{Y}_j = y_j q_j'$ and $y_j \in C_j$ (rank-one and monotonicity restrictions)

- (Single) numerical
  $\underline{Y}_j = y_j q_j'$ and $y_j \in L_j$ (rank-one and linearity restrictions)

For each variable these levels can be chosen independently. The general requirement in the "single" options is $\underline{Y}_j = y_j q_j'$, i.e., $\underline{Y}_j$ is of rank one; for identification purposes y_j is always normalized so that $y_j' D_j y_j = n$, which implies that the variance of the quantified variable $q_j = G_j y_j$ is 1. In the ordinal case the additional restriction $y_j \in C_j$ means that y_j must be located in the convex cone of all k_j-vectors with nondecreasing elements; in the numerical case the additional restriction $y_j \in L_j$ means that y_j must be located in the subspace of all k_j-vectors that are a linear transformation of the vector consisting of k_j successive integers (= normalized data vector).

Optimization is achieved by executing the following iteration scheme:

(1) Initialization I or II

(2) Loop across sets and variables

(3) Eliminate contributions of other variables

(4) Update category quantifications

(5) Update object scores

(6) Orthonormalization

(7) Convergence test: repeat (2)–(6) or continue

(8) Rotation

Steps (1) to (8) are explained below.

(1) Initialization

I. Random

The object scores X are initialized with random numbers, which are normalized so that $u'M_*X = 0$ and $X'M_*X = Kn\, I$, yielding $\tilde{X}$. For multiple variables the initial category quantifications are set equal to zero. For single variables the initial category quantifications $\tilde{y}_j$ are defined as the first k_j successive integers normalized in such a way that $u'D_j\tilde{y}_j = 0$ and $\tilde{y}_j D_j \tilde{y}_j = n$, and the initial variable weights are set equal to zero.

II. Nested

In this case the above iteration scheme is executed twice. In the first cycle (initialized with initialization I) all single variables are temporarily treated as single numerical, so that for the second, proper cycle all relevant quantities can be copied from the results of the first one.

(2) Loop across sets and variables

The next two steps are repeated for $k = 1, \ldots, K$ and all $j \in J(k)$. During the updating of variable j all parameters of the remaining variables are fixed at their current values.

(3) Eliminate contributions of other variables

For quantifying variable j in set k, we define the auxiliary matrix

$$V_{(k)j} = \sum_{j \in J(k)} G_j \underline{Y}_j - G_j \underline{Y}_j$$

which accumulates the contributions of the other variables in set k; then in $(X - V_{(k)j})$ the contributions of the other variables are eliminated from the object scores. This device enables us to write the loss $\sigma(X;\underline{Y}_j)$ as a function of X and $\underline{Y}_j$ only:

$$\sigma(X;\underline{Y}_j) = \text{constant} + 1/K \operatorname{tr}\left(\left((X - V_{(k)j}) - G_j\underline{Y}_j\right)' M_k\left((X - V_{(k)j}) - G_j\underline{Y}_j\right)\right)$$

With fixed current values $\tilde{X}$ the unconstrained minimum over $\underline{Y}_j$ is attained for the matrix

$$\tilde{Y}_j = (G_j' M_k G_j)^{-1} G_j' M_k (\tilde{X} - V_{(k)j})$$

which forms the basis of the further computations. When switching to another variable l in the same set, the matrix $V_{(k)l}$ is not computed from scratch, but updated:

$$V_{(k)l} \leftarrow V_{(k)j} + G_j\underline{Y}_j - G_l\underline{Y}_l$$

(4) Update category quantifications

(a) For multiple nominal variables the new category quantifications are simply

$$\underline{Y}_j^+ = \tilde{Y}_j$$

(b) For single variables one cycle of an ALS algorithm (De Leeuw et al., 1976) is executed for computing the rank-one decomposition of $\tilde{Y}_j$, with restrictions on the left-hand vector.

This cycle starts from the previous category quantifications $\tilde{y}_j$ with

$$a_j^+ = \tilde{Y}_j' D_j \tilde{y}_j$$

When the current variable is numerical we are ready; else we compute

$$y_j^* = \tilde{Y}_j a_j^+.$$

Now, when the current variable is single nominal we can simply obtain y_j^+ by normalizing y_j^* in the way indicated below; else the variable must be ordinal, and we have to insert the weighted monotonic regression process

$$y_j^* \leftarrow WMON(y_j^*)$$

which makes y_j^* monotonically increasing. The weights used are the diagonal elements of D_j and the subalgorithm used is the up-and-down-blocks minimum violators algorithm (Kruskal, 1964; Barlow et al., 1972). The result is normalized:

$$y_j^+ = n^{1/2} y_j^* (y_j^{*\prime} D_j y_j^*)^{-1/2}$$

Finally, we set

$$\underline{Y}_j^+ = y_j^+ a_j^{+\prime}$$

(5) Update object scores

During the loop across sets, the auxiliary score matrix W is accumulated as

$$W \leftarrow W + M_k \sum_{j \in J(k)} G_j \underline{Y}_j^+$$

and centered with respect to M_*:

$$X^* = \{I - M_* uu' / u' M_* u\} W$$

From these two steps $M_*^{-1} X^*$ would yield the locally best update without orthogonality constraints.

(6) Orthonormalization

The orthonormalization problem is to find an M_*-orthonormal X^+ that is closest to $M_*^{-1}X^*$ in the M_*-weighted least squares sense. In OVERALS this is done by setting

$$X^+ \leftarrow m^{1/2}M_*^{-1/2}\text{PROCRU}\,(M_*^{-1/2}X^*)$$

The notation PROCRU( ) is used to denote the Procrustes orthonormalization process. If the singular value decomposition of the input matrix $M_*^{-1/2}X^*$ is denoted by $K\Lambda L'$, with $K'K = I, L'L = I$, and Λ diagonal, then the output matrix $KL' = M_*^{-1/2}X^* L\Lambda^{-1}L'$ satisfies orthonormality in the unit metric (Cliff, 1966). The matrix X^+ defined above satisfies orthonormality in the metric M_*. The calculation of L and Λ is based on tridiagonalization with Householder transformations followed by the implicit QL algorithm (Wilkinson, 1965).

(7) Convergence test

The difference between consecutive values of tr Λ^4 is compared with the user-specified convergence criterion ε — a small positive number. After convergence the badness-of-fit value $\sigma(X;\underline{Y}) = p - \text{tr}\,\Lambda^4$ is also given. Steps (2) to (6) are repeated as long as the loss difference exceeds ε.

(8) Rotation

The OVERALS loss function $\sigma(X;\underline{Y})$ is invariant under simultaneous rotations of X and $\underline{Y}$. It can be shown that the solution is related to the principal axes of the average projection operator

$$Q_* = 1/K\sum_k M_k Q_k (Q_k' M_k Q_k)^{-1} Q_k' M_k$$

In order to achieve principal axes orientation, which is useful for purposes of interpretation and comparison, it is sufficient to find a rotation matrix that makes the cross products of the matrix $M_*^{-1/2}X^*$ diagonal — a matrix identical to the one used in the Procrustes orthonormalization in step (6). In the terminology of that section we rotate the matrices X^+, $\underline{Y}^+$, and the vectors a_j with the matrix L. The rotation matrix L is taken from the last PROCRU operation as described in step (6).

Diagnostics

Maximum Rank

The maximum rank ρ_{max} indicates the maximum number of dimensions that can be computed for any data set (if exceeded, OVERALS adjusts the number of dimensions if possible and issues a message). In general we have:

$$\rho_{max} = \begin{cases} \min\{(n-1), r_1, r_2\} & \text{if } K = 2 \\ \min\{(n-1), \max r_k\} & \text{if } K > 2 \end{cases}$$

where the quantities r_k are defined as

$$r_k = \sum_{j \in JM(k)} k_j + m_{k1} - m_{k2}.$$

Here m_{k1} is the number of multiple variables with no missing values in set k, m_{k2} the number of single variables in set k, and $JM(k)$ an index set recording which variables are multiple in set k. Furthermore, OVERALS stops when either one of the following conditions is not satisfied.

(1) $r_k < n_k - 1$

(2) $n_k > 2$

(3) $\sum_k r_k \leq \sum_k (n_k - 1) - (n_{\max} - 1)$.

Here n_k denotes the number of nonmissing objects in set k, and $n_{\max}$ the maximum across all of n_k.

Marginal Frequencies

The frequencies table gives the univariate marginals and the number of missing values (i.e., values that are regarded as out of range for the current analysis) for each variable. These are computed as the column sums of D_j and the total sum of M_k for $j \in J(k)$.

Fit and Loss Measures

In the *Summary of Analysis*, loss and fit measures are reported:

- Loss per set

This is K times $\sigma(X;\underline{Y})$, partitioned with respect to sets and dimensions; the means per dimension are also given.

- Eigenvalue

The values listed here are 1 minus the means per dimension defined above, forming a partitioning of FIT, which is $\rho - \sigma(X;\underline{Y})$ when convergence is reached. These quantities are the eigenvalues of Q_* defined in section (8).

Other fit and loss measures reported are

- Multiple fit

This measure is computed as the diagonal of the matrix $\underline{Y}_j' D_j \underline{Y}_j$, computed for all variables (rows) with dimensions given in the columns.

- Single fit

This table gives the squared weights, computed only for variables that are single. The sum of squares of the weights: $a_j' a_j$.

- Single loss

Single loss is equal to multiple fit minus single fit for single variables only. It is the loss incurred by the imposition of the rank-one measurement level restrictions.

Component Loadings and Qualifications

After the *Summary of Analysis*, the weights are reported, then the quantities:

- Component loadings for single variables

  Loadings are the lengths of the projections of the quantified (single) variables onto the object space: $q_j' X$. When there are no missing data, the loadings are equal to the correlations between the quantified variables and the object scores (the principal components).

- Component loadings for multiple variables

  In this case the loadings are computed for each of the multiple quantifications, i.e., each column of Y_j. For dimension s we have

  $$(ny_{(j)s}' \ D_j y_{(j)s})^{-1/2} y_{(j)s}' G_j' X$$

  Next the object scores are reported. The following results are arranged by variable:

- Category quantifications (either Y_j or y_j)

- Single coordinates

  For single variables only: $\underline{Y}_j = y_j a_j'$.

- Multiple coordinates

  These are $\tilde{Y}_j$ defined previously, i.e., the unconstrained minimizers of the loss function, for multiple variables equal to the category quantifications.

- Category centroids

  The centroids of all objects that share the same category, $D_j^{-1} G_j' X$. Note that they are not necessarily equal to the multiple coordinates.

- Projected category centroids

  For single variables only, $y_j b_j'$. These are the points on a line in the direction given by the loadings b_j that result from projection of the category centroids with weights D_j.

References

Barlow, Bartholomew, Bremner, & Brunk (1972)

Cliff (1966)

De Leeuw (1973)

De Leeuw, Young, & Takane(1976)

Gifi (1981)

Kruskal (1964)

Van de Geer (1987)

Van der Burg (1988)

Van der Burg, De Leeuw, & Verdegaal (1984)

Van der Burg, De Leeuw, & Verdegaal (1988)

Verdegaal (1986)
Wilkinson (1965)

PARTIAL CORR

Notation

N	number of cases
X_{kl}	value of variable k for case l
w_l	weight for case l
W_{ij}	sum of the weights of cases used in computation of statistics for variables i and j
W_i	sum of the weights of cases used in computation of statistics for variable i

Statistics

- Zero Order Correlations

$$r_{ij} = \frac{\sum_{l=1}^{N} w_l X_{il} X_{jl} - \left(\sum_{l=1}^{N} w_l X_{il}\right)\left(\sum_{l=1}^{N} w_l X_{jl}\right) / W_{ij}}{\sqrt{\left[\sum_{l=1}^{N} w_l X_{il}^2 - \frac{\left(\sum_{l=1}^{N} w_l X_{il}\right)^2}{W_{ij}}\right]\left[\sum_{l=1}^{N} w_l X_{jl}^2 - \frac{\left(\sum_{l=1}^{N} w_l X_{jl}\right)^2}{W_{ij}}\right]}}$$

Noncomputable coefficients are set to system missing. The significance level for r_{ij} is based on

$$t = r_{ij}\sqrt{\frac{W_{ij} - 2}{1 - r_{ij}^2}}$$

which, under the null hypothesis, is distributed as a t with $W_{ij} - 2$ degrees of freedom. By default, one-tail significance levels are printed.

- Means and Standard Deviations

$$\bar{X}_j = \sum_{i=1}^{N} w_i X_{ji} / W_j$$

$$S_j = \sqrt{\left(\sum_{i=1}^{N} w_i X_{ji}^2 - \bar{X}_j^2 W_j\right) / (W_j - 1)}$$

If pairwise deletion is selected, means and standard deviations are based on *all* nonmissing cases. For listwise deletion, only cases with no missing values on any specified variable are included.

- Partial Correlations

Partial correlations are calculated recursively from the lower-order coefficients using

$$r_{ij.k} = \frac{r_{ij} - r_{ki} r_{kj}}{\sqrt{(1 - r_{ki}^2)(1 - r_{kj}^2)}} \qquad \text{(first order)}$$

$$r_{ij.kl} = \frac{r_{ij.k} - r_{il.k} r_{jl.k}}{\sqrt{(1 - r_{il.k}^2)(1 - r_{jl.k}^2)}} \qquad \text{(second order)}$$

and similarly for higher orders (Morrison (1976), p. 94).

If the denominator is less than 10^{-20}, or if any of the lower-order coefficients necessary for calculations are system missing, the coefficient is set to system missing. If a coefficient in absolute value is greater than one, it is set to system missing. (This may occur with pair-wise deletion.)

- Significance Level

The significance level is based on

$$t = r \sqrt{\frac{df}{1 - r^2}}$$

The degrees of freedom are

$$df = M - \theta - 2,$$

where θ is the order of the coefficient and M is the minimum sum of weights from which the zero-order coefficients involved in the computations were calculated. Thus, for $r_{ij.kl}$

$$M = \min\,(W_{ij}, W_{ki}, W_{kj}, W_{il}, W_{lk}, W_{jl})$$

where W_{ij} is the sum of weights of the cases used to calculate r_{ij}. If listwise deletion of missing values (default) was used, all W_{ij} are equal. By default, the significance level is one-tailed.

Reference

Morrison (1976)

PRINCALS

General

The PRINCALS algorithm was first described in Van Rijckevorsel & De Leeuw (1979) and De Leeuw & Van Rijckevorsel (1980); also see Gifi (1981,1985). Characteristic features of PRINCALS are the ability to specify any of a number of measurement levels for each variable separately and the treatment of missing values by setting weights in the loss function equal to zero.

Notation

n number of cases (objects)

m number of variables

p number of dimensions.

For variable j, $j = 1, ..., m$

h_j n-vector with categorical observations

k_j number of categories (distinct values) of variable j

G_j indicator matrix for variable j, of order $n \times k_j$

The elements of G_j are defined as $i = 1, ..., n$; $r = 1, ..., k_j$

$g_{(j)ir} = 1$ when the ith object is in the rth category of variable j

$g_{(j)ir} = 0$ when the ith object is not in the rth category of variable j

M_j binary, diagonal $n \times n$ matrix

The diagonal elements of M_j are

$m_{(j)ii} = 1$ when the ith observation is within the range $[1, k_j]$

$m_{(j)ii} = 0$ when the ith observation is outside the range $[1, k_j]$

D_j diagonal matrix containing the univariate marginals, i.e., the column sums of G_j

The quantification matrices and parameter vectors are

X object scores, of order $n \times p$

Y_j multiple category quantifications, of order $k_j \times p$

y_j single category quantifications, of order k_j

a_j variable weights (equal to component loadings) of order p

Q	transformed data matrix of order $n \times m$ with columns $q_j = G_j y_j$
$\underline{Y}$	collection of multiple and single category quantifications.

Note: the matrices G_j, M_j, and D_j are exclusively notational devices; they are stored in reduced form, and the program fully profits from their sparseness by replacing matrix multiplications with selective accumulation.

Objective Function Optimization

The PRINCALS objective is to find object scores X and a set of $\underline{Y}_j$ (for $j = 1, ..., m$) — the underlining indicates that they are possibly restricted — so that the function

$$\sigma(X;\underline{Y}) = 1/m \sum_j \mathrm{tr}\,(X - G_j\underline{Y}_j)'M_j(X - G_j\underline{Y}_j)$$

is minimal, under the normalization restriction $X'M_*X = mnI$, where the matrix $M_* = \sum_j M_j$, and I is the $p \times p$ identity matrix. The inclusion of M_j in $\sigma(X;\underline{Y})$ ensures that there is no influence of data values outside the range $[1, k_j]$, which may be really missing or merely regarded as such; M_* contains the number of "active" data values for each object. The object scores are also centered, i.e., they satisfy $u'M_*X = 0$ with u denoting an n-vector with ones.

The following measurement levels are distinguished in PRINCALS:

- Multiple Nominal
  $\underline{Y}_j = Y_j$ unrestricted

- Single Nominal
  $\underline{Y}_j = y_j a_j'$ rank-one restrictions only

- (Single) Ordinal
  $\underline{Y}_j = y_j a_j'$ and $y_j \in C_j$ rank-one and monotonicity restrictions

- (Single) Numerical
  $\underline{Y}_j = y_j a_j'$ and $y_j \in L_j$ rank-one and linearity restrictions

For each variable, these levels can be chosen independently. The general requirement in the "single" options is $\underline{Y}_j = y_j a_j'$, i.e., $\underline{Y}_j$ is of rank one; for identification purposes y_j is always normalized so that $y_j' D_j y_j = n$, which implies that the variance of the quantified variable $q_j = G_j y_j$ is 1. In the ordinal case the additional restriction $y_j \in C_j$ means that y_j must be located in the convex cone of all k_j -vectors with nondecreasing elements. In the numerical case the additional restriction $y_j \in L_j$ means that y_j must be located in the subspace of all k_j -vectors that are a linear transformation of the vector consisting of k_j successive integers.

Optimization is achieved by executing the following iteration scheme twice:
(1) Initialization (a) or (b)
(2) Update object scores
(3) Orthonormalization
(4) Update category quantifications

(5) Convergence test: repeat (2) - (4) or continue
(6) Rotation

The first time (for the initial configuration) initialization (a) described below is used and all single variables are temporarily treated as single numerical. Multiple nominal variables are treated as multiple nominal. The second time (for the final configuration) initialization (b) is used. Steps (1) to (6) are explained below.

(1) Initialization

(a) The object scores X are initialized with random numbers, which are normalized so that $u'M_*X = 0$ and $X'M_*X = mnI$, yielding $\tilde{X}$. For multiple variables the initial category quantifications are obtained as $\tilde{Y}_j = D_j^{-1}G_j'\tilde{X}$. For single variables the initial category quantifications are defined as the first k_j successive integers, normalized so that $u'D_j\tilde{y}_j = 0$ and $\tilde{y}'_jD_j\tilde{y}_j = n$, and the initial variable weights are calculated as the vector $\tilde{a}_j = \tilde{X}'G_j\tilde{y}_j$, rescaled to unit length.

(b) All relevant quantities are copied from the results of the first cycle.

(2) Updated object scores

First the auxiliary score matrix Z is computed as

$$Z \leftarrow \sum_j M_jG_j\tilde{Y}_j$$

and centered with respect to M_*:

$$\tilde{Z} \leftarrow \{M_* - (M_*uu'M_*/u'M_*u)\}Z$$

These two steps yield locally the best updates when there are no orthogonality constraints.

(3) Orthonormalization

The orthonormalization problem is to find an M_*-orthonormal X^+ that is closest to $\tilde{Z}$ in the least squares sense. In PRINCALS this is done by setting

$$X^+ \leftarrow m^{1/2}M_*^{-1/2}\text{GRAM}\,(M_*^{-1/2}\tilde{Z})$$

which is equal to the genuine least squares estimate up to a rotation — see (6). The notation GRAM ( ) is used to denote the Gram-Schmidt transformation (Björk & Golub, 1973).

(4) Update category quantifications; loop across variable $j = 1, \ldots, m$:

(a) For multiple nominal variables the new category quantifications are computed as:

$$Y_j^+ = D^{-1}{}_jG_j'X^+$$

(b) For single variables first an unconstrained update is computed in the same way:

$$\tilde{Y}_j = D^{-1}_j G_j' X^+$$

Next, one cycle of an ALS algorithm (De Leeuw et al., 1976) is executed for computing a rank-one decomposition of $\tilde{Y}_j$, with restrictions on the left-hand vector. This cycle starts from the previous single quantifications $\tilde{y}_j$ with

$$a_j^+ = \tilde{Y}_j'D_j\tilde{y}_j$$

When the current variable is numerical, we are ready; else we compute

$$y_j^* = \tilde{Y}_j a_j^+$$

Now, when the current variable is single nominal we can simply obtain y_j^+ by normalizing y_j^* in the way indicated below; else the variable must be ordinal, and we have to insert the weighted monotonic regression process

$$y_j^* \leftarrow \text{WMON}\,(y_j^*)$$

which makes y_j^* monotonically increasing. The weights used are the diagonal elements of D_j, and the subalgorithm used is the up-and-down-blocks minimum violators algorithm (Kruskal, 1964; Barlow et al., 1972). The result is normalized:

$$y_j^+ = n^{1/2} y_j^* \, (y_j'^* D_j y_j^*)^{-1/2}$$

Finally, we set

$$\underline{Y}_j^+ = y_j^+ a_j'^+$$

(5) Convergence test

The difference between consecutive values of the quantity

$$\text{TFIT} = 1/m \sum_s \left[\sum_{j \in J} y'_{(j)\,s} D_j y_{(j)\,s} + \sum_{j \notin J} a_j' a_j \right]$$

where $y_{(j)\,s}$ denotes the sth column of Y_j and where J is an index set recording which variables are multiple, is compared with the user-specified convergence criterion ε—a small positive number. It can be shown that TFIT $= p - \sigma(X;\underline{Y})$. Steps (2) to (4) are repeated as long as the loss difference exceeds ε.

(6) Rotation

As remarked in (3), during iteration the orientation of X and Y with respect to the coordinate system is not necessarily correct; this also reflects the fact that $\sigma(X;\underline{Y})$ is invariant under simultaneous rotations of X and Y. From the theory of principal components it is known that if all variables would be single the matrix A — which can be formed by stacking the row vectors a_j' — has the property that $A'A$ is diagonal. Therefore we may rotate so that the matrix

$$1/mA'A = 1/m \sum_j a_j a_j' = 1/m \sum_j Y_j' D_j Y_j$$

becomes diagonal. The corresponding eigenvalues are printed after the convergence message of the program. The calculation involves tridiagonalization with Householder transformations followed by the implicit QL algorithm (Wilkinson, 1965).

Diagnostics

- Maximum Rank (May be issued as a warning when exceeded)

The maximum rank p_{max} indicates the maximum number of dimensions that can be computed for any data set. In general we have:

$$p_{max} = \min \{ (n-1), ((\sum_{j \in J} k_j + m_2) - \max(m_1, \max(0, 1 - m_2))) \}$$

where m_1 is the number of multiple variables with no missing values, m_2 the number of single variables, and J an index set recording which variables are multiple. Although the number of non-trivial dimensions may be less than p_{max} when $m = 2$, PRINCALS does allow dimensionalities all the way up to p_{max}. When, due to empty categories in the actual data, the rank deteriorates below the specified dimensionality, the program stops.

- Marginal Frequencies

The frequencies table gives the univariate marginals and the number of missing values (i.e., values that are regarded as out of range for the current analysis) for each variable. These are computed as the column sums of D_j and the total sum of M_j.

- Fit and Loss Measures

When the HISTORY option is in effect, the following fit and loss measures are reported:

(a) Total fit. This is the quantity TFIT defined in (5).

(b) Total loss. This is $\sigma(X;\underline{Y})$, computed as the sum of multiple loss and single loss defined below.

(c) Multiple loss. This measure is computed as

$$\text{TMLOSS} = p - 1/m \sum_j \text{tr}\, Y_j' D_j Y_j$$

(d) Single loss. This measure is computed only when some of the variables are single:

$$\text{SLOSS} = 1/m \sum_{j \notin J} \text{tr}\, Y_j' D_j Y_j + \sum_{j \notin J} a_j' a_j$$

- Eigenvalues and Correlations Between Optimally Scaled Variables

If there are no missing data, the eigenvalues printed by PRINCALS are those of $1/mR(Q)$, where $R(Q)$ denotes the matrix of correlations between the optimally scaled variables in the columns of Q. For multiple variables, q_j is defined here as $G_j y_{(j)1}$. When all variables are single or when $p = 1$, $R(Q)$ itself is also printed. If there are missing data, then the eigenvalues are those of the matrix with elements $q_j' M_*^{-1} q_1$, which is not necessarily a correlation matrix, although it is positive semi-definite.

References

Barlow, Bartholomew, Bremner, & Brunk (1972)

Björk & Golub (1973)

De Leeuw & Van Rijckevorsel (1980)

De Leeuw, Young, & Takane (1976)

Gifi (1981)

Gifi (1985)

Kruskal (1964)

Van Rijckevorsel & De Leeuw (1979)

Wilkinson (1965)

PROBIT

Notation

n	number of subjects
r	number of responses
k	number of levels of the grouping variables
c	natural response rate (=0 if not given)
p	% response $= \begin{cases} r/n & \text{if natural response rate not given} \\ (r/n - c)/(1-c) & \text{if natural response rate given} \end{cases}$
n_c	number of subjects in control group if natural response rate is to be estimated
x	matrix of x's $(x_1, x_2, \ldots x_k)$
b	vector of slopes $(b_1, b_2, \ldots b_k)$

Maximum Likelihood Estimation

- Starting value for maximum likelihood iteration

$$p^* = \begin{cases} 0.95 & \text{if } p=1 \\ 0.05 & \text{if } p=0 \\ p & \text{otherwise} \end{cases}$$

$$Y = \begin{cases} \text{Probit}\,(p^*) + 5 & \text{Probit Model} \\ \dfrac{\log\,(p^* / (1-p^*))}{2} + 5 & \text{Logit Model} \end{cases}$$

$$C = c$$

- Using the current value of Y, calculate

Probit Model:

$$P = \frac{1}{\sqrt{(2\pi)}} \int_{-\infty}^{(Y-5)} e^{-u^2/2} du$$

$$Z = \frac{1}{\sqrt{(2\pi)}} e^{-(Y-5)^2/2}$$

Logit Model:

$$P = \frac{e^{2(Y-5)}}{1 + e^{2(Y-5)}}$$

$$Z = 2P(1-P)$$

Both Models:

$$Q = 1 - P$$

$$w = \frac{Z^2}{[P + C / (1 - C)]Q}$$

$$p = (r / n - c) / (1 - c)$$

- Compute

$$y = Y + \frac{p - P}{PQ}$$

- Using weights of nw, solve the weighted least squares regression of y on the x's to get b_i and $V(b_i)$. If natural response is to be estimated:

$$b_i = b_i + \frac{n_c(1 - C)}{C}$$

$$V(b_i) = V(b_i) + \frac{n_c(c - C)}{C}$$

$$\delta c_i = b_i(1 - C)$$

Compute the intercepts for each group

$$a_i = \bar{y}_i - \sum_{j=1}^{k} b_j x_j$$

Compute the new Ys

$$Y_i = a_i + \sum_{j=1}^{k} b_j x_j$$

Update C

$$C = C + \delta c$$

- Using the new values of Y, continue iteration until the largest change in a Y between successive iterations is less than .001, or the maximum number of iterations (20) is reached. (Note that either of these criteria may be changed.)

Goodness of Fit and Frequency Table

$$T = a_i + \sum_{i=1}^{k} b_j x_j - 5$$

$$P = \frac{1}{\sqrt{(2\pi)}} \int_{-\infty}^{T} e^{-u^2/2} du \quad \text{Probit Model}$$

$$= \frac{e^{2T}}{1 + e^{2T}} \quad \text{Logit Model}$$

O = observed frequency (For logit model, the observed frequency is always 0 or 1.)

$E = nP$

$$\chi^2 = \sum \frac{(O - E)^2}{E} \quad \text{for Probit}$$

$$\chi^2 = \sum \frac{(O - E)^2}{E(1 - E)} \quad \text{for Logit}$$

Relative Median Potency

Heterogeneity factor

$$h = \chi^2 / df$$

where χ^2 and df are from the model fit

Notation

$$t = \begin{cases} 1.96 & \text{without heterogeneity factor} \\ t_{(0.025,\, df)} & \text{with heterogeneity factor} \end{cases}$$

$$g = \begin{cases} \dfrac{t^2 V(b)}{b^2} & \text{without heterogeneity factor} \\ \dfrac{t^2 V(b)}{b^2} h & \text{with heterogeneity factor} \end{cases}$$

$$Snw_k = \sum_{i=1}^{n_k} nw = \text{sum of weighting coefficients for the kth group}$$

Estimate of relative median potency for group i vs group j

$$M_{ij} = (a_i - a_j) / b$$

Estimate of variance of M_{ij}

$$V(M_{ij}) = \begin{cases} \dfrac{1}{b^2}\left[\dfrac{1}{Snw_i} + \dfrac{1}{Snw_j} + (M_{ij} - \bar{x}_i + \bar{x}_j)^2\right] V(b) & \text{without heterogeneity factor} \\ \dfrac{h}{b^2}\left[\dfrac{1}{Snw_i} + \dfrac{1}{Snw_j} + (M_{ij} - \bar{x}_i + \bar{x}_j)^2\right] V(b) & \text{with heterogeneity factor} \end{cases}$$

95% confidence limits

$$M_{ij} + \frac{g}{1-g}(M_{ij} - \bar{x}_i + \bar{x}_j) \pm \frac{t}{1-g}\sqrt{[V(M_{ij})\,(1-g)]}$$

Fiducial Limits for Effective *X*

For group i

Snw = sum of weighting coefficients for group i

$$VarA = V(a_i)\,\bar{x}_i^2 + \frac{1}{Snw}$$

$$CovAB = V(b)\,\bar{x}_i$$

For models which include natural response

$$VarA = V(a_i)\,\bar{x}_i^2 + \frac{1}{Snw} + V(C)\,\bar{x}_i^2 / (1-C) + 2\bar{x}_i^2 \text{Cov}\,(b, C) / (1-C)$$

$$CovAB = V(b)\,\bar{x}_i + \text{Cov}\,(b, C)\,\bar{x}_i / (1-C)$$

Compute effective X by

$$Y = \begin{cases} \text{Probit}\,(p) + 5 & \text{Probit Model} \\ \dfrac{\text{Log}\,(p/(1-p))}{2} + 5 & \text{Logit Model} \end{cases}$$

$$X = (Y - a_i) / b$$

and $V(X)$

$$V(X) = VarA - 2(X)(CovAB) + X^2 VarB - g(VarA - CovAB^2 / V(b))$$

95% fiducial limits for X

$$X + g(X - CovAB / V(b)) / (1 - g) \pm t\sqrt{V(X) / (b(1 - g))}$$

References

Finney (1971)

PROXIMITIES

Standardizing Cases or Variables

Either cases or variables can be standardized. The following methods of standardization are available:

- Z

  PROXIMITIES subtracts the mean from each value for the variable or case being standardized and then divides by the standard deviation of the values. If a standard deviation is zero, PROXIMITIES sets all values for the case or variable to zero.

- RANGE

  PROXIMITIES divides each value for the variable or case being standardized by the range of the values. If the range is zero, PROXIMITIES leaves all values unchanged.

- RESCALE

  From each value for the variable or case being standardized, PROXIMITIES subtracts the minimum value and then divides by the range. If a range is zero, PROXIMITIES sets all values for the case or variable to .50.

- MAX

  PROXIMITIES divides each value for the variable or case being standardized by the maximum of the values. If the maximum of a set of values is zero, PROXIMITIES uses an alternate process to produce a comparable standardization: it divides by the absolute magnitude of the smallest value and adds one.

- MEAN

  PROXIMITIES divides each value for the variable or case being standardized by the mean of the values. If a mean is zero, PROXIMITIES adds one to all values for the case or variable to produce a mean of one.

- SD

  PROXIMITIES divides each value for the variable or case being standardized by the standard deviation of the values. PROXIMITIES does not change the values if their standard deviation is zero.

Transformations

Three transformations are available for the values PROXIMITIES computes or reads:

- ABSOLUTE

  Take the absolute values of the proximities.

- REVERSE

Transform similarity values into dissimilarities, or vice versa, by changing the signs of the coefficients.

- RESCALE

RESCALE standardizes the proximities by first subtracting the value of the smallest and then dividing by the range.

If you specify more than one transformation, PROXIMITIES does them in the order listed above: first ABSOLUTE, then REVERSE, then RESCALE.

Proximities Measures

Measures for Continuous Data

- EUCLID

The distance between two items, x and y, is the square root of the sum of the squared differences between the values for the items.

$$\text{EUCLID}\ (x, y) = \sqrt{\Sigma_i (x_i - y_i)^2}$$

- SEUCLID

The distance between two items is the sum of the squared differences between the values for the items.

$$\text{SEUCLID}\ (x, y) = \Sigma_i (x_i - y_i)^2$$

- CORRELATION

This is a pattern similarity measure.

$$\text{CORRELATION}\ (x, y) = \frac{\Sigma_i (Z_{xi} Z_{yi})}{N}$$

where Z_{xi} is the (standardized) Z-score value of x for the ith case or variable, and N is the number of cases or variables.

- COSINE

This is a pattern similarity measure.

$$\text{COSINE}\ (x, y) = \frac{\Sigma_i (x_i y_i)}{\sqrt{((\Sigma_i x_i^2)(\Sigma_i y_i^2))}}$$

- CHEBYCHEV

The distance between two items is the maximum absolute difference between the values for the items.

$$\text{CHEBYCHEV}\ (x, y) = \max_i |x_i - y_i|$$

- BLOCK

The distance between two items is the sum of the absolute differences between the values for the items.

$$\text{BLOCK}\,(x, y) = \Sigma_i |x_i - y_i|$$

- MINKOWSKI(p)

The distance between two items is the pth root of the sum of the absolute differences to the pth power between the values for the items.

$$\text{MINKOWSKI}\,(x, y) = (\Sigma_i |x_i - y_i|^p)^{1/p}$$

- POWER (p,r)

The distance between two items is the rth root of the sum of the absolute differences to the pth power between the values for the items.

$$\text{POWER}\,(x, y) = (\Sigma_i |x_i - y_i|^p)^{1/r}$$

Measures for Frequency Count Data

- CHISQ

The magnitude of this similarity measure depends on the total frequencies of the two cases or variables whose proximity is computed. Expected values are from the model of independence of cases (or variables), x and y.

$$\text{CHISQ}\,(x, y) = \sqrt{\sum_i \frac{(x_i - E(x_i))^2}{E(x_i)} + \sum_i \frac{(y_i - E(y_i))^2}{E(y_i)}}$$

- PH2

This is the CHISQ measure normalized by the square root of the combined frequency. Therefore, its value does not depend on the total frequencies of the two cases or variables whose proximity is computed.

$$\text{PH2}\,(x, y) = \frac{\text{CHISQ}\,(x, y)}{\sqrt{N}}$$

Measures for Binary Data

PROXIMITIES constructs a 2×2 contingency table for each pair of items in turn. It uses this table to compute a proximity measure for the pair.

		Item 2	
		Present	Absent
	Present	a	b
Item 1	Absent	c	d

PROXIMITIES computes all binary measures from the values of a, b, c, and d. These values are tallies across variables (when the items are cases) or tallies across cases (when the items are variables).

- Russel and Rao Similarity Measure

This is the binary dot product.

$$\text{RR}\,(x, y) = \frac{a}{a + b + c + d}$$

- Simple Matching Similarity Measure

  This is the ratio of the number of matches to the total number of characteristics.

  $$\mathrm{SM}\ (x, y) = \frac{a+d}{a+b+c+d}$$

- Jaccard Similarity Measure

  This is also known as the similarity ratio.

  $$\mathrm{JACCARD}\ (x, y) = \frac{a}{a+b+c}$$

- Dice or Czekanowski or Sorenson Similarity Measure

  $$\mathrm{DICE}\ (x, y) = \frac{2a}{2a+b+c}$$

- Sokal and Sneath Similarity Measure 1

  $$\mathrm{SS1}\ (x, y) = \frac{2\,(a+d)}{2\,(a+d)\ +b+c}$$

- Rogers and Tanimoto Similarity Measure

  $$\mathrm{RT}\ (x, y) = \frac{a+d}{a+d+2\,(b+c)}$$

- Sokal and Sneath Similarity Measure 2

  $$\mathrm{SS2}\ (x, y) = \frac{a}{a+2\,(b+c)}$$

- Kulczynski Similarity Measure 1

  This measure has a minimum value of 0 and no upper limit. It is undefined when there are no nonmatches ($b = 0$ and $c = 0$). Therefore, PROXIMITIES assigns an artificial upper limit of 9999.999 to K1 when it is undefined or exceeds this value.

  $$\mathrm{K1}\ (x, y) = \frac{a}{b+c}$$

- Sokal and Sneath Similarity Measure 3

  This measure also has a minimum value of 0, has no upper limit, and is undefined when there are no nonmatches ($b = 0$ and $c = 0$). As with K1, PROXIMITIES assigns an artificial upper limit of 9999.999 to SS3 when it is undefined or exceeds this value.

  $$SS3\ (x, y) = \frac{a+d}{b+c}$$

Conditional Probabilities

The following three binary measures yield values that you can interpret in terms of conditional probability. All three are similarity measures.

- Kulczynski Similarity Measure 2

This yields the average conditional probability that a characteristic is present in one item given that the characteristic is present in the other item. The measure is an average over both items acting as predictors. It has a range of 0 to 1.

$$\text{K2}(x, y) = \frac{a/(a+b) + a/(a+c)}{2}$$

- Sokal and Sneath Similarity Measure 4

This yields the conditional probability that a characteristic of one item is in the same state (present or absent) as the characteristic of the other item. The measure is an average over both items acting as predictors. It has a range of 0 to 1.

$$\text{SS4}(x, y) = \frac{a/(a+b) + a/(a+c) + d/(b+d) + d/(c+d)}{4}$$

- Hamann Similarity Measure

This measure gives the probability that a characteristic has the same state in both items (present in both or absent from both) minus the probability that a characteristic has different states in the two items (present in one and absent from the other). HAMANN has a range of -1 to +1 and is monotonically related to SM, SS1, and RT.

$$\text{HAMANN}(x, y) = \frac{(a+d) - (b+c)}{a+b+c+d}$$

Predictability Measures

The following four binary measures assess the association between items as the predictability of one given the other. All four measures yield similarities.

- Goodman and Kruskal Lambda (Similarity)

This coefficient assesses the predictability of the state of a characteristic on one item (presence or absence) given the state on the other item. Specifically, lambda measures the proportional reduction in error using one item to predict the other, when the directions of prediction are of equal importance. Lambda has a range of 0 to 1.

$$t_1 = \max(a, b) + \max(c, d) + \max(a, c) + \max(b, d)$$

$$t_2 = \max(a+c, b+d) + \max(a+b, c+d)$$

$$\text{LAMBDA}(x, y) = \frac{t_1 - t_2}{2(a+b+c+d) - t_2}$$

- Anderberg's *D* (Similarity)

This coefficient assesses the predictability of the state of a characteristic on one item (presence or absence) given the state on the other. D measures the actual reduction in the error probability when one item is used to predict the other. The range of D is 0 to 1.

$$t_1 = \max(a, b) + \max(c, d) + \max(a, c) + \max(b, d)$$

$$t_2 = \max(a+c, b+d) + \max(a+b, c+d)$$

$$\text{D}(x, y) = \frac{t_1 - t_2}{2(a+b+c+d)}$$

- Yule's *Y* Coefficient of Colligation (Similarity)

This is a function of the cross ratio for a 2×2 table. It has a range of -1 to +1.

$$Y(x, y) = \frac{\sqrt{ad} - \sqrt{bc}}{\sqrt{ad} + \sqrt{bc}}$$

- Yule's *Q* (Similarity)

This is the 2×2 version of Goodman and Kruskal's ordinal measure *gamma*. Like Yule's Y, Q is a function of the cross-product ratio for a 2×2 table and has a range of -1 to +1.

$$Q(x, y) = \frac{ad - bc}{ad + bc}$$

Other Binary Measures

The remaining binary measures available in PROXIMITIES are either binary equivalents of association measures for continuous variables or measures of special properties of the relation between items.

- Ochiai Similarity Measure

This is the binary form of the cosine. It has a range of 0 to 1 and is a similarity measure.

$$\text{OCHIAI}(x, y) = \sqrt{\left(\frac{a}{a+b}\right)\left(\frac{a}{a+c}\right)}$$

- Sokol and Sneath Similarity Measure 5

This is a similarity measure. Its range is 0 to 1.

$$\text{SS5}(x, y) = \frac{ad}{\sqrt{(a+b)(a+c)(b+d)(c+d)}}$$

- Fourfold Point Correlation (Similarity)

This is the binary form of the Pearson product-moment correlation coefficient. Phi is a similarity measure, and its range is 0 to 1.

$$\text{PHI}(x, y) = \frac{ad - bc}{\sqrt{(a+b)(a+c)(b+d)(c+d)}}$$

- Binary Euclidean Distance

This is a distance measure. Its minimum value is 0, and it has no upper limit.

$$\text{BEUCLID}(x, y) = \sqrt{b+c}$$

- Binary Squared Euclidean Distance

This is also a distance measure. Its minimum value is 0, and it has no upper limit.

$$\text{BSEUCLID}(x, y) = b + c$$

- Size Difference

This is a dissimilarity measure with a minimum value of 0 and no upper limit.

$$\text{SIZE}(x, y) = \frac{(b-c)^2}{(a+b+c+d)^2}$$

- Pattern Difference

This is also a dissimilarity measure. Its range is 0 to 1.

$$\text{PATTERN}(x, y) = \frac{bc}{(a+b+c+d)^2}$$

- Binary Shape Difference

This dissimilarity measure has no upper or lower limit.

$$\text{BSHAPE}(x, y) = \frac{(a+b+c+d)(b+c) - (b-c)^2}{(a+b+c+d)^2}$$

- Dispersion Similarity Measure

This similarity measure has a range of -1 to +1.

$$\text{DISPER}(x, y) = \frac{ad - bc}{(a+b+c+d)^2}$$

- Variance Dissimilarity Measure

This dissimilarity measure has a minimum value of 0 and no upper limit.

$$\text{VARIANCE}(x, y) = \frac{b+c}{4(a+b+c+d)}$$

- Binary Lance-and-Williams Nonmetric Dissimilarity Measure

Also known as the Bray-Curtis nonmetric coefficient, this dissimilarity measure has a range of 0 to 1.

$$\text{BLWMN}(x, y) = \frac{b+c}{2a+b+c}$$

References

Anderberg (1973)

Romesburg (1984)

QUICK CLUSTER

When the desired number of clusters is known, QUICK CLUSTER groups cases efficiently into clusters.

Notation

NC	number of clusters requested
$\underline{M}_i$	mean of *i*th cluster
$\underline{x}_k$	vector of *k*th observation
$d(\underline{x}_i, \underline{x}_j)$	Euclidean distance between vectors $\underline{x}_i$ and $\underline{x}_j$
d_{mn}	$\min_{i,j} d(\underline{M}_i, \underline{M}_j)$
ε	convergence criteria

Algorithm

The first iteration involves three steps:

- Step 1: Select initial cluster centers.

(a) If $\min_i d(\underline{x}_k, \underline{M}_i) > d_{mn}$ and $d(\underline{x}_k, \underline{M}_m) > d(\underline{x}_k, \underline{M}_n)$, then $\underline{x}_k$ replaces $\underline{M}_n$. If $\min_i d(\underline{x}_k, \underline{M}_i) > d_{mn}$ and $d(\underline{x}_k, \underline{M}_m) < d(\underline{x}_k, \underline{M}_n)$, then $\underline{x}_k$ replaces $\underline{M}_m$; i.e., if the distance between $\underline{x}_k$ and its closest cluster mean is greater than the distance between the two closest means ($\underline{M}_m$ and $\underline{M}_n$), then $\underline{x}_k$ replaces either $\underline{M}_m$ or $\underline{M}_n$, whichever is closer to $\underline{x}_k$.

(b) If $\underline{x}_k$ does not replace a cluster mean in (a), a second test is made:

Let $d_q = \min_i d(\underline{x}_k, \underline{M}_i)$.

If $d_q > \min_i d(\underline{M}_q, \underline{M}_i)$, then $\underline{M}_q = \underline{x}_k$;

i.e., $\underline{x}_k$ is closest to $\underline{M}_q$ with a distance of d_q.

If that distance (d_q) is greater than the distance between $\underline{M}_q$ and its closest $\underline{M}_i$, then $\underline{x}_k$ replaces $\underline{M}_q$.

At the end of one pass through the data, the initial means of all *NC* clusters are set.

Note that if NOINITIAL is specified, the first *NC* cases with no missing values are the initial cluster means.

- Step 2: Update of initial cluster centers.

Starting with the first case, each case in turn is assigned to the nearest cluster and that cluster mean is updated. Note that the initial cluster center is included in this mean. The updated cluster means are the classification cluster centers.

Note that if NOUPDATE is specified, this step is skipped.

- Step 3: Assign cases to the nearest cluster.

The third pass through the data assigns each case to the nearest cluster, where distance from a cluster is the Euclidean distance between that case and the (updated) classification centers. Final cluster means are then calculated as the average values of clustering variables for cases assigned to each cluster. Final cluster means do not contain classification centers.

When the number of iterations is greater than one, the final cluster means in Step 3 are set to the classification cluster means in the end of Step 2, and QUICK CLUSTER repeats Step 3 again. The algorithm stops when either the maximum number of iterations is reached or the maximum change of cluster centers in two successive iterations is smaller than ε times the minimum distance among the initial cluster centers.

References

Hartigan (1975)

RANK

Notation

Let $y_1 < y_2 < \ldots < y_m$ be m distinct ordered observations for the sample and $C_1, C_2, \ldots, C_m$ be the corresponding sum of caseweights for each value. Define

$$CC_i = \sum_{k=1}^{i} C_k = \text{cumulative sum of caseweights up to } y_i$$

$$W = CC_m = \sum_{k=1}^{m} C_k = \text{total sum of caseweights}$$

Statistics

- Rank (R_i)

  A rank is assigned to each case based on four different ways of treating ties or caseweights not equal to 1.

  For every i, $i = 1, \ldots, m$,

  (a) if $C_i \geq 1$

  $R_i = CC_{i-1} + 1$ if TIES = LOW

  $R_i = CC_i$ if TIES = HIGH

  $R_i = CC_{i-1} + (C_i + 1)/2$ if TIES = MEAN

  $R_i = i$ if TIES = CONDENSE

  (b) if $C_i < 1$

  $R_i = CC_{i-1}$ if TIES = LOW

  $R_i = CC_i$ if TIES = HIGH

  $R_i = CC_{i-1} + C_i/2$ if TIES = MEAN

  $R_i = i$ if TIES = CONDENSE

  Note: $CC_0 = 0$

- RFRACTION (RF_i)

  Fractional rank
  $RF_i = R_i/W$, $i = 1, \ldots, m$

- PERCENT (P_i)

Fractional rank as a percent

$$P_i = \frac{R_i}{W} * 100 \qquad , i = 1, \ldots, m$$

- PROPORTION (F_i): Estimate for cumulative proportion

The proportion is calculated for each case based on four different methods of estimating fractional rank.

$$F_i = (R_i - \frac{3}{8}) / (W + \frac{1}{4}) \quad \text{(BLOM)}$$

$$F_i = (R_i - \frac{1}{2}) / W \quad \text{(RANKIT)}$$

$$F_i = (R_i - \frac{1}{3}) / (W + \frac{1}{3}) \quad \text{(TUKEY)}$$

$$F_i = R_i / (W + 1) \quad \text{(Van der Waerden)}$$

Note: F_i will be set to SYSMIS if the calculated value of F_i by the formula

is negative.

- NORMAL (a):

Normal scores that are the z-scores from the standard normal distribution which corresponds to the estimated cumulative proportion F. The normal score is defined by

$$a_i = \Psi(F_i) \ , \qquad i = 1, \ldots, m \ ,$$

where Ψ is the inverse cumulative standard normal distribution (PROBIT).

- NTILES (K):

Assign group membership for the requested number of groups. If K groups are requested, the n-tile (N_i) for case i is defined by

$$N_i = \left[\frac{R_i K}{W+1}\right] + 1 \ ,$$

where $\left[\frac{R_i K}{W+1}\right]$ is the greatest integer that is less than or equal to $R_i K / (W+1)$.

- SAVAGE (S) :

Savage scores based on exponential distribution.

The Savage score is calculated by

$$S_i = \begin{cases} \left[(1 - g_{i_1}) l_{i_1+1} + g_{i_2} l_{i_2+1} + \sum_{j=i_1+2}^{i_2} l_j \right] / C_i - 1 & i_1 + 2 \le i_2 \\ [(1 - g_{i_1}) l_{i_1+1} + g_{i_2} l_{i_2+1}] / C_i - 1 & i_1 + 1 = i_2 \\ l_{i_1+1} - 1 & i_1 = i_2 \end{cases}$$

where

$$i_1 = [CC_{i-1}], \quad i_2 = [CC_i], \quad W^* = \begin{cases} W & \text{if } W \text{ is an integer} \\ [W] + 1 & \text{if } W \text{ is not an integer} \end{cases}$$

$$g_{i_1} = CC_{i-1} - i_1 \ , \ g_{i_2} = CC_i - i_2$$

and $l_1, \ldots, l_{w^*}$ are defined as the expected values of the order statistics from an exponential distribution; that is,

$$l_j = \sum_{K=1}^{j} \frac{1}{W^* - K + 1}$$

References

Blom (1958)

Chambers et al. (1983)

Lehmann (1975)

Tukey (1962)

REGRESSION

General

This procedure performs multiple linear regression with five methods for entry and removal of variables. It also provides extensive analysis of residual and influential cases. Caseweight (CASEWEIGHT) and regression weight (REGWGT) can be specified in the model fitting.

Notation

y_i	Dependent variable for case i with variance σ^2/g_i
c_i	Caseweight for case i; $c_i = 1$ if CASEWEIGHT is not specified
g_i	Regression weight for case i; $g_i = 1$ if REGWGT is not specified
l	Number of distinct cases
w_i	$c_i g_i$
W	$\sum_{i=1}^{l} w_i$
p	Number of independent variables
C	Sum of caseweights: $\sum_{i=1}^{l} c_i$
x_{ki}	The kth independent variable for case i
$\bar{X}_k$	Sample mean for the kth independent variable: $\bar{X}_k = \left(\sum_{i=1}^{l} w_i x_{ki}\right)/W$
$\bar{Y}$	Sample mean for the dependent variable: $\bar{Y} = \left(\sum_{i=1}^{l} w_i y_i\right)/W$
h_i	Leverage for case i
$\tilde{h}_i$	$\tilde{h}_i = \frac{g_i}{W} + h_i$
S_{kj}	Sample covariance for X_k and X_j
S_{yy}	Sample variance for Y
S_{ky}	Sample covariance for X_k and Y
p^*	Number of coefficients in the model. $p^*=p$ if the intercept is not included;

otherwise $p^* = p+1$

R The sample correlation matrix for $X_1, \ldots, X_p$ and Y

Descriptive Statistics

$$R = \begin{bmatrix} r_{11} & \cdots & r_{1p} & r_{1y} \\ r_{21} & \cdots & r_{2p} & r_{2y} \\ \cdot & \cdots & \cdot & \cdot \\ r_{y1} & \cdots & r_{yp} & r_{yy} \end{bmatrix}$$

where

$$r_{kj} = \frac{S_{kj}}{\sqrt{S_{kk}S_{jj}}}$$

and

$$r_{ky} = \frac{S_{ky}}{\sqrt{S_{kk}S_{yy}}}$$

The sample mean $\bar{X}_i$ and covariance S_{ij} are computed by a provisional means algorithm. Define

$$W_k = \sum_{i=1}^{k} w_i = \text{cumulative weight up to case } k$$

then

$$\bar{X}_{i(k)} = \bar{X}_{i(k-1)} + (x_{ik} - \bar{X}_{i(k-1)}) \frac{w_k}{W_k}$$

and, if the intercept is included,

$$C_{ij(k)} = C_{ij(k-1)} + (x_{ik} - \bar{X}_{i(k-1)})(x_{jk} - \bar{X}_{j(k-1)}) \left(w_k - \frac{w_k^2}{W_k}\right)$$

Otherwise,

$$C_{ij(k)} = C_{ij(k-1)} + w_k x_{ik} x_{jk}$$

where

$$\bar{X}_{i(1)} = x_{i1}$$

and

$$C_{ij(1)} = 0$$

The sample covariance S_{ij} is computed as the final C_{ij} divided by $C-1$.

Sweep Operations (Dempster 1969)

For a regression model of the form

$$Y_i = \beta_0 + \beta_1 X_{1i} + \beta_2 X_{2i} + \ldots + \beta_p X_{pi} + e_i$$

sweep operations are used to compute the least squares estimates b of β and the associated regression statistics. The sweeping starts with the correlation matrix R. Let $\tilde{R}$ be the new matrix produced by sweeping on the kth row and column of R. The elements of $\tilde{R}$ are

$$\tilde{r}_{kk} = \frac{1}{r_{kk}}$$

$$\tilde{r}_{ik} = \frac{r_{ik}}{r_{kk}}, \quad i \neq k$$

$$\tilde{r}_{kj} = -\frac{r_{kj}}{r_{kk}}, \quad j \neq k$$

and

$$\tilde{r}_{ij} = \frac{r_{ij}r_{kk} - r_{ik}r_{kj}}{r_{kk}}, \quad i \neq k, j \neq k$$

If the above sweep operations are repeatedly applied to each row of R_{11} in

$$R = \begin{pmatrix} R_{11} & R_{12} \\ R_{21} & R_{22} \end{pmatrix}$$

where R_{11} contains independent variables in the equation at the current step, the result is

$$\tilde{R} = \begin{pmatrix} R_{11}^{-1} & -R_{11}^{-1}R_{12} \\ R_{21}R_{11}^{-1} & R_{22} - R_{21}R_{11}^{-1}R_{12} \end{pmatrix}$$

The last row of

$$R_{21}R_{11}^{-1}$$

contains the standardized coefficients (also called BETA), and

$$R_{22} - R_{21}R_{11}^{-1}R_{12}$$

can be used to obtain the partial correlations for the variables not in the equation, controlling for the variables already in the equation. Note that this routine is its own inverse; that is, exactly the same operations are performed to remove a variable as to enter a variable.

Variable Selection Criteria

Let r_{ij} be the element in the current swept matrix associated with X_i and X_j. Variables are entered or removed one at a time. X_k is eligible for entry if it is an independent variable not currently in the model with

$r_{kk} \geq t$ (Tolerance with a default of 0.0001)

and also, for each variable X_j that is currently in the model,

$$\left(r_{jj} - \frac{r_{jk}r_{kj}}{r_{kk}} \right) t \leq 1$$

The above condition is imposed so that entry of the variable does not reduce the tolerance of variables already in the model to unacceptable levels.

The F-to-enter value for X_k is computed as

$$F-to-enter_k = \frac{(C - p^* - 1)\, V_k}{r_{yy} - V_k}$$

with *1* and $C - p^* - 1$ degrees of freedom, where p^* is the number of coefficients currently in the model and

$$V_k = \frac{r_{yk} r_{ky}}{r_{kk}}$$

The F-to-remove value for X_k is computed as

$$F-to-remove_k = \frac{(C-p^*)\,|V_k|}{r_{yy}}$$

with *1* and $C - p^*$ degrees of freedom.

Methods for Variable Entry and Removal

Five methods for entry and removal of variable are available. The selection process is repeated until (1) the maximum number of steps (MAXSTEP) is reached or (2) no more independent variables qualify for entry/removal. The algorithms for these five methods are described below.

Stepwise

If there are independent variables currently entered in the model, choose X_k such that $F-to-remove_k$ is minimum. X_k is removed if $F-to-remove_k < F_{out}$ (default=2.71) or, if probability criteria are used, $P(F-to-remove_k) > P_{out}$ (default=0.1). If the inequality does not hold, no variable is removed from the model.

If there are no independent variables currently entered in the model or if no entered variable is to be removed, choose X_k such that $F-to-enter_k$ is maximum. X_k is entered if $F-to-enter_k > F_{in}$(default=3.84) or, $P(F-to-enter_k) < P_{in}$ (default=0.05). If the inequality does not hold, no variable is entered.

At each step, all eligible variables are considered for removal and entry.

Forward

This procedure is the entry phase of the stepwise procedure.

Backward

This procedure is the removal phase of the stepwise procedure and can be used only after at least one independent variable has been entered in the model.

Enter (Forced Entry)

Choose X_k such that r_{kk} is maximum and enter X_k. Repeat for all variables to be entered.

Remove (Forced Removal)

Choose X_k such that r_{kk} is minimum and remove X_k. Repeat for all variables to be removed.

Summary Statistics

For the summary statistics, assume p independent variables are currently entered in the equation, of which a block of q variables have been entered/removed in the current step.

- Multiple R

$$R = \sqrt{1 - r_{yy}}$$

- R Square

$$R^2 = 1 - r_{yy}$$

- Adjusted R Square

$$R^2_{adj} = R^2 - \frac{(1 - R^2)\,p}{C - p^*}$$

- R Square Change, when a block of q independent variables was added or removed

$$\Delta R^2 = R^2_{current} - R^2_{previous}$$

- F Change and Significance of F Change

$$\Delta F = \begin{cases} \dfrac{\Delta R^2 (C - p^*)}{q\,(1 - R^2_{current})} & \text{for the removal of } q \text{ independent variable} \\ \dfrac{\Delta R^2 (C - p^* - q)}{q\,(R^2_{previous} - 1)} & \text{for the addition of } q \text{ independent variable} \end{cases}$$

the degrees of freedom for the addition are q and $C - p^*$, while the degrees of freedom for the removal are q and $C - p^* - q$.

- Residual Sum of Squares

$$SS_e = r_{yy}(C - 1)\,S_{yy}$$

with degrees of freedom $C - p^*$.

- Sum of Squares Due to Regression

$$SS_R = R^2 (C - 1)\,S_{yy}$$

with degrees of freedom p.

- ANOVA Table

Analysis of Variance	df	Sum of Squares	Mean Square
Regression	p	SS_R	$(SS_R)/p$
Residual	$C - p^*$	SS_e	$(SS_e)/(C - p^*)$

- Variance-Covariance Matrix for Unstandardized Regression Coefficient Estimates

A square matrix of size p with diagonal elements equal to the variance, the below diagonal elements equal to the covariance, and the above diagonal elements equal to the correlations:

$$VAR(b_k) = \frac{r_{kk} r_{yy} S_{yy}}{S_{kk}(C - p^*)}$$

$$COV(b_k, b_j) = \frac{r_{kj} r_{yy} S_{yy}}{\sqrt{S_{kk} S_{jj}}(C - p^*)}$$

$$COR(b_k, b_j) = \frac{r_{kj}}{\sqrt{r_{kk} r_{jj}}}$$

Selection Criteria

- Akaike Information Criterion (AIC)

$$AIC = C\left(ln\left(\frac{SS_e}{C}\right)\right) + 2p^*$$

- Ameniya's Prediction Criterion (PC)

$$PC = \frac{(1 - R^2)(C + p^*)}{C - p^*}$$

- Mallow's C_p (CP)

$$CP = \frac{SS_e}{\hat{\sigma}^2} + 2p^* - C$$

where $\hat{\sigma}^2$ is the mean square error from fitting the model that includes all the variables in the variable list.

- Schwarz Bayesian Criterion (SBC)

$$SBC = C\left(ln\left(\frac{SS_e}{C}\right)\right) + p^* \, ln(C)$$

Collinearity

- Variance Inflation Factors

$$VIF_i = \frac{1}{r_{ii}}$$

- Tolerance

$$\text{Tolerance}_i = r_{ii}$$

- Eigenvalues, λ_k

The eigenvalues of scaled and uncentered cross-product matrix for the independent variables in the equation are computed by the QL method (Wilkinson & Reinsch, 1971).

- Condition Indices

$$\eta_k = \frac{max\,\lambda_j}{\lambda_k}$$

- Variance-Decomposition Proportions

Let

$$v_i = (v_{i1}, \ldots, v_{ip})$$

be the eigenvector associated with eigenvalue λ_i. Also, let

$$\Phi_{ij} = v_{ij}^2/\lambda_i \quad \text{and} \; \Phi_j = \sum_{i=1}^{p} \Phi_{ij}$$

The variance-decomposition proportion for the jth regression coefficient associated with the ith component is defined as

$$\pi_{ij} = \Phi_{ij}/\Phi_j$$

Statistics for Variables in the Equation

- Regression Coefficient b_k

$$b_k = \frac{r_{yk}\sqrt{S_{yy}}}{\sqrt{S_{kk}}} \quad \text{for } k=1,\ldots,p.$$

The standard error of b_k is computed as

$$\hat{\sigma}_{b_k} = \sqrt{\frac{r_{kk}r_{yy}S_{yy}}{S_{kk}(C-p^*)}}$$

- A 95% confidence interval for β_k is constructed from

$$b_k \pm \hat{\sigma}_{b_k} t_{0.025,\,C-p^*}$$

- If the model includes the intercept, the intercept is estimated as

$$b_0 = \bar{y} - \sum_{k=1}^{p} b_k \bar{X}_k$$

The variance of b_0 is estimated by

$$\hat{\sigma}_{b_0}^2 = \frac{(C-1)\,r_{yy}S_{yy}}{C(C-p^*)} + \sum_{k=1}^{p} \bar{X}_k^2 \hat{\sigma}_{b_k}^2 + 2 \sum_{k=j+1}^{p} \sum_{j=1}^{p-1} \bar{X}_k \bar{X}_j est.COV(b_k, b_j)$$

- Beta Coefficients

$$Beta_k = r_{yk}$$

The standard error of $Beta_k$ is estimated by

$$\hat{\sigma}_{Beta_k} = \sqrt{\frac{r_{yy}r_{kk}}{C-p^*}}$$

F-test for $Beta_k$

$$F = \left(\frac{Beta_k}{\hat{\sigma}_{Beta_k}}\right)^2$$

with 1 and $C - p^*$ degrees of freedom.

- Part Correlation of X_k with Y

$$Part - Corr(X_k) = \frac{r_{yk}}{\sqrt{r_{kk}}}$$

- Partial Correlation of X_k with Y

$$Partial - Corr(X_k) = \frac{r_{yk}}{\sqrt{r_{kk}r_{yy} - r_{yk}r_{ky}}}$$

Statistics for Variables Not in the Equation

- Standardized regression coefficient $Beta_k{}^*$ if X_k enters the equation at the next step

$$Beta_k{}^* = \frac{r_{yk}}{r_{kk}}$$

The F-test for $Beta_k{}^*$

$$F = \frac{(C - p^* - 1)\, r_{yk}^2}{r_{kk}r_{yy} - r_{yk}^2}$$

with 1 and $C - p^*$ degrees of freedom

- Partial Correlation of X_k and Y

$$Partial(X_k) = \frac{r_{yk}}{\sqrt{r_{yy}r_{kk}}}$$

- Tolerance of X_k

$$Tolerance_k = r_{kk}$$

- Minimum tolerance among variables already in the equation if X_k enters at the next step is

$$\min_{1 \le j \le p} \left(\frac{1}{r_{jj} - (r_{kj}r_{jk})/r_{kk}}, r_{kk}\right)$$

Residuals and Associated Statistics

There are nineteen temporary variables which can be added to the active system file. These variables can be requested with the RESIDUAL subcommand.

- Centered Leverage Values

For all cases compute

$$h_i = \begin{cases} \dfrac{g_i}{(C-1)} \displaystyle\sum_{j=1}^{p} \sum_{k=1}^{p} \dfrac{(X_{ji} - \bar{X}_j)(X_{ki} - \bar{X}_k) r_{jk}}{\sqrt{S_{jj} S_{kk}}} & \text{if intercept is included} \\ \dfrac{g_i}{(C-1)} \displaystyle\sum_{j=1}^{p} \sum_{k=1}^{p} \dfrac{X_{ji} X_{ki} r_{jk}}{\sqrt{S_{jj} S_{kk}}} & \text{otherwise} \end{cases}$$

For selected cases, leverage is h_i; for unselected case i with positive caseweight, leverage is

$$h'_i = \begin{cases} \left(\dfrac{1}{W} + h_i\right) / \left(1 + \dfrac{1}{W} + h_i\right) - \dfrac{1}{W+1} & \text{if intercept is included} \\ h_i / (1 + h_i) & \text{otherwise} \end{cases}$$

- Unstandardized Predicted Values

$$\hat{Y}_i = \begin{cases} \displaystyle\sum_{k=1}^{p} b_k X_{ki} & \text{if no intercept} \\ b_0 + \displaystyle\sum_{k=1}^{p} b_k X_{ki} & \text{otherwise} \end{cases}$$

- Unstandardized Residuals

$$e_i = Y_i - \hat{Y}_i$$

- Standardized Residuals

$$ZRESID_i = \begin{cases} \dfrac{e_i}{s} & \text{if no regression weight is specified} \\ \text{SYSMIS} & \text{otherwise} \end{cases}$$

where s is the square root of the residual mean square.

- Standardized Predicted Values

$$ZPRED_i = \begin{cases} \dfrac{\hat{Y}_i - \bar{Y}}{sd} & \text{if no regression weight is specified} \\ \text{SYSMIS} & \text{otherwise} \end{cases}$$

where sd is computed as

$$sd = \sqrt{\sum_{i=1}^{l} \frac{c_i (\hat{Y}_i - \bar{Y})^2}{C-1}}$$

- Studentized Residuals

$$SRES_i = \begin{cases} \dfrac{e_i/s}{\sqrt{(1-\tilde{h}_i)/g_i}} & \text{for selected cases with } c_i > 0 \\ \dfrac{e_i/s}{\sqrt{(1+\tilde{h}_i)/g_i}} & \text{otherwise} \end{cases}$$

- Deleted Residuals

$$DRESID_i = \begin{cases} e_i/(1-\tilde{h}_i) & \text{for selected cases with } c_i > 0 \\ e_i & \text{otherwise} \end{cases}$$

- Studentized Deleted Residuals

$$SDRESID_i = \begin{cases} \dfrac{DRESID_i}{s_{(i)}} & \text{for selected cases with } c_i > 0 \\ \dfrac{e_i}{s\sqrt{(1+\tilde{h}_i)/g_i}} & \text{otherwise} \end{cases}$$

where $s_{(i)}$ is computed as

$$s_{(i)} = \frac{1}{\sqrt{C-p^* - 1}}\sqrt{\frac{(C-p^*)\,s^2}{1-\tilde{h}_i} - DRESID_i^2}$$

- Adjusted Predicted Values

$$ADJPRED_i = Y_i - DRESID_i$$

- Dfbeta

$$DFBETA_i = b - b(i) = \frac{g_i e_i (X^t W X)^{-1} X_i^t}{1-\tilde{h}_i}$$

where

$$X_i^t = \begin{cases} (1, X_{1i}, \ldots, X_{pi}) & \text{if intercept is included} \\ (X_{1i}, \ldots, X_{pi}) & \text{otherwise} \end{cases}$$

and $W = diag(w_1, \ldots, w_l)$.

- Standardized Dfbeta

$$SDBETA_{ij} = \frac{b_j - b_j(i)}{s_{(i)}\sqrt{(X^t W X)_{jj}^{-1}}}$$

where $b_j - b_j(i)$ is the jth component of $b - b(i)$

• Dffit

$$DFFIT_i = X_i [b - b(i)] = \frac{\tilde{h}_i e_i}{1 - \tilde{h}_i}$$

• Standardized Dffit

$$SDFIT_i = \frac{DFFIT_i}{s_{(i)} \sqrt{\tilde{h}_i}}$$

• Covratio

$$COVRATIO_i = \left(\frac{s_{(i)}}{s}\right)^{2p^*} \times \frac{1}{1 - \tilde{h}_i}$$

• Mahalanobis' Distance

For selected cases with $c_i > 0$,

$$MAHAL_i = \begin{cases} (C-1)\, h_i & \text{if intercept is included} \\ (C)\, h_i & \text{otherwise} \end{cases}$$

For unselected cases with $c_i > 0$

$$MAHAL_i = \begin{cases} Ch'_i & \text{if intercept is included} \\ (C+1)\, h'_i & \text{otherwise} \end{cases}$$

• Cook's Distance (Cook 1977)

For selected cases with $c_i > 0$

$$COOK_i = \begin{cases} (DRESID_i^2 \tilde{h}_i g_i) / [s^2 (p+1)] & \text{if intercept is included} \\ (DRESID_i^2 h_i g_i) / (s^2 p) & \text{otherwise} \end{cases}$$

For unselected cases with $c_i > 0$

$$COOK_i = \begin{cases} (DRESID_i^2 (h'_i + \frac{1}{W})) / [\tilde{s}^2 (p+1)] & \text{if intercept is included} \\ (DRESID_i^2 h'_i) / (\tilde{s}^2 p) & \text{otherwise} \end{cases}$$

where h'_i is the leverage for unselected case i, and $\tilde{s}^2$ is computed as

$$\tilde{s}^2 = \begin{cases} \frac{1}{C-p} \left[SS_e + e_i^2 (1 - h'_i - \frac{1}{1+W}) \right] & \text{if intercept is included} \\ \frac{1}{C-p+1} [SS_e + e_i^2 (1 - h'_i)] & \text{otherwise} \end{cases}$$

• Standard Errors of the mean predicted values

For all the cases with positive caseweight,

$$SEPRED_i = \begin{cases} s\sqrt{\tilde{h}_i/g_i} & \text{if intercept is included} \\ s\sqrt{h_i/g_i} & \text{otherwise} \end{cases}$$

- 95% Confidence Interval for Mean Predicted Response

$$LMCIN_i = \hat{Y}_i - t_{0.025,\, C-p^*}\; SEPRED_i$$

$$UMCIN_i = \hat{Y}_i + t_{0.025,\, C-p^*}\; SEPRED_i$$

- 95% Confidence Interval for a single observation

$$LICIN_i = \begin{cases} \hat{Y}_i - t_{0.025,\, C-p^*}\, s\sqrt{(\tilde{h}_i + 1)/g_i} & \text{if intercept is included} \\ \hat{Y}_i - t_{0.025,\, C-p}\, s\sqrt{(h_i + 1)/g_i} & \text{otherwise} \end{cases}$$

$$UICIN_i = \begin{cases} \hat{Y}_i + t_{0.025,\, C-p^*}\, s\sqrt{(\tilde{h}_i + 1)/g_i} & \text{if intercept is included} \\ \hat{Y}_i + t_{0.025,\, C-p}\, s\sqrt{(h_i + 1)/g_i} & \text{otherwise} \end{cases}$$

- Durbin-Watson statistic

$$DW = \frac{\sum_{i=2}^{l} (\tilde{e}_i - \tilde{e}_{i-1})^2}{\sum_{i=1}^{l} c_i \tilde{e}_i^2}$$

where $\tilde{e}_i = e_i\sqrt{g_i}$.

Partial Residual Plots

The scatterplots of the residuals of the dependent variable and an independent variable when both of these variables are regressed on the rest of the independent variables can be requested in the RESIDUAL branch. The algorithm for these residuals is described in Velleman & Welsch (1981).

Missing Values

By default, a case that has a missing value for any variable is deleted from the computation of the correlation matrix on which all consequent computations are based. Users are allowed to change the treatment of cases with missing values.

References

Cook (1977)

Dempster (1969)

Velleman & Welsch (1981)

Wilkinson & Reisch (1971)

RELIABILITY

GENERAL

The RELIABILITY procedure employs one of two different computing methods, depending upon the MODEL specification and options and statistics requested.

Method 1 does not involve computing a covariance matrix. It is faster than method 2 and, for large problems, requires much less workspace. However, it can compute coefficients only for ALPHA and SPLIT models, and it does not allow computation of a number of optional statistics, nor does it allow matrix input or output. Method 1 is used only when alpha or split models are requested and only FRIEDMAN, COCHRAN, DESCRIPTIVES, SCALE, and/or ANOVA are specified on the STATISTICS subcommand and/or TOTAL is specified on the SUMMARY subcommand.

Method 2 requires computing a covariance matrix of the variables. It is slower than method 1 and requires more space. However, it can process all models, statistics, and options.

The two methods differ in one other important respect. Method 1 will continue processing a scale containing variables with zero variance and leave them in the scale. Method 2 will delete variables with zero variance and continue processing if at least 2 variables remain in the scale. If item deletion is required, method 2 can be selected by requesting the covariance method.

NOTATION

There are N persons taking a test that consists of k items. A score X_{ji} is given to the jth person on the ith item.

$i \rightarrow$ items

		1	2 …	i …	k	
	1 ⋮	X_{11}	X_{12}		X_{1k}	P_1
$j\downarrow$ person	j ⋮			X_{ji}		
	N	X_{N1}	X_{N2}		X_{Nk}	P_N
		T_1	T_2 …	T_i …	T_k	G

If the model is SPLIT, k_1 items are in part 1, $k_2 = k - k_1$ in part 2. If the number of items in each part is not specified and k is even, the program sets $k_1 = k_2 = k/2$. If k is odd, $k_1 = (k+1)/2$. It is assumed that the first k_1 items are part 1.

$$W = \sum_{j=1}^{N} w_j$$ Sum of the weights, where w_j is the weight for case j

$$P_j = \sum_{i=1}^{k} X_{ji}$$ The total score of the jth person

$$\bar{P}_j = P_j/k$$ Mean of the observations for the jth person

$$T_i = \sum_{j=1}^{N} X_{ji}w_j$$ The total score for the ith item

$$G = \sum_{i=1}^{k}\sum_{j=1}^{N} X_{ji}w_j$$ Grand sum of the scores

$$\bar{G} = \frac{G}{Wk}$$ Grand mean of the observations

Scale and Item Statistics—Method 1

Item Means and Standard Deviations

- Mean for i^{th} item

$$\bar{T}_i = T_i/W$$

- Standard deviation for the ith item

$$S_i = \sqrt{\frac{\sum_{j=1}^{N} w_j X_{ji}^2 - W\bar{T}_i^2}{W-1}}$$

Scale Mean and Scale Variance

- Scale mean

$$M = G/W$$

For the split model:

- Mean part 1

$$M_1 = \sum_{i=1}^{k_1} \bar{T}_i$$

- Mean part 2

$$M_2 = \sum_{i=k_1+1}^{k} \bar{T}_i$$

- Scale variance

$$S_p^2 = \frac{1}{(W-1)}\left[\sum_{j=1}^{N} P_j^2 w_j - W\left(\sum_{i=1}^{k}\bar{T}_i\right)\right]^2$$

For the split model:

- Variance part 1

$$S_{p1}^2 = \frac{1}{W-1}\left[\sum_{j=1}^{N} w_j\left(\sum_{i=1}^{k_1} X_{ji}\right) - W\left(\sum_{i=1}^{k_1}\bar{T}_i\right)\right]^2$$

- Variance part 2

$$S_{p2}^2 = \frac{1}{W-1}\left[\sum_{j=1}^{N} w_j\left(\sum_{i=k_1+1}^{k} X_{ji}\right)^2 - W\left(\sum_{i=k_1+1}^{k}\bar{T}_i\right)\right]^2$$

Item-Total Statistics

- Scale mean if i^{th} item deleted

$$\tilde{M}_i = M - \bar{T}_i$$

- Scale variance if i^{th} item deleted

$$\tilde{S}_i^2 = S_p^2 + S_i^2 - 2\text{cov}\,(X_i, P)$$

where the covariance between item i and the case score is

$$\text{cov}\,(X_i, P) = \frac{1}{W-1}\left(\sum_{j=1}^{N} P_j X_{ji} w_j - \sum_{l=1}^{k}\bar{T}_l T_i\right)$$

- Alpha if i^{th} item deleted

$$\bar{A}_i = \frac{k-1}{k-2}\left(1 - \sum_{\substack{l=1\\ l\neq i}}^{k} S_l^2/\tilde{S}_i^2\right)$$

- Correlation between i^{th} item and sum of others

$$R_i = \frac{\text{cov}\,(X_i, P) - S_i^2}{S_i\tilde{S}_i}$$

The ANOVA Table (Winer (1971))

Source of Variation	Sum of Squares	df
Between people	$\sum_{j=1}^{N} P_j^2 w_j / k - G^2/\text{Wk}$	$W-1$
Within people	$\sum_{i=1}^{k}\sum_{j=1}^{N} w_j X_{ji}^2 - \sum_{j=1}^{N} P_j^2 w_j / k$	$W(k-1)$
Between measures	$\sum_{i=1}^{k} T_i^2 / W - G^2/\text{Wk}$	$k-1$
Residual	$\sum_{i=1}^{k}\sum_{j=1}^{N} w_j X_{ji}^2 - \sum_{j=1}^{N} P_j^2 w_j / k$ $-\sum_{i=1}^{k} T_i^2 / W - G^2/\text{Wk}$	$(W-1)\ (k-1)$
Total	$\sum_{i=1}^{k}\sum_{j=1}^{N} w_j X_{ji}^2 - G^2/\text{Wk}$	$Wk-1$

Each of the mean squares is obtained by dividing the sum of squares by the corresponding degrees of freedom. The F ratio for between measures is

$$F = \frac{MS_{\text{between measures}}}{MS_{residual}},\ df = (k-1,\ (W-1)\ (k-1))$$

Friedman Test or Cochran Test

$$\chi^2 = \frac{SS_{\text{between measures}}}{MS_{\text{within people}}},\ df = k-1$$

Note: data must be ranks for Friedman test, a dichotomy for Cochran test.

Kendall's Coefficient of Concordance

$$W = \frac{SS_{\text{between measures}}}{SS_{\text{total}}}$$

(Will not be printed if Cochran is also specified.)

Tukey's Test for Nonadditivity

- The residual sums of squares are further subdivided to

  $SS_{\text{nonadd}} = M^2/D,\ df = 1$

where

$$D = (SS_{\text{bet. meas}} SS_{\text{bet. people}}) / (Wk)$$

$$\left(= \left[\sum_{i=1}^{k} (\bar{T}_i - \bar{G})^2 \right] \left[\sum_{j=1}^{N} w_j (\bar{P}_j - \bar{G})^2 \right] \right)$$

$$M = \sum_{i=1}^{k} \bar{T}_i \sum_{j=1}^{N} \bar{P}_j X_{ji} w_j - \bar{G} \sum_{j=1}^{N} P_j^2 w_j / k - \bar{G} SS_{\text{bet. meas}}$$

$$\left(= \sum_{j=1}^{N} w_j (\bar{P}_j - \bar{G}) \left[\sum_{i=1}^{k} X_{ji} (\bar{T}_i - \bar{G}) \right] \right)$$

$$SS_{\text{bal}} = SS_{\text{res}} - SS_{\text{nonadd}}, df = (W-1)(k-1) - 1$$

- The test for nonadditivity is

$$F = \frac{MS_{\text{nonadd}}}{MS_{\text{balance}}} \qquad df = (1, (W-1)(k-1) - 1)$$

- The regression coefficient for the nonadditivity term is

$$\hat{B} = M/D,$$

and the power to transform to additivity is

$$\hat{p} = 1 - \hat{B}\bar{G}$$

Scale Statistics

Reliability Coefficient Alpha (Cronbach (1951))

$$A = \frac{k}{k-1} \left(1 - \frac{\sum_{i=1}^{k} S_i^2}{S_p^2} \right)$$

If the model is split, separate alphas are computed:

$$A_1 = \frac{k_1}{k_1 - 1} \left(1 - \sum_{i=1}^{k_1} \frac{S_i^2}{S_{p1}^2} \right)$$

$$A_2 = \frac{k_2}{k_2 - 1} \left(1 - \sum_{i=k_1+1}^{k_2} \frac{S_i^2}{S_{p2}^2} \right)$$

For Split Model Only

- Correlation between the two parts of the test

$$R = \frac{\frac{1}{2} (S_p^2 - S_{p1}^2 - S_{p2}^2)}{S_{p1} S_{p2}}$$

- Equal length Spearman-Brown coefficient

$$Y = \frac{2R}{1+R}$$

- Guttman split half

$$G = \frac{2\,(S_p^2 - S_{p1}^2 - S_{p2}^2)}{S_p^2}$$

- Unequal length Spearman-Brown

$$ULY = \frac{-R^2 + \sqrt{R^4 + 4R^2\,(1-R^2)\,k_1 k_2 / k^2}}{2\,(1-R^2)\,k_1 k_2 / k^2}$$

Basic Computations—Method 2

Items with zero variance are deleted from the scale and from k, k_1 and k_2. The inverses of matrices, when needed, are computed using the sweep operator described by Dempster (1969). If $|V| < 10^{-30}$ a warning is printed and statistics which require V^{-1} are skipped.

Covariance Matrix V and Correlation Matrix R

$$v_{ij} = \begin{cases} \left(\frac{1}{W-1}\left(\sum_{l=1}^{N} X_{li}X_{lj}w_j - W\bar{T}_i\bar{T}_j\right), i, j = 1, \ldots, k\right) & \text{if raw data input} \\ r_{ij}S_iS_j & \text{if corr matrix \& SD input} \end{cases}$$

$$r_{ij} = \frac{v_{ij}}{S_iS_i}, \text{ where } S_i^2 = \frac{v_{ij}}{W-1}$$

Scale Variance

$$S_p^2 = \sum_{i=1}^{k} S_i^2 + 2\sum_{i<j}^{k}\sum^{k} v_{ij}$$

If the model is split,

$$S_{p1}^2 = \sum_{i=1}^{k_1} S_i^2 + 2\sum_{i<j}^{k_1}\sum^{k_1} v_{ij}$$

$$S_{p2}^2 = \sum_{i=k_1+1}^{k} S_i^2 + 2\sum_{i=k_1+1}^{k}\sum_{j>i}^{k} v_{ij}$$

where the first k_1 items are in part 1.

Scale Statistics—Method 2

Alpha Model

- Estimated reliability

$$\frac{k}{k-1}\left(1 - \frac{\sum_{i=1}^{k} S_i^2}{S_p^2}\right)$$

- Standardized item alpha

$$\frac{k\overline{\text{Corr}}}{1 + (k-1)\overline{\text{Corr}}}$$

where

$$\overline{\text{Corr}} = \frac{2}{k(k-1)} \sum_{i<j}^{k} \sum^{k} r_{ij}$$

Split Model

- Correlation between forms

$$\frac{\sum_{i=1}^{k_1} \sum_{j=k_1+1}^{k} v_{ij}}{S_{p1} S_{p2}}$$

- Guttman Split-Half

$$G = \frac{\sum_{i=1}^{k_1} \sum_{j=k_1+1}^{k} v_{ij}}{S_p^2}$$

Alpha and Spearman-Brown equal and unequal length are computed as in method 1.

Guttman Model (Guttman (1945))

$$L_1 = 1 - \frac{\sum_{i=1}^{k} S_i^2}{S_p^2}$$

$$L_2 = L_1 + \frac{\sqrt{\frac{2k}{k-1} \sum_{i<j}^{k} \sum^{k} v_{ij}^2}}{S_p^2}$$

$$L_3 = \frac{k}{k-1} L_1$$

$$L_4 = \frac{4 \sum_{i<j}^{k} \sum^{k} v_{ij}}{S_p^2}$$

$$L_5 = L_1 + \frac{2\sqrt{\max_i \sum_{j \neq i}^{k} v_{ij}^2}}{S_p^2}$$

$$L_6 = 1 - \sum_{i=1}^{k} \varepsilon_i^2 / S_p^2; \text{where } \varepsilon_i^2 = (V^{-1})_{ii}^{-1}$$

Parallel Model (Kristof (1963))

- Common variance

$$CV = \overline{\text{var}} = \frac{1}{k}\sum_{i=1}^{k} S_i^2$$

- True variance

$$TV = \overline{\text{cov}} = \frac{2}{k(k-1)}\sum_{i<j}^{k}\sum^{k} v_{ij}$$

- Error variance

$$EV = \overline{\text{var}} - \overline{\text{cov}}$$

- Common inter-item correlation

$$\hat{R} = \overline{\text{cov}} / \overline{\text{var}}$$

- Reliability of the scale

$$A = \frac{k}{k-1}\left(1 - \frac{\sum_{i=1}^{k} S_i^2}{S_p^2}\right)$$

- Unbiased estimate of the reliability

$$\hat{A} = \frac{2 + (W-3)A}{(W-1)}$$

where A is defined above.

- Test for goodness of fit

$$\chi^2 = -(W-1)\left(1 - \frac{k(k+1)^2(2k-3)}{12(k-1)\left(\frac{k(k+1)}{2} - 2\right)(W-1)}\right)\log L$$

where

$$L = \frac{|V|}{(\overline{\text{var}} - \overline{\text{cov}})^{k-1}(\overline{\text{var}} + (k-1)\overline{\text{cov}})}$$

$$df = \frac{k(k+1)}{2} - 2$$

- Log of the determinant of the unconstrained matrix

$$\log UC = \log|V|$$

- Log of the determinant of the constrained matrix

$$\log C = \log\left((\overline{\text{var}} - \overline{\text{cov}})^{k-1}(\overline{\text{var}} + (k-1)\overline{\text{cov}})\right)$$

Strict Parallel (Kristof (1963))

- Common variance

$$CV = \overline{\mathrm{var}} + \frac{1}{k}\sum_{i=1}^{k}(\bar{T}_i - \bar{G})^2$$

- Error variance

$$EV = MS_{\text{within people}}$$

All mean squares are calculated as described later in the analysis of variance table.

- True variance

$$TV = \overline{\mathrm{var}} + \frac{1}{k}\sum_{i=1}^{k}(\bar{T}_i - \bar{G})^2 - EV$$

- Common inter-item correlation

$$\hat{R} = \frac{\overline{\mathrm{cov}} - \frac{1}{(k-1)k}\sum_{i=1}^{k}(\bar{T}_i - \bar{G})^2}{\overline{\mathrm{var}} + \frac{1}{k}\sum_{i=1}^{k}(\bar{T}_i - \bar{G})^2}$$

- Reliability of the scale

$$Rel = \frac{k\hat{R}}{1 + (k-1)\hat{R}}$$

- Unbiased estimate of the reliability

$$Rel = \frac{3 + (W-3)Rel}{W}$$

- Test for goodness of fit

$$\chi^2 = -(W-1)\left(1 - \frac{k(k+1)^2(2k-3)}{12(k-1)(k(k+3)/2-3)(W-1)}\right)\log L$$

where

$$L = \frac{|V|}{(\overline{\mathrm{var}} + (k-1)\overline{\mathrm{cov}})\left(\overline{\mathrm{var}} - \overline{\mathrm{cov}} + \frac{1}{k}\sum_{i=1}^{k}(\bar{T}_i - \bar{G})^2\right)^{k-1}}$$

$$df = k(k+3)/2 - 3$$

- Log of the determinant of the unconstrained matrix

$$\log UC = \log|V|$$

- Log of the determinant of the constrained matrix

$$\log C = \log\left(\overline{\text{var}} + (k-1)\,\overline{\text{cov}}\right)\left(\overline{\text{var}} - \overline{\text{cov}} + \frac{1}{k-1}\sum_{i=1}^{k}\left(\bar{T}_i - \bar{G}\right)^2\right)^{k-1}$$

Additional Statistics—Method 2

Descriptive and scale statistics and Tukey's test are calculated as in method 1. Multiple R^2 if an item is deleted is calculated as

$$\tilde{R}_i^2 = 1 - \frac{\varepsilon_i^2}{S_i^2} \qquad \varepsilon_i^2 = \frac{1}{(V^{-1})_{ii}}$$

Analysis of Variance Table

Source of Variation	Sum of Squares	df
Between People	$(W-1)\left[\frac{1}{k}\left(\sum_{i=1}^{k} S_i^2 - \frac{2}{k-1}\sum\sum_{i<j} v_{ij}\right)\right] + \frac{2}{(k-1)}\sum_{i<j} v_{ij}$	$W-1$
Within People	$\frac{(W-1)\,(k-1)}{k}\left[\sum_{i=1}^{k} S_i^2 - \frac{2}{k-1}\sum\sum_{i<j} v_{ij}\right] + (W-1)\,SS_{\text{bet. people}}$	$W(k-1)$
Between Measures	$W\left(\sum_{i=1}^{k}\bar{T}_i^2 - \frac{1}{k}\left(\sum_{i=1}^{k}\bar{T}_i\right)^2\right)$	$k-1$
Residual	$\frac{(W-1)\,(k-1)}{k}\left[\sum_{i=1}^{k} S_i^2 - \frac{2}{k-1}\sum\sum_{i<j} v_{ij}\right]$	$(W-1)\,(k-1)$
Total	Between SS + Within SS	$Wk-1$

Hotelling's T^2 (Winer, 1971)

- $T^2 = WY'B^{-1}Y$

where

$$Y = \begin{bmatrix} \bar{T}_1 - \bar{T}_k \\ \bar{T}_2 - \bar{T}_k \\ \vdots \\ \bar{T}_{k-1} - \bar{T}_k \end{bmatrix}$$

$$B = CVC'$$

where C is an identity matrix of rank $k-1$ augmented with a column of -1 on the right.

$$b_{ij} = v_{ij} - v_{ik} - v_{jk} + S_k^2$$

The test will not be done if $W < k$ or $|B| < 10^{-30}$.

- The significance level of T^2 is based on

$$F = \frac{W-k+1}{(W-1)(k-1)} T^2, \text{ with } df = (k-1, W-k+1)$$

Item Mean Summaries

- Mean = $\sum_{i=1}^{k} \bar{T}_i / k$

- Variance = $\dfrac{\sum_{i=1}^{k} \bar{T}_i^2 - \left(\sum_{i=1}^{k} \bar{T}_i\right)^2 / k}{(k-1)}$

- Maximum = $\max_i \bar{T}_i$

- Minimum = $\min_i \bar{T}_i$

- Range = Maximum - Minimum

- Ratio = $\dfrac{\text{Maximum}}{\text{Minimum}}$

Item Variance Summaries

Same as for item means except that S_i^2 is substituted for $\bar{T}_i$ in all calculations.

Inter-Item Covariance Summaries

- Mean = $\dfrac{\sum\sum_{i<j} v_{ij}}{k(k-1)}$

- Variance = $\dfrac{1}{k(k-1)-1}\left[\sum\sum_{i<j} v_{ij}^2 - \dfrac{1}{k(k-1)}\left(\sum\sum_{i<j} v_{ij}\right)^2\right]$

- Maximum = $\max_{i,j} v_{ij}$

- Minimum = $\min_{i,j} v_{ij}$

- Range = maximum - minimum

- Ratio = $\dfrac{\text{maximum}}{\text{minimum}}$

Inter-Item Correlations

Same as for inter-item covariances, with v_{ij} being replaced by r_{ij}.

If the model is split, statistics are also calculated separately for each scale.

References

Cronbach (1951)

Dempster (1969)

Guttman (1945)

Kristof (1963, 1969)

Novick & Lewis (1967)

Winer (1971)

Replace Missing Values (RMV)

General

Missing values in a time series are estimated.

Notation

$X = (X_1, \ldots, X_n)$	original series
$\hat{X}_i$	estimate for missing value
p	number of spans
k	the number of consecutive missing values
X_i to X_{i+k-1}	set of consecutive missing values

Methods for Estimating Missing Values

- Linear Interpolation ($LINT(X)$)

$$\hat{X}_{i+l} = \begin{cases} X_{i-1} + \dfrac{l+1}{k+1}(X_{i+k} - X_{i-1}) & l = 0, \ldots, k-1 \\ SYSMIS & i = 1 \text{ or } i+k-1 = n \end{cases}$$

If $k=1$ (that is, only one consecutive missing observation), then

$$\hat{X}_i = \begin{cases} \dfrac{1}{2}(X_{i-1} + X_{i+1}) & i = 2, \ldots, n-1 \\ SYSMIS & i = 1 \text{ or } i = n \end{cases}$$

- Mean of p Nearest Preceding and p Subsequent Values ($MEAN(X, p)$)

  If the number of nonmissing observations in $(X_1, \ldots, X_{i-1})$ or $(X_{i+k}, \ldots, X_n)$ is less than p, then set $\hat{X}_{i+l} = SYSMIS$; otherwise, set $\hat{X}_{i+l}$ = average of p nonmissing observations preceeding X_i and p nonmissing observations following X_{i+k-1}.

- Median of p Nearest Preceding and p Subsequent Values ($MEDIAN(X, p)$)

  If the number of nonmissing observations in $(X_1, \ldots, X_{i-1})$ or $(X_{i+k}, \ldots, X_n)$ is less than p, then set $\hat{X}_{i+l} = SYSMIS$; otherwise, set $\hat{X}_{i+l}$ = median of p nonmissing observations preceeding X_i and p nonmissing observations following X_{i+k-1}.

- Series Mean ($SMEAN(X)$)

  $\hat{X}_{i+l}$= average of all nonmissing observations in the series

- Linear Trend ($TREND(X)$)

  (1) Use all the nonmissing observations in the series to fit the regression line of the form

  $$\hat{X}_t = a + bt$$

  The least squares estimates are

  $$b = \frac{\sum (X_t - \bar{X})(t - \bar{t})}{\sum (t - \bar{t})^2}$$

  $$a = \bar{X} - b\bar{t}$$

  (2) Apply the regression equation to replace the missing values

  $$\hat{X}_{i+l} = a + b(i + l)$$

SAMPLE

Selection of Random Samples

Selection of a Proportion *p*

For each case, a random uniform number in the range 0 to 1 is generated. If it is less than p, the case is included in the sample.

Selection of a Sample of n_1 Cases out of a Total of *n*

$$(a)\ p = \frac{n_1}{n}$$

$$n = n - 1$$

Select a case if its uniform (0,1) number is less than p. If selected, $n_1 = n_1 - 1$, and return to (a).

Selection of Cases in Nonparametric Procedures

The sampling procedure is as follows:

Each time a case is encountered after the limit imposed by the size of the workspace has been reached, the program decides whether to include it in the sample or not at random. The probability that the new cases will enter the sample is equal to the number of cases which can be held in the workspace divided by the number of cases so far encountered.

If the program decides to accept a case, it then picks at random one of the cases previously stored in the workspace and drops it from the analysis, replacing it with the new case. Each case has the same probability of being in the sample.

If case weighting is used, the nonparametric procedures may use a case more than once. For example, if the weight of a case is 2.3, the program will use that case twice, and may choose at random, with a probability of 0.3, to use it a third time. If sampling is in effect, each of these two or three cases is a candidate for sampling.

SEASON

General

Based on the Multiplicative or Additive model, procedure SEASON decomposes the existing series into three components: Trend-Cycle, Seasonal, and Irregular.

Model

- Multiplicative model
  $X_t = TC_t S_t I_t, t = 1, \ldots, n$

- Additive model
  $X_t = TC_t + S_t + I_t, t = 1, \ldots, n$

where TC_t is the "trend-cycle" component, S_t is the "seasonal" component, and I_t is the "irregular" or "random" component.

The procedure for estimating the seasonal component is:

(1) Smooth the series by the moving average method; the moving average series reflects the trend-cycle component.

(2) Obtain the seasonal-irregular component by dividing the original series by the smoothed values if the model is multiplicative, or by subtracting the smoothed values from the original series if the model is additive.

(3) Isolate the seasonal component from the seasonal-irregular component by computing the medial average (average) of the specific seasonal relatives for each unit of periods if the model is multiplicative (additive).

Moving Average Series

Based on the specified method and period p, the moving average series Z_t for X_t is defined as follows:

- p is even, weight all points equally

$$Z_t = \begin{cases} \displaystyle\sum_{j=t-\frac{p}{2}}^{t+\frac{p}{2}-1} X_j/p & t = \frac{p}{2}+1, \ldots, n-\frac{p}{2}+1 \\ \text{SYSMIS} & \text{otherwise} \end{cases}$$

- p is even, weights unequal

$$Z_t = \begin{cases} (X_{t-\frac{p}{2}} + X_{t+\frac{p}{2}})/2p + \left(\sum_{j=t-\frac{p}{2}+1}^{t+\frac{p}{2}-1} X_j \right) / p \ , & t = \frac{p}{2}+1, \ldots, n-\frac{p}{2} \\ \text{SYSMIS} \ , & \text{otherwise} \end{cases}$$

- p is odd

$$Z_t = \begin{cases} \left(\sum_{j=t-\left[\frac{p}{2}\right]}^{t+\left[\frac{p}{2}\right]} X_j \right) / p \ , & t = \left[\frac{p}{2}\right]+1, \ldots, n-\left[\frac{p}{2}\right] \\ \text{SYSMIS} \ , & \text{otherwise} \end{cases}$$

Ratios or Differences (Seasonal-Irregular Component)

- Multiplicative Model

$$SI_t = \begin{cases} \text{SYSMIS} \ , & \text{if } Z_t = \text{sysmis} \\ (X_t / Z_t)\, 100 \ , & \text{otherwise} \end{cases}$$

- Additive Model

$$SI_t = \begin{cases} \text{SYSMIS} \ , & \text{if } Z_t = \text{sysmis} \\ X_t - Z_t \ , & \text{otherwise} \end{cases}$$

Seasonal Factors (Seasonal Components)

- Multiplicative Model

$$F_t = \begin{cases} \text{medial average } (SI_{t+p}, SI_{t+2p}, \ldots, SI_{t+qp}) \ , & 1 \le t \le L - \left[\frac{L}{p}\right]p \\ \text{medial average } (SI_{t+p}, SI_{t+2p}, \ldots, SI_{t+(q-1)p}) \ , & L - \left[\frac{L}{p}\right]p < t \le \left[\frac{p}{2}\right] \\ \text{medial average } (SI_t, SI_{t+p}, \ldots, SI_{t+(q-1)p}) \ , & \left[\frac{p}{2}\right] < t \le p \end{cases}$$

where

$$L = n - \frac{p}{2} + 1, q = \left[\frac{L}{p}\right], \quad \text{if p is even and all points are weighted equally}$$

$$L = n - \left[\frac{p}{2}\right], q = [(n - p/2)/p] \ , \quad \text{otherwise}$$

and the medial average of a series is the mean value of the series after the smallest and the largest values are excluded. The seasonal factor is defined as

$$SAF_t = F_t \frac{100p}{\sum_{t=1}^{p} F_t} \ , \quad t = 1, \ldots, p$$

- Additive Model

  F_t is defined as the arithmetic average of the series shown above. Then

  $$SAF_t = F_t - \bar{F} \ , \quad \text{where}$$

  $$\bar{F} = \sum_{t=1}^{p} F_t / p$$

Seasonally Adjusted Series (SAS)

$$SAS_t = \begin{cases} (X_t / SAF_m)\,100 \ , & \text{if model is multiplicative} \\ X_t - SAF_m \ , & \text{if model is additive} \end{cases}$$

where

$$m = t - [t/p]\,p$$

Smoothed Trend-Cycle Series

The smoothed trend-cycle series (STC) is obtained by applying a 3×3 moving average on seasonally adjusted series (SAS). Thus,

$$STC_t = \frac{1}{9}[(SAS)_{t-2} + 2(SAS)_{t-1} + 3(SAS)_t + 2(SAS)_{t+1} + (SAS)_{t+2}] \ ,$$

$$t = 2, \ldots, n-2$$

and for the two end points on the beginning and end of the series

$$(STC)_2 = \frac{1}{3}[(SAS)_1 + (SAS)_2 + (SAS)_3]$$

$$(STC)_{n-1} = \frac{1}{3}[(SAS)_{n-2} + (SAS)_{n-1} + (SAS)_n]$$

$$(STC)_1 = (STC)_2 + \frac{1}{2}[(STC)_2 - (STC)_3]$$

$$(STC)_n = (STC)_{n-1} + \frac{1}{2}[(STC)_{n-1} - (STC)_{n-2}]$$

Irregular Component

For $t = 1, \ldots, n$

$$I_t = \begin{cases} (SAS)_t / (STC)_t \ , & \text{if model is multiplicative} \\ (SAS)_t - (STC)_t \ , & \text{if model is additive} \end{cases}$$

References

Makridakis et al. (1983)

SPECTRA

Univariate Series

For $\forall t$, the series X_t can be represented by

$$X_t = a_o^x + \left\{ \sum_{K=1}^{q} a_K^x \cos 2\pi f_K (t-1) + b_K^x \sin 2\pi f_K (t-1) \right\}$$

where

$$t = 1, 2, \ldots N$$

$$a_o^x = \bar{X}, \bar{X} = \sum_{t=1}^{N} X_t / N$$

$$a_K^x = \frac{2}{N} \left[\sum_{t=1}^{N} X_t \cos 2\pi f_K (t-1) \right]$$

$$b_K^x = \frac{2}{N} \left[\sum_{t=1}^{N} X_t \sin 2\pi f_K (t-1) \right]$$

$$f_K = K/N$$

$$q = \left\{ \begin{array}{ll} N/2 & , \text{ if } N \text{ is even} \\ (N-1)/2 & , \text{ if } N \text{ is odd} \end{array} \right.$$

The following statistics are calculated:

- Frequency

  $f_K = K/N, K = 1, \ldots, q$

- Period

  $1/f_K = N/K, K = 1, \ldots, q$

- Fourier cosine coefficient

  $a_K^x, K = 1, \ldots, q$

- Fourier sine coefficient

  $b_K^x = (a_K^x - ib_K^x)\ (a_K^x + ib_K^x)$

- Periodogram

  $I_K^x = [\,(a_K^x)^2 + (b_K^x)^2]\ N/2, K = 1, \ldots, q$

  spectral density estimate

  $s_K^x = \sum_{j=p}^{p} w_j\ I_{K+j}^x$, where $2p + 1 = m$ (number of spans)

and

$l^x_{-K} = l^x_K,\ K = 1, \ldots, q$

$l^x_o = l^x_1$

$l^x_K = l_{N+1-K}$ for $K > q$

$w_{-p}, w_{-p+1}, \ldots, w_o, w_1, \ldots, w_p$ are the periodogram weights defined by different data windows.

Bivariate Series

For the bivariate series X_t and Y_t

$$X_t = a^x_o + \sum_{K=1}^{q} (a^x_K \cos 2\pi f_K t + b^x_K \sin 2\pi f_K t) \qquad t = 1, \ldots, N$$

$$Y_t = a^y_o + \sum_{K=1}^{q} (a^y_K \cos 2\pi f_K t + b^y_K \sin 2\pi f_K t)$$

- Cross-periodogram of X and Y

$$= 1^{xy}_K = \frac{N}{2}(a^x_K - ib^x_K)(a^y_K + ib^y_K)$$

$$= \frac{N}{2}\{(a^x_K a^y_K + b^x_K b^y_K) + i(a^x_K b^y_K - b^x_K a^y_K)\}$$

- Real (1^{xy}_K)

$$\frac{N}{2}(a^x_K a^y_K + b^x_K b^y_K) = (RC)_K$$

- Imaginary (1^{xy}_K)

$$\frac{N}{2}(a^x_K b^y_K - b^x_K a^y_K) = (IC)_K$$

- Cospectral density estimate

$$C_K = \sum_{j=-p}^{p} w_j (RC)_{K+j}$$

- Quadrature spectrum estimate

$$Q_K = \sum_{j=-p}^{p} w_j (IC)_{K+j}$$

- Cross amplitude values

$$A_K = (Q^2_K + C^2_K)^{1/2}$$

- Squared coherency values

$$K_K = \frac{A^2_K}{S^X_K S^Y_K}$$

- Gain values

$$G_K = \begin{cases} A_K/S_K^Y & \text{(gain of } Y_t \text{ over } X_t \text{ at } f_K) \\ A_K/S_K^Y & \text{(gain of } X_t \text{ over } Y_t \text{ at } f_K) \end{cases}$$

- Phase spectrum estimate

$$\psi_K = \begin{cases} \tan^{-1}(Q_K/C_K) & \text{if } \begin{array}{l} Q_K > 0, C_K > 0 \\ Q_K < 0, C_K > 0 \end{array} \\ \tan^{-1}(Q_K/C_K) + \pi & \text{if } Q_K > 0, C_K < 0 \\ \tan^{-1}(Q_K/C_K) - \pi & \text{if } Q_K < 0, C_K < 0 \end{cases}$$

Data Windows

m = number of spans, $p = (m-1)/2$

- HAMMING (Tukey-Hamming Window)

$$w(j) = 0.54 + 0.46\cos\pi j/p, \quad j = 0, \ldots, p$$
$$w(-j) = w(j), j \neq 0$$

- TUKEY (Tukey Window)

$$w(j) = 0.5 + 0.5\cos\pi j/p, \quad j = 0, \ldots, p$$
$$w(-j) = w(j), j \neq 0$$

- PARZEN (Parzen Window)

$$w(j) = 1 - 6(j/p)^2 + 6(j/p)^3, \quad j = 0, 1, \ldots, [p/2]$$
$$w(j) = 2(1 - j/p)^3, \quad j = [p/2] + 1, \ldots, p$$
$$w(-j) = w(j), j \neq 0$$

- BARTLETT (Bartlett Window)

$$w(j) = 1 - j/p, \quad j = 0, \ldots, p$$
$$w(-j) = w(j), j \neq 0$$

- UNIT (Equal Weight Window)

$$w(j) = 1, \quad j = -p, -p+1, \ldots, 0, 1, \ldots, p$$

- User-specified weights

$$w(-p), w(-p+1), \ldots, w(0), w(1), \ldots, w(p)$$

If normalized weights are used for any of the methods,

$$w_{(j)}^* = w_{(j)} / \sum_{j=-p}^{p} w(j), j = -p, \ldots, 0, 1, \ldots, p$$

References

Bloomfield (1976)

Fuller (1976)

SURVIVAL

General

Although life table analysis may be useful in many differing situations and disciplines, for simplicity, the usual survival-time-to-death terminology will be used here.

Notation

X_j	time from starting event to terminal event or censoring for case j
w_j	weight for case j
k	total number of intervals
t_i	beginning time for ith interval
h_i	width of interval i
c_i	sum of weights of cases censored in interval i
d_i	sum of weights of cases experiencing the terminal event in interval i

Construction of Life Table (Gehan, 1975)

Computation of Intervals

The widths of the intervals for the actuarial calculations must be defined by the user. In addition to the last interval specified, an additional interval is automatically created to take care of any times exceeding the last. If the upper limits are not in ascending order, a message is printed and the procedure stops. If the interval width does not divide the time range into an integral number of intervals, a warning is printed and the interval width is reset so that the number of intervals will be the nearest integer to that resulting from the user specification.

Count of Events and Censoring

For each case the interval i into which the survival time falls is determined.

$$t_i \le X_j < t_{i+1}$$

If X_j exceeds t_k, the starting time for the last interval, it is included in the last interval. The status code is examined to determine whether the observed time is time to event or time to censoring. If it is time to censoring, that is, the terminal event did not occur, c_i is incremented by the case weight. If it is time to event, d_i is incremented by the case weight.

Calculation of Survival Functions

For each interval the following are calculated:

- Number alive at the beginning

$$l_i = l_{i-1} - c_{i-1} - d_{i-1}$$

where l_1 is the sum of weights of all cases in the table

- Number exposed to risk of an event

$$r_i = l_i - c_i/2$$

- Proportion terminating

$$q_i = \frac{d_i}{r_i}$$

- Proportion surviving

$$p_i = 1 - q_i$$

- Cumulative proportion surviving at end of interval

$$P_i = P_{i-1}p_i$$

where

$$P_o = 1$$

- Probability density function

$$f_i = \frac{P_i - P_{i+1}}{h_i}$$

- Hazard rate

$$\lambda_i = \frac{2q_i}{h_i(1+p_i)}$$

- Standard error of probability surviving

$$SE(P_i) = P_i \sqrt{\sum_{j=1}^{i} q_j/(r_j p_j)}$$

- Standard error of probability density

$$SE(f_i) = \frac{P_i q_i}{h_i} \sqrt{\sum_{j=1}^{i-1} q_j/(r_j p_j) + p_i/(r_i q_i)}$$

For the first interval

$$SE(f_1) = \frac{P_1 q_1}{h_1} \sqrt{\frac{p_1}{r_1 q_1}}$$

- Standard error of the hazard rate

$$SE(\lambda_i) = \sqrt{\frac{\lambda_i^2}{r_i q_i}\{1 - (\frac{\lambda_i h_i}{2})^2\}}$$

If $q_i = 0$, the standard error for interval i is set to zero.

- Median survival time

If $P_k > 0.5$ the value printed for median survival time is

t_k+

Otherwise, let i be the interval for which $P_i < 0.5$ and $P_{i-1} \geq 0.5$. The estimate of the median survival time is then

$$Md = (t_i) + \frac{h_{i-1}(P_{i-1} - 0.5)}{P_{i-1} - P_i}$$

Comparison of Survival Distributions

The survival times from the groups to be compared are jointly sorted into ascending order. If survival times are equal, the uncensored is taken to be less than the censored. When approximate comparisons are done, they are based on the lifetables, with the beginning of the interval determining the length of survival for cases censored or experiencing the event in that interval.

Notation

N	number of cases
$X_{(k)}$	survival time for case k, where times are sorted into ascending order so that case 1 has the shortest time and case N the longest
w_k	weight for case k
g	number of nonempty groups in the comparison
W_j	sum of weights of cases in group j
W_c	sum of weights of censored cases
W_u	sum of weights of uncensored cases
W	sum of weights of all cases

Computations

For each case the following are computed:

- ULE_k

Sum of weights of uncensored cases with survival times less than or equal to that of case k.

- CLE_k

Same as above but for censored cases.

- UE_k

Sum of weights of uncensored cases with survival times equal to that of case k.

- CE_k

Same as above, but for censored cases.

The score for case k is:

$$S_k = \begin{cases} ULE_k & \text{if } X_k \text{ is censored} \\ A_1 - A_2 - A_3 & \text{if } X_k \text{ is uncensored} \end{cases}$$

- If X_k is censored:

  $$S_k = ULE_k$$

- If X_k is uncensored:

  $$S_k = A_1 - A_2 - A_3$$

where

$A_1 = ULE_k - UE_k$ uncensored cases surviving shorter than case k

$A_2 = W_c - CLE_k + CE_k$ censored cases surviving longer than or equal to case k

$A_3 = W_u - ULE_k$ uncensored cases surviving longer than case k

Test Statistic and Significance (Lee and Desu, 1972)

The test statistic is

$$D = \frac{(W-1)B}{T}$$

where

$$B = \sum_{j=1}^{g} SS_j^2 / W_j$$

SS_j = the sum of scores of cases in group j

$$T = \sum_{i=1}^{N} S_i^2$$

Under the hypothesis that the groups are samples from the same survival distribution, D is asymptotically distributed as a chi square with $(g-1)$ degrees of freedom.

References

Gehan (1975)

Lee & Desu (1972)

T-TEST

General

T-TEST compares the means of two groups.

Two Independent Samples

Notation

X_{ki}	value for *i*th case of group *k*
w_{ki}	weight for *i*th case of group *k*
n_k	number of cases in group *k*
W_k	sum of weights of cases in group *k*

Basic Statistics

- Means

$$\bar{X}_k = \frac{\sum_{i=1}^{n_k} X_{ki} w_{ki}}{W_k} \qquad k = 1, 2$$

- Variances

$$S_k^2 = \frac{\sum_{i=1}^{n_k} X_{ki}^2 w_{ki} - \left(\sum_{i=1}^{n_k} X_{ki} w_{ki}\right)^2 / W_k}{(W_k - 1)}$$

- Standard Errors of the Mean

$$SEM_k = S_k / \sqrt{W_k}$$

- Differences of the Means for Groups 1 and 2

$$D = \bar{X}_1 - \bar{X}_2$$

- Unpooled (Separate Variance) Standard Error of the Difference

$$S_D = \sqrt{\frac{S_1^2}{W_1} + \frac{S_2^2}{W_2}}$$

The 95% confidence interval for mean difference is

$$D \pm t_{df'} S_D$$

where $t_{df'}$ is the upper 2.5% critical value for the t distribution with df' degrees of freedom.

- Pooled Standard Error of the Difference

$$S'_D = S_p \sqrt{\frac{1}{W_1} + \frac{1}{W_2}}$$

where the pooled estimate of the variance is

$$S_p^2 = \frac{(W_1 - 1) S_1^2 + (W_2 - 1) S_2^2}{W_1 + W_2 - 2}$$

The 95% confidence interval for mean difference

$$D \pm t_{df} S'_D$$

where df is defined in the following.

The *t*-statistics for Equality of Means

- Separate Variance

$$t = D / S_D$$

$$df' = \frac{1}{Z_1 + Z_2}$$

where

$$Z_k = \left(\frac{S_k^2 / W_k}{S_1^2 / W_1 + S_2^2 / W_2} \right)^2 / (W_k - 1)$$

- Pooled Variance

$$t' = D / S'_D$$

$$df = W_1 + W_2 - 2$$

The two-tailed significance levels are obtained from the t distribution separately for each of the computed t-values.

The Test for Equality of Variances

Before Release 5, F statistic is used for testing the homogeneity.

$$F = \max \left(\frac{S_1^2}{S_2^2}, \frac{S_2^2}{S_1^2} \right)$$

The degrees of freedom are

$$(W_1 - 1, W_2 - 1) \text{ if } S_1^2 / S_2^2 \geq S_2^2 / S_1^2$$

$$(W_2 - 1, W_1 - 1) \text{ if } S_2^2 / S_1^2 > S_1^2 / S_2^2$$

In Release 5, the Levene statistic is used and defined as

$$L = \frac{(W - 2) \sum_{i=1}^{2} W_i (\bar{Z}_i - \bar{Z})^2}{\sum_{i=1}^{2} \sum_{l=1}^{n_i} W_{il} (Z_{il} - \bar{Z}_i)^2}$$

where

$$Z_{il} = \left|X_{il} - \bar{X}_i\right|$$

$$\bar{Z}_i = \frac{\sum_{l=1}^{n_i} W_{il} Z_{il}}{\ldots}$$

Th

...se i

...se i

- Variances

$$S_X^2 = \frac{\sum_{i=1}^{N} w_i X_i^2 - \left(\sum_{i=1}^{N} w_i X_i\right)^2 / W}{W - 1}$$

Similarly for S_Y^2.

- Covariance between X and Y

$$S_{XY} = \frac{1}{W-1}\left[\sum_{k=1}^{N} X_k Y_k w_k - \left(\sum_{k=1}^{N} w_k X_k\right)\left(\sum_{k=1}^{N} w_k Y_k\right)/ W\right]$$

- Difference of the Means

$$D = \bar{X} - \bar{Y}$$

- Standard Error of the Difference

$$S_D = \sqrt{(S_X^2 + S_Y^2 - 2S_{XY}) / W}$$

- t-statistic for Equality of Means

$$t = D / S_D$$

with $(W - 1)$ degrees of freedom. A two-tailed significance level is printed.

- 95% Confidence Interval for Mean Difference

$$D \pm t_{W-1} S_D$$

- Correlation Coefficient between X and Y

$$r = \frac{S_{XY}}{S_X S_Y}$$

The two-tailed significance level is based on

$$t = r \sqrt{\frac{W - 2}{1 - r^2}}$$

with $(W - 2)$ degrees of freedom.

References

Blalock (1972)

WLS

General

WLS estimates regression model with different weights for different cases.

Notation

n	the number of cases
p	the number of parameters for the model
y_i	the observed dependent variable for case i
X_i	a vector of the observed independent variables
β	a vector of the parameters
w_i	the weight for case i

Model

The linear regression model has the form of

$$y_i = X'_i \beta + \varepsilon_i , \qquad i = 1, \ldots, n \tag{1}$$

where $E(\varepsilon_i) = 0$ and $V(\varepsilon_i) = w_i^{-1}\sigma^2$. Assuming that $\varepsilon_1, \ldots, \varepsilon_n$ follow a normal distribution, the log-likelihood function of model (1) is

$$L = 0.5\left\{ - nln2\pi - nln\sigma^2 + \sum_{i=1}^{n} lnw_i - \frac{\sum_{i=1}^{n} w_i (y_i - X'_i \beta)^2}{\sigma^2} \right\} \tag{2}$$

Computational Details

The algorithm used to obtain the weighted least-square estimates for the parameters in the model is the same as the REGRESSION procedure with regression weight. For details of the algorithm and statistics (the ANOVA table and the variables in the equation), see REGRESSION.

After the estimation is finished, the log-likelihood function shown in (2) is estimated by

$$\hat{L} = 0.5\left\{ - nln2\pi - nln\hat{\sigma}^2 + \sum_{i=1}^{n} lnw_i - (n-p) \right\}$$

where $\hat{\sigma}^2$ is the mean square error in the ANOVA table.

2SLS

General

2SLS produces the two-stage least-squares estimation for a structure of simultaneous linear equations.

Notation

p	the number of predictors
p_1	the number of endogenous variables among p predictors
k	the number of instrument variables
n	the number of cases
w_i	the weight for case i
y	an $n \times 1$ vector which consists of a sample of the dependent variable
Z	an $n \times p$ matrix which represents observed predictors
δ	a $p \times 1$ parameter vector
X	an $n \times k$ matrix with element X_{ij}, which represents the observed value of the jth instrumental variable for case i
Z_1	a submatrix of Z with dimension $n \times p_1$, which represents observed endogenous variables
δ_1	a subvector of δ with parameters associated with Z_1

Model

The structure equations of interest are written in the form

$$y = Z\delta = [Z_1, Z_2]\begin{bmatrix}\delta_1\\ \delta_2\end{bmatrix} + \varepsilon_1 \tag{1}$$

$$Z_1 = X\beta + \varepsilon_2$$

where

$$Z = [Z_1, Z_2]\,,\ \delta = \begin{bmatrix}\delta_1\\ \delta_2\end{bmatrix}$$

and ε_1 and ε_2 are the disturbances with zero means and covariance matrices $\sigma_1^2 I_n$ and $\sigma_2^2 I_n$, respectively.

Estimation

The estimation technique used was developed by Theil (1953, a,b). Let us first premultiply both sides of equation (1) by X' to obtain

$$X'y = X'Z\delta + X'\varepsilon_1 \qquad (2)$$

Since the disturbance vector has zero mean and covariance matrix $\sigma_1^2(X'X)$, it is easy to see that $(X'X)^{-\frac{1}{2}} X'\varepsilon_1$ would have a covariance matrix $\sigma_1^2 I_n$. Thus, multiplying $(X'X)^{-\frac{1}{2}}$ to both sides of equation (2) results in a multiple linear regression model

$$(X'X)^{-\frac{1}{2}} X'y = (X'X)^{-\frac{1}{2}} X'Z\delta + (X'X)^{-\frac{1}{2}} X'\varepsilon_1 (3)$$

The ordinary least-square estimator $\hat{\delta}$ for δ is

$$\hat{\delta} = (Z'X(X'X)^{-1}X'Z)^{-1} Z'X(X'X)^{-1}X'y$$

Computation Details

- 2SLS constructs a matrix R,

  $$R = \begin{bmatrix} 1 & V' \\ V & M \end{bmatrix}$$

  where

  $$M = C_{zx}(C_{xx})^{-1}C'_{zx}$$
  $$V = C_{zx}(C_{xx})^{-1}C_{xy}$$

  and C_{zx} is the correlation matrix between Z and X, and C_{xx} is the correlation matrix among instrumental variables.

- Sweep the matrix R to obtain regression coefficient estimate for δ.

- Compute sum of the squares of residuals (SSE) by

  $$y'y - uZ'y - y'Zu' + uZ'Zu'$$

  where

  $$u = y'X(X'X)^{-1}X'z[z'X(X'X)^{-1}X'z]^{-1}$$

- Compute the statistics for the ANOVA table and for variables in the equation. Details can be found in REGRESSION.

References

Theil (1953, a, b)

Appendix 1: Significance Level of a Standard Normal Deviate

General

The significance level is based on a polynomial approximation.

Notation

X	value of the standard normal deviate
Q	one-sided significance level

Computation (Abramowitz and Stegun (1965))

$$Q(X) = 0.5\{1 + Z(a_1 + Z(a_2 + Z(a_3 + Z(a_4 + Z(a_5 + Z(a_6))))))\}^{-16}$$

where

$$Z = \begin{cases} 0.7071067812|X| & \text{if } |X| \le 14.14 \\ 10 & \text{otherwise} \end{cases}$$

$a_1 = 0.070523078\ldots$ $\quad a_4 = 0.0001520143$

$a_2 = 0.0422820123$ $\quad a_5 = 0.0002765672$

$a_3 = 0.0092705272$ $\quad a_6 = 0.0000430638$

References

For discussion of the accuracy of most of the significance-level algorithms used, see Ling (1978).

Appendix 2: Significance of a *t* Statistic

General

An exact formula is used for 30 or fewer degrees of freedom, the Cornish-Fisher approximation otherwise.

Notation

X	absolute value of the t variable
k	degrees of freedom
Q	two-sided significance level

Computation (Abramowitz and Stegun (1965))

- (1) For $k \le 30$,

$$Q = 1 - A(k)$$

where, for k odd

$$A(k) = \begin{cases} \frac{2}{\pi}\left\{\theta + \sin\theta\left[\cos\theta + \frac{2}{3}\cos^3\theta + \ldots + \frac{2 \cdot 4 \ldots (k-3)}{3 \cdot 5 \ldots (k-2)}\cos^{k-2}\theta\right]\right\} & k \ne 1 \\ \frac{2\theta}{\pi} & k = 1 \end{cases}$$

For k even,

$$A(k) = \sin\theta\left\{1 + \frac{1}{2}\cos^2\theta + \frac{1 \cdot 3}{2 \cdot 4}\cos^4\theta + \ldots + \frac{1 \cdot 3 \ldots (k-3)}{2 \cdot 4 \ldots (k-2)}\cos^{k-2}\theta\right\}$$

and

$$\theta = \arctan\frac{X}{\sqrt{k}}$$

$$\sin(\theta) = \frac{\tilde{\theta}}{\sqrt{1 + \tilde{\theta}^2}}$$

$$\cos(\theta) = \frac{1}{\sqrt{1 + \tilde{\theta}^2}}$$

where

$$\tilde{\theta} = \frac{X}{\sqrt{k}}$$

- (2) If $k > 30$ and $X < 5 \times 10^{-5}$,

$$Q = 1$$

If $k > 30$ and $X \geq 5 \times 10^{-5}$,

$$Q = 2\left(Q_N(X) + \frac{XR\exp\left(\frac{-X^2}{2}\right)}{\sqrt{2\pi}} \right)$$

where $Q_N(X)$ is the normal one-tailed significance probability, and

$$R = \frac{(x^2+1)}{4k} + \frac{-3 + x^2(-5 + x^2(-7 + 3x^2))}{96k^2}$$

$$+ \frac{(-15) + x^2(-3 + x^2(6 + x^2(14 + x^2(-11 + x^2))))}{384k^3}$$

$$+ \frac{945 + x^2(-915 + x^2(-213 + x^2(-939 + x^2(-2141 + x^2(2225 + x^2(-375 + 15x^2))))))}{92160k^4}$$

$$+ \frac{17955 + x^2(5355 + x^2(180 + x^2(1140 + x^2(2490 + x^2(5994 + x^2(-7516 + x^2(1764 + x^2(-133 + 3x^2))))))))}{368640k^5}$$

Appendix 3: Significance of a Chi-Square Statistic

General

For 30 or fewer degrees of freedom, an exact series expansion is used; otherwise the Peizer-Pratt approximation is used.

Notation

X	value of the chi-square statistic
k	degrees of freedom
Q	significance level (right-tail probability)

Computation

- If $X \le 0$ or $k < 1$,

  $Q = 1$

- If $k = 1$,

  $Q = 2Q_N(\sqrt{X})$

  where $Q_N(\sqrt{X})$ is the standard normal one-tailed significance probability.

- For $k \le 30$, an exact series expansion is used (Abramowitz and Stegun (1965), eqs. 26.4.4 and 26.4.5)

$$Q = \begin{cases} 2Q_N(\sqrt{X}) + R\sqrt{\frac{2}{\pi}}exp\left(\frac{-X}{2}\right) & k \text{ odd} \\ exp\left(\frac{-X}{2}\right) \times (1+R) & k \text{ even} \end{cases}$$

where

$$R = \begin{cases} \sum_{r=1}^{(k-1)/2} \frac{X^{r-1/2}}{1 \cdot 3 \ldots (2r-1)} & k \text{ odd} \\ \sum_{r=1}^{(k-2)/2} \frac{X^r}{2 \cdot 4 \ldots 2r} & k \text{ even} \end{cases}$$

- If $k > 30$, the Peizer-Pratt approximation is used (Peizer and Pratt (1968), eq 2.24a).

- If $X \geq 150$,

  $Q = 0$

  otherwise

  $Q = Q_N(Z)$

  where

$$
Z = \begin{cases} (-(\frac{1}{3} + \frac{0.08}{k}))/(\sqrt{2k-2}) & \text{if } X = k-1 \\ (d\sqrt{(k-1)\log(\frac{k-1}{X}) + X - (k-1)})/|X-(k-1)| & \text{if } X \neq k-1 \end{cases}
$$

  where

  $d = X - k + 2/3 - 0.08/k$

- If $Z < 0$,

  $Q = 1 - Q_N(Z)$

Appendix 4: Significance of an F Statistic

General

Either the Peizer-Pratt approximation or an exact algorithm suggested by O.G. Ludwig(1963) and improved by Bosten and Battiste is used.

Notation

F	value of the F statistic
k_1	numerator degrees of freedom
k_2	denominator degrees of freedom
Q_F	one-tailed significance level

Computation

- If $k_1 \geq 20$ and $k_2 \geq 20$ and if $F > 12, Q_F = 0$
- Peizer-Pratt (1968, p.1420)

  The Peizer-Pratt approximation is used if $k_1 \geq 20$ and $k_2 \geq 20$ and $F \leq 12$, or $\min(k_1, k_2) \geq 6$ and $\max(k_1, k_2) > 2000$,

  $$Q_F = Q_N(Z)$$

  where

  $$Z = d \times \sqrt{\frac{1 + qg\left(\frac{S}{np}\right) + pg\left(\frac{T}{nq}\right)}{\left(n + \frac{1}{6}\right)pq}}$$

  and

  $$d = S + \frac{1}{6} - \left(n + \frac{1}{3}\right)p + 0.04\left(\frac{q}{k_2} - \frac{p}{k_1} + \frac{q - 0.5}{k_1 + k_2}\right)$$

  $$S = \frac{k_2 - 1}{2} \qquad T = \frac{k_1 - 1}{2}$$

  $$n = \frac{k_1 + k_2 - 2}{2} \qquad p = \frac{k_2}{k_1 F + k_2} \qquad q = 1 - p$$

  $$g(X) = \left(1 - X^2 + 2X\log(X)\right) / (1 - X)^2 \quad \text{for } X \neq 1, X > 0$$

  $$g(0) = 1, g(1) = 0$$

If $Z < 0$, $Q_F = 1 - Q_N(Z)$. If $Z > 10$, $Q_F = 0$.

- Exact Algorithm

Determine the parameters for the incomplete beta functions

$$X = \frac{k_2}{k_2 + k_1 F}$$

$$a = \begin{cases} k_2/2 & X \le 0.5 \\ k_1/2 & X > 0.5 \end{cases}$$

$$b = \begin{cases} k_1/2 & X \le 0.5 \\ k_2/2 & X > 0.5 \end{cases}$$

$$Y = \begin{cases} X & X \le 0.5 \\ 1 - X & X > 0.5 \end{cases}$$

The F and incomplete beta functions are related as

$$Q_F(F, k_1, k_2) = \begin{cases} I_X(k_2/2, k_1/2) & X \le 0.5 \\ 1 - I_{1-X}(k_1/2, k_2/2) & X > 0.5 \end{cases}$$

The following is used for the computations:

$$I_Y(a, b) = INFSUM \times \frac{Y^a}{\Gamma(a+1)} \times \frac{\Gamma(PS + a)}{\Gamma(PS)} + FINSUM \times \frac{\Gamma(a+b)}{\Gamma(a)\Gamma(b+1)} \times Y^a (1 - Y)^b$$

where

$$INFSUM = \sum_{i=0}^{\infty} \frac{(1 - PS)_i a}{a + i} \frac{Y^i}{i!}$$

$$(1 - PS)_i = \begin{cases} 1 & i = 0 \\ \dfrac{1 + i - PS}{1 - PS} & i > 0 \end{cases}$$

$$PS = \begin{cases} 1 & b \text{ is an integer} \\ b - [b] & \text{otherwise} \end{cases}$$

and

$[b]$ = largest integer less than or equal to b

$$FINSUM = \sum_{i=1}^{[b]} \frac{b(b-1)\dots(b-i+1)}{(a+b-1)(a+b-2)\dots(a+b-i)} \frac{1}{(1-Y)^i}$$

Summation of INFSUM terminates when a summand is less than 10^{-78} or less than $FINSUM \times 10^{-6}$.

Appendix 5:Significance Level for Fisher's Exact Test

General

For a 2×2 table, the exact one tailed probability of the observed or more extreme configuration under the assumption of independence of rows and columns and conditioned on the marginal totals is calculated. All cell contents are rounded to the nearest integers.

Computations

The rows and columns are interchanged so that the first cell contains the smallest entry. The table is then

a	b	$(a+b)$
c	d	$(c+d)$
$(a+c)$	$(b+d)$	N

If $bc < ad$, the table is again rearranged so that the first cell contains min(b, c), maintaining row and column totals. This results in the tail with the smaller probability being calculated. The probability of this table is

$$Pr(a, b, c, d) = \frac{(a+b)!\,(c+d)!\,(a+c)!\,(b+d)!}{N!\,a!\,b!\,c!\,d!}$$

The one-tailed probability is the probability that the first cell is less than or equal to a, that is

$$\sum_{x=0}^{a} Pr(a-x, b+x, c+x, d-x)$$

If $N \leq 30$, the probability that the first cell is zero is calculated as

$$P_0 = \frac{(c+d)!\,(b+d)!}{N!\,(d-a)!}$$

using a stored table of factorials. If $N > 30$,

$$P_0 = \begin{cases} \dfrac{(d-a+1)\cdots(d+b)}{(c+d+1)\,(c+d+2)\cdots N}, & \text{if } c+d \leq b+d \\ \dfrac{(d-a+1)\cdots(d+c)}{(b+d+1)\,(b+d+2)\cdots N}, & \text{otherwise} \end{cases}$$

Subsequent probabilities are calculated recursively using

$$P_i = P_{i-1} \times \frac{(a+b-i+1)\,(a+c-i+1)}{i\,(d-a+i)}$$

The two-tailed probability is the one-tailed probability plus the probability that the first cell is greater than a and less than or equal to $a + b$. That is

$$\sum_{y=1}^{b} P_r(a+y, b-y, c-y, d+y)$$

Appendix 6: Sorting and Searching

General

Sorting and searching have a significant impact on the performance of a number of procedures. For those procedures, the methods used are identified here.

Breakdown

In the general mode, BREAKDOWN constructs a list of cells in storage ordered by the table number and the values of the independent variables, indexed by a precedence vector. For each case, it is searched by traversing the list once, adding to an existing cell or creating a new one once for each table. When all the data have been read, the list is converted to a table physically ordered by table number and values of independent variables using the precedence vector. The precedence vector is searched to find the precedence of the cell which falls physically first; this cell is then exchanged with the cell which falls logically first. This procedure is repeated for each cell.

CROSSTABS

In the general mode, the table of cells is searched using an unordered open scatter table search and insertion algorithm similar to Knuth's Algorithm L (Knuth (1973), p. 518). The scatter table contains only pointers to the actual cell contents and is twice as large as it need be (i.e., if there is room for m cells, the scatter table has room for $2m$ pointers). This means it can never be more than half full. Collisions are resolved by sequential search from the initial location until an empty pointer is found.

The hash function used is given by the following algorithm:

Let

k be the table number

p be the dimension of the table

v_i $(i = 1, \ldots, p)$ be the bit string used to represent the value of the ith variable defining table k

m be the length of the scatter table

n be the resulting hash value, to be used as an index in the scatter table

$j := k$

for $i := 1$ to p

$j := j$ rotated left 3 bits

$j := j$ EXCLUSIVE OR v_i

end

$n := (j \text{ modulo } m) + 1$

When the tables have been completed, the cells are sorted by table numbers and the values of the defining variables using the algorithm described by Singleton (1969).

FREQUENCIES

In general mode, FREQUENCIES uses the same search and sort algorithms as CROSSTABS, except that its hashing function is given by:

$$h=(((k + 16807v) \text{ modulo } 2^{31}) \text{ modulo } m) + 1$$

where

h is the hash value, to be used as an index in the scatter table

k is the table number

v is the integer value of the bits representing the value to be tabulated

m is the length of the scatter table

NONPAR CORR and NPAR TESTS

Both use the method of Singleton to sort cases for computing ranks.

SURVIVAL

SURVIVAL uses a modified Quicksort similar to Knuth's algorithm Q (Knuth (1973), p. 116) to sort cases.

References

Knuth (1973)

Singleton (1969)

Appendix 7: Generation of Random Numbers

Normal deviates are generated using an algorithm of Brent (1974). Uniform numbers are generated using the algorithm of Lewis, Goodman, and Miller (1969). There is a single stream of random numbers used for the entire system.

References

Abraham, B., and Ledolter, J. (1983). *Statistical Methods of Forecasting.* New York:John Wiley and sons.

Abramowitz, N., and Stegun, I. (1965). *Handbook of Mathematical Functions.* National Bureau of Standards, Applied Mathematics Series 55. Washington, D.C.: U.S. Government Printing Office.

Addelman, S. (1962). Symmetrical and asymmetrical fractional factorial plans. *Technometrics,* 4:47-58.

Anderberg, M.R. (1973). *Cluster Analysis for Applications.* New York: Academic Press.

Anderson, T.W. (1958). *Introduction to Multivariate Statistical Analysis.* New York: John Wiley & Sons.

Andrews, F., Morgan, J., Sonquist, J., and Klem, L. (1973). *Multiple Classification Analysis.* Ann Arbor: University of Michigan.

Barlow, R.E., Bartholomew, D.J., Bremner, J.M., and Brunk, H.D. (1972). *Statistical Inference under Order Restrictions.* New York: John Wiley & Sons.

Bartlett, M.S. (1946). On the Theoretical Specification of Sampling Properties of Autocorrelated Time Series. *Jour. Royal Stat. Soc.*, B8, 27.

Benzécri, J.P. (1969). Statistical Analysis As a Tool to Make Patterns Emerge from Data. In *Methodologies of Pattern Recognition*, edited by S. Watanabe. New York: Academic Press.

Bishop, Y.M.M., Fienberg, S.E., and Holland, P.W. (1975). *Discrete Multivariate Analysis: Theory and Practice.* Cambridge: MIT Press.

Blalock, H.M. (1972). *Social Statistics.* New York: McGraw-Hill.

Bliss, C.I. (1967). *Statistics in Biology*, Vol. 1. New York: McGraw-Hill.

Blom, G. (1958). *Statistical Estimates and Transformed Beta Variables.* New York: John Wiley and Sons.

Bloomfield, P. (1976). *Fourier Analysis of Time Series.* New York: John Wiley and Sons.

Bloxom, B. (1978). Constrained Multidimensional Scaling in *n* Spaces. *Psychometrika*, 43, 397-408.

Bock, R.D. (1975). *Multivariate Statistical Methods in Behavioral Research.* New York: McGraw-Hill.

Bosten, N.E., and Battiste, E.L. Remark on Algorithm 179. *Collected Algorithms of the ACM*, 179-P 2-R1.

Bowdler, H.J., Martin, R.S., Reinch, C., and Wilkinson, J.H. (1968). The QR and OL Algorithm for Symmetric Matrices. *Numerische Mathematik*, 11, 293-306.

Box, G.E.P., and Jenkins, G.M. (1976). *Time Series Analysis: Forecasting and Control.* San Francisco: Holden-Day.

Brent, R. (1974). Algorithm 488. *Comm. ACM*, 17 (12).

Breslow, N.E. (1974). Covariance analysis of censored survival data. *Biometrics,* 30, 89-99.

Brigham, E.O. (1974). *The Fast Fourier Transform.* Englewood Cliffs: Prentice-Hall.

Brown, M.B. (1975). The Asymptotic Standard Errors of Some Estimates of Uncertainty in the Two-Way Contingency Table. *Psychometrika*, 40(3), 291.

Brown, M.B., and Benedetti, J.K. (1977). Sampling Behavior of Tests for Correlation in Two-Way Contingency Tables. *Journal of the American Statistical Association*, 72, 309-315.

Brownlee, K.A. (1965). *Statistical Theory and Methodology in Science and Engineering.* New York: John Wiley & Sons.

Björk, A., and Golub, G.H. (1973). Numerical Methods for Computing Angles between Linear Subspaces. *Mathematics of Computation*, 27, 579-594.

Cain, K.C., and Lange, N.T. (1984). Approximate case influence for the proportional hazards regression model with consored data.*Biometrics,* 40, 493-99.

Carroll, J.D., and Chang, J.J. (1970). Analysis of Individual Differences in Multidimensional Scaling via an N-Way Generalization of "Eckart-Young" Decomposition. *Psychometrika,* 35, 238-319.

Carroll, J.D., and Chang, J.J. (1972). IDIOSCAL (Individual Differences in Orientation Scaling). Paper presented at the spring meeting of the Psychometric Society, Princeton, NJ.

Carroll, J.D., Pruzansky, S., and Kruskal, J.B. (1980). CANDELINC: A General Approach to Multidimensional Analysis with Linear Constraints on Parameters. *Psychometrika*, 45, 3-24.

Chambers, J.M., Cleveland, W.S., Kleiner, B., and Tukey, P.A. (1983). *Graphical Methods for Data Analysis.* Belmont, Ca.: Wadsworth International Group; Boston: Duxbury Press.

Cook, R.D. (1977). Detection of Influential Observations in Linear Regression. *Technometrics*, 19, 15-18.

Cliff, N. (1966). Orthogonal Rotation to Congruence. *Psychometrika*, 31, 33-42.

Cooley, W.W., and Lohnes, P.R. (1971). *Multivariate Data Analysis.* New York: John Wiley & Sons.

Cox, D.R. (1972). Regression Models and Life-Tables (with Discussion). *Jour. Royal Stat. Soc.*, B34, 187-220.

Cronbach, L.J. (1951). Coefficient Alpha and the Internal Structure of Tests. *Psychometrika*, 16, 297-334.

Cryer, J.D.(1986). *Time Series Analysis.* Boston: Duxbury Press.

Dallal, G.E., and Wilkinson, L. (1986). An analytic approximation to the distribution of Lilliefors's test statistic for normality. *The American Statistician*, 40, No. 4.

De Leeuw, J. (1973). *Canonical Analysis of Categorical Data.* Doctoral dissertation, University of Leiden. Reissued by DSWO Press (Leiden, 1984).

De Leeuw, J., Young, F.W., and Takane, Y. (1976). Additive Structure in Qualitative Data: An Alternating Least Squares Method with Optimal Scaling Features. *Psychometrika*, 31, 33-42.

De Leeuw, J., and Van Rijckevorsel, J. (1980). HOMALS and PRINCALS—Some Generalizations of Principal Components Analysis. In *Data Analysis and Informatics*, edited by E. Diday et al. Amsterdam: North-Holland.

Dempster, A.P. (1969). *Elements of Continuous Multivariate Analysis.* Reading, MA: Addison-Wesley.

Dineen, L.C., and Blakesley, B.C. (1973). Algorithm AS 62: A Generator for the Sampling Distribution of the Mann-Whitney U Statistic. *Applied Statistics*, 22, 269-273.

Dixon, W.J., editor (1973). *BMD Biomedical Computer Programs.* Los Angeles: University of California Press.

Draper, N.R., and Smith, H. (1969). *Applied Regression Analysis.* New York: John Wiley & Sons.

Duncan, D.B. (1955). Multiple Range and Multiple F-Tests. *Biometrics*, 11, 1-42.

Dziuban, C.D., and Shirkey, E.C. (1974). When Is a Correlation Matrix Appropriate for Factor Analysis? *Psychological Bulletin*, 81, 358-361.

Eckart, C., and Young, G. (1936). The Approximation of One Matrix by Another One of Lower Rank. *Psychometrika*, 1, 211-218.

Edwards, A.L. (1954). *Techniques of Attitude and Scale Construction.* New York: Appleton.

Eisenhart, C. (1947). Significance of the Largest of a Set of Sample Estimates of Variance. In *Techniques of Statistical Analysis*, edited by C. Eisenhart, M.W. Hastay, and N.A. Wallis. New York: McGraw-Hill.

Emerson, P.L. (1968). Numerical Construction of Orthogonal Polynomials from a General Recurrence Formula. *Biometrics*, 24, 695-701.

Faddeeva, V.N. (1959). *Computational Methods of Linear Algebra.* New York: Dover.

Fienberg, S.E. (1977). *The Analysis of Cross-Classified Categorical Data.* Cambridge, MA: The MIT Press.

Finn, J.D. (1977). Multivariate Analysis of Variance and Covariance. In *Statistical Methods for Digital Computers*, Vol. 3, edited by K. Enslein, A. Ralston, and H. Wilf. New York: John Wiley & Sons.

Finney, D.J. (1971). *Probit Analysis.* Cambridge:Cambridge University Press.

Frigge, M., Hoaglin, D.C., and Iglewicz, B. (1987). Some implementations for the boxplot. in Heiberger, R.M., and Martin, M., eds. *Computer Science and Statistics Proceedings of the 19th Symposium on the Interface.* Alexandria, Va.:American Statistical Association.

Fuller, W.A. (1976). *Introduction to Statistical Time Series.* New York: John Wiley and Sons.

Gardner, E.S., (1985). Exponential smooting: The state of the art. *Journal of Forecasting,* 4:1-28.

Gebhardt, F. (1966). Approximation to the Critical Values for Duncan's Multiple Range Test. *Biometrics*, 22, 179-182.

Gehan, E.A. (1975). Statistical Methods for Survival Time Studies. In *Cancer Therapy: Prognostic Factors and Criteria*. New York: Raven Press, 7-35.

Gifi, A. (1981). *Nonlinear Multivariate Analysis.* Leiden: Department of Data Theory.

Gifi, A. (1985). *PRINCALS.* Leiden: Department of Data Theory, Internal Report UG-85-02.

Gill, P.E., Murray, W.M., Saunders, M.A., and Wright, M.H. (1984). Procedures for optimization problems with a mixture of bounds and general linear constraints. *ACM Transactions on Mathematical Software*, 10 (3), 282-96.

Gill, P.E., Murray, W.M., Saunders, M.A., and Wright, M.H. (1986). *User's Guide for NPSOL (version 4.0): A Fortran Package for Nonlinear Programming.* Technical Report SOL 86-2, Department of Operations Research, Stanford University.

Gill, P.E., Murray, W.M., and Wright, M.H. (1981). *Practical Optimization.* London: Academic Press.

Golub, G.H. (1969). Matrix Decompositions and Statistical Calculations. In *Statistical Computation*, edited by R.C. Milton and J.A. Nelder. New York: Academic Press.

Golub, G.H., and Reinsch, C. (1971). Linear Algebra, Chapter I.10. In Vol. II of *Handbook for Automatic Computation*, edited by J.H. Wilkinson and C. Rheinsch. New York: Springer-Verlag.

Goodenough, W.H. (1944). A Technique for Scale Analysis. *Educ. Psych. Meas.*, 179-190.

Goodman, L.A., and Kruskal, W.H. (1954). Measures of Association for Cross-Classification. *Journal of the American Statistical Association*, 49, 732-764.

Goodman, L.A., and Kruskal, W.H. (1972). Measures of association for cross classifications, IV:Simplification of asymptotic variances. *JASA,* 67:415-21.

Green, P. (1977). *Analyzing Multivariate Data.* New York: John Wiley & Sons.

Greenacre, M.J. (1984). *Theory and Applications of Correspondence Analysis.* London: Academic Press.

Guilford, J.R. (1954). *Psychometric Methods.* New York: McGraw-Hill.

Guttman, L. (1941). The quantification of a class of attributes: A theory and method of scale construction. In P. Horst et al., eds, *The Prediction of Personal Adjustment.* New York: Social Science Research Council.

Guttman, L. (1945). A Basis for Analysing Test-Retest Reliability. *Psychometrika*, 10(4), 255-282.

Haberman, S.J. (1977). Maximum Likelihood Estimates in Exponential Response Models. *Ann. Stat.*, 5, 815-841.

Haberman, S.J. (1978). *Analysis of Qualitative Data*, Vol. 1. New York: Academic Press.

Haberman, S.J. (1979). *Analysis of Qualitative Data*, Vol. 2. New York: Academic Press.

Haberman, S.J. (1982). Analysis of Dispersion of Multinomial Responses. *JASA*, 77, 568-580.

Harman, H.H. (1976). *Modern Factor Analysis*, 3rd ed. Chicago: University of Chicago Press.

Harshman, R.A. (1970). Foundations of the PARAFAC Procedure: Models and Conditions for an Explanatory Multi-model Factor Analysis. Working Papers in Phonetics No. 16. Los Angeles: University of California.

Hartigan, J.A. (1975). *Clustering Algorithms.* New York: John Wiley & Sons.

Hays, W.L. (1973). *Statistics for the Social Sciences.* New York: Holt, Rinehart & Winston.

Heiser (1981). *Unfolding Analysis of Proximal Data.* Doctoral dissertation. Department of Data Theory, University of Leiden.

Hoaglin, D.C., Mosteller, F., and Tukey, J.W. (1983). *Understanding Robust and Exploratory Data Analysis.* New York: John Wiley and Sons.

Hoaglin, D.C., Mosteller, F., and Tukey, J.W. (1985). *Exploring Data Tables, Trends and Shapes.* New York: John Wiley and Sons.

Hoaglin, D.C., and Welsch, R.E. (1978). The Hat Matrix in Regression and ANOVA. *American Statistician*, 32, 17-22.

Horst, P. (1963). *Matrix Algebra for Social Scientists.* New York: Holt, Rinehart and Winston.

Israëls, A. (1987). *Eigenvalue Techniques for Qualitative Data.* Leiden: DSWO Press.

Jenrich, R.I., and Sampson, P.F. (1966). Rotation for Simple Loading. *Psychometrika*, 31(3), 313-323.

Joreskog, K.G. (1977). Factor Analysis by Least-Square and Maximum Likelihood Methods. In *Statistical Methods for Digital Computers*, Vol. 3, edited by K. Enslein, A. Ralston, and R.S. Wilf. New York: John Wiley & Sons.

Jones, L.E., and Young, F.W. (1972). Structure of a Social Environment: Longitudinal Individual Differences Scaling of an Intact Group. *Journal of Personality and Social Psychology*, 24, 108-121.

Kaiser, H.F. (1963). Image Analysis. In *Problems in Measuring Change*, edited by C.W. Harris. Madison: University of Wisconsin Press.

Kendall, M.G. (1955). *Rank Correlation Methods.* London: Charles Griffin.

Kendall, M.G., and Stuart, A. (1961). *The Advanced Theory of Statistics*, Vol. 2. London: Charles Griffin.

Kim, Jae-On (1971). Predictive Measures of Ordinal Association. *American Journal of Sociology*, 76(5), 891.

Knuth, D.E. (1973). *The Art of Computer Programming*, Vol. 3: Sorting and Searching. Reading, MA: Addison-Wesley.

Kramer, C.Y. (1956). Extension of Multiple Range Tests to Group Means with Unequal Numbers of Replication. *Biometrics*, 12, 307-310.

Kristof, W. (1963). The statistical theory of stepped-up reliability coefficients when the test has been divided into several equivalent parts. *Psychometrica,* 28:221-38.

Kristof, W. (1969). Estimation of True Score and Error Variance under Various Equivalent Assumptions. *Psychometrika*, 34, 489-507.

Kruskal, J.B. (1964). Nonmetric Multidimensional Scaling: A Numerical Method. *Psychometrika*, 29, 115-129.

Lawless, J.F. (1982). *Statistical Models and Methods for Lifetime Data.* New York: Wiley.

Ledolter, J., and Abraham, B. (1984). Some comments on the initialization of exponential smoothing. *Journal of Forecasting*, 3:79-84.

Lee, E., and Desu, M. (1972). A Computer Program for Comparing *k* Samples with Right Censored Data. *Computer Programs in Biomedicine*, 315-321.

Lehmann, E.L. (1975). *Nonparametrics: Statistical Methods Based on Ranks.* San Franscisco: Holden-Day.

Lewis, Goodman, Miller (1969). A Pseudo-Random Number Generator for the System 360. *IBM Systems Journal*, 8(2), 136-145.

Lilliefors, H.W. (1967). On the Kolmogorov-Smirnov tests for normality with mean and variance unknown. *Journal of the American Statistical Association,* 62:399-402.

Ling, R.E. (1978). A Study of the Accuracy of Some Approximations for t, x^2 and F Tail Probabilities. *Journal of the American Statistical Association*, 73, 274-283.

Loether, H.J., and McTavish, D.G. (1975). *Descriptive and Inferential Statistics.* Boston: Allyn and Bacon.

Ludwig, O.G. (1963). Algorithm 179: Incomplete Beta Ratio. *Comm. ACM*, 6, 314.

MacCallum, R.C. (1977). Effects of Conditionality on INDSCAL and ALSCAL Weights. *Psychometrika*, 42, 297-305.

Makridakis, S., Wheelwright, S.C., and McGee, V.E. (1983). *Forecasting: Methods and Applications.* 2nd ed. New York: John Wiley and Sons.

Mardia, K.V. (1972). *Statistics of Directional Data.* New York: Academic Press.

Mardia, K.V., Kent, J.T., and Bibby, J.M. (1979). *Multivariate Analysis.* New York: Academic Press.

Meulman, J. (1982). *Homogeneity Analysis of Incomplete Data.* Leiden:DSWO Press.

Miller, R.G., Jr. (1966). *Simultaneous Statistical Inference.* New York: McGraw-Hill.

Minpack. Argonne National Labs Report ANL-80-74.

Monro, D.M. (1975). Algorithm AS 83: Complex discrete fast Fourier transform. *Applied Statistics,* 24:153-60.

Monro, D.M., and Branch, J.L. (1977). Algorithm AS 117: The Chirp discrete Fourier transform of general length.*Applied Statistics,* 26:351-61.

More, J.J. (1977). The Levenberg-Marquardt algorithm:Implementation and theory in numerical analysis. In Watson, G.A., ed., *Lecture Notes in Math 630*, 105-116. Berlin:Springer-Verlag.

Morrison, D.F. (1967). *Multivariate Statistical Methods.* New York: McGraw-Hill.

Mudholkar, G.S., Chaubey, Y.P., and Lin, Ching-Choung (1976). Some Approximations for the Non-Central-F Distribution. *Technometrics*, 18, 351-358.

Muller, K.E., and Peterson, B.L. (1984). Practical Methods for Computing Power in Testing the Multivariate General Linear Hypothesis. *Computational Statistics and Data Analysis*, 2, 143-158.

Nishisato, S. (1980). *Analysis of Categorical Data: Dual Scaling and Its Applications.* Toronto: University of Toronto Press.

Novick, M.R., and Lewis, C. (1967). Coefficient Alpha and the Reliability of Composite Measurements. *Psychometrika*, 32, 1-13.

Null, C.H., and Sarle, W.S. (1982). Multidimensional scaling by least squares. Proceedings of the 7th Annual SAS User's Group International.

Overall, J.E., and Klett, C.F. (1972). *Applied Multivariate Analysis.* New York: McGraw-Hill.

Pillai, K.C.S. (1967). Upper Percentage Points of the Largest Root of a Matrix in Multivariate Analysis. *Biometrika*, 54, 189-194.

Peizer, D.B., and Pratt, J.W. (1968). A Normal Approximation for Binomial F, Beta and Other

Common, Related Tail Probabilities. *Journal of the American Statistical Association*, 63, 1416-1456.

Plackett, R.L., and Burman, J.P. (1946). The design of optimum multifactorial experiments. *Biometrika,* 33:305-325.

Quenouville, M.H. (1949). Approximate Tests of Correlation in Time Series. *Jour. Royal Stat. Soc.*, B11, 68.

Rao, C.R. (1952). *Advanced Statistical Methods in Biometric Research.* New York: John Wiley & Sons.

Rao, C.R. (1955). Estimation and Test of Significance in Factor Analysis. *Psychometrika*, 20(2), 93-111.

Rao, C.R. (1973). *Linear Statistical Inference and Its Applications.* New York: John Wiley & Sons.

Rao, C.R. (1980). Matrix Approximations and Reduction of Dimensionality in Multivariate Statistical Analysis. In *Multivariate Analysis*, Vol. 5, edited by P.R. Krishnaiah. Amsterdam: North-Holland.

Robson, D.S. (1959). A Simple Method for Construction of Orthogonal Polynomials When the Independent Variable Is Unequally Spaced. *Biometrics*, 15, 187-191.

Romesburg, H.C. (1984). *Cluster Analysis for Researchers.* Belmont, CA: Lifetime Learning Publications.

Rummel, R.J. (1970). *Applied Factor Analysis.* Evanston, IL: Northwestern University Press.

Scheffé, H.A. (1959). *The Analysis of Variance.* New York: John Wiley & Sons.

Schiffman, S.S., Reynolds, M.L., and Young, F.W. (1981). *Introduction to Multidimensional Scaling: Theory, Methods, and Applications.* New York: Academic Press.

Searle, S.R. (1966). *Matrix Algebra for the Biological Sciences.* New York: John Wiley & Sons.

Searle, S.R. (1971). *Linear Models.* New York: John Wiley & Sons.

Siegel, S. (1956). *Nonparametric Statistics for the Behavioral Sciences.* New York: McGraw-Hill.

Singleton, R.C. (1969). Algorithm 347: Efficient Sorting in Minimal Storage. *Communications of the ACM*, 12, 185-187.

Smirnov, N.V. (1948). Table for Estimating the Goodness of Fit of Empirical Distributions. *Annals of Mathematical Statistics*, 19, 279-281.

Snedecor, G.W., and Cochran, W.G. (1967). *Statistical Methods.* Ames, IA: Iowa State University Press.

Speed, M.F. (1976). Response Curves in the One-Way Classification with Unequal Numbers of Observations per Cell. *Proceedings of the Statistical Computing Section, American Statistical Association.*

Spicer, C.C. (1972). Algorithm AS 52: Calculation of Power Sums of Deviations about the Mean. *Applied Statistics*, 21, 226-227.

Stewart, G.W. (1973). *Introduction to Matrix Computations.* New York: Academic Press.

Storer, B.E., and Crowley, J. (1985). A diagnostic for Cox regression and general conditional likelihoods. *Jour. of the American Statistical Association,* Vol. 80, No. 389.

Takane, Y., de Leeuw, J., and Young, F.W. (1977). Nonmetric Individual Differences Multidimensional Scaling: An Alternating Least Squares Method with Optimal Scaling Features. *Psychometrika*, 42, 7-67.

Tarone, R. (1975). Tests for trend in life table analysis. *Biometrika,* 62:3.

Tarone, R., and Ware, J. (1977). On distribution-free tests for equality of survival distributions. *Biometrika,* 64:1:156-60.

Tatsuoka, M.M. (1971). *Multivariate Analysis.* New York: John Wiley & Sons.

Theil, H. (1953a). *Repeated Least-Square Applied to Complete Equation Systems.* The Hague: Central Planning Bureau.

Theil, H. (1953b). *Estimation and Simultaneous Correlation in complete Equation Systems.* The Hague: Central Planning Bureau.

Timm, N.H. (1975). *Multivariate Analysis with Applications in Education and Psychology.* Monterey, CA: Brooks/Cole.

Tucker, L.R. (1972). Relations between Multidimensional Scaling and Three-Mode Factor Analysis. *Psychometrika*, 37, 3-28.

Tukey, J.W. (1962). The future of data analysis.*Annals of Mathematical Statistics,* 33: 22.

Tukey, J.W. (1977). *Exploratory Data Analysis.* Reading, Mass.: Addison-Wesley.

Van de Geer, J.P. (1971). *Introduction to Multivariate Analysis for the Social Sciences.* San Francisco: W.H. Freeman.

Van de Geer, J.P. (1987). *Algebra and Geometry of OVERALS.* Leiden: Internal Report RR-87-

13, Department of Data Theory.

Van der Burg, E. (1988). *Nonlinear Canonical Correlation and Some Related Techniques.* Leiden: DSWO Press.

Van der Burg, E., De Leeuw, J., and Verdegaal, R. (1984). *Non-linear Canonical Correlation Analysis.* Leiden: Internal Report RR-84-12, Department of Data Theory.

Van der Burg, E., De Leeuw, J., and Verdegaal, R. (1988). Homogeneity Analysis with *k* Sets of Variables: An Alternating Least Squares Method with Optimal Scaling Features. *Psychometrika*, 53, 177-197.

Van Rijckevorsel, J., and De Leeuw, J. (1979). *An Outline of PRINCALS.* Leiden: Department of Data Theory, Internal Report RB 002-'79.

Velleman, P.F., and Hoaglin, D.C. (1981). *Applications, Basics, and Computing of Exploratory Data Analysis.* Boston:Duxbury Press.

Velleman, P.E., and Welsch, R.E. (1981). Efficient Computing of Regression Diagnostics. *The American Statistician*, 35, 234-242.

Verdegaal, R. (1986). *OVERALS.* Leiden: Internal Report UG-86-01, Department of Data Theory.

Wilkinson, J.H. (1965). *The Algebraic Eigenvalue Problem.* Oxford: Clarendon Press.

Wilkinson, J.H., and Reisch, C. (1971). Linear Algebra. In Vol. II of *Handbook for Automatic Computation*, edited by J.H. Wilkinson and C. Rheinsch. New York: Springer-Verlag.

Winer, B.J. (1971). *Statistical Principles in Experimental Design*, 2nd ed. New York: McGraw-Hill.

Wolter, K.M. (1985). *Introduction to Variance Estimation.* Berlin: Springer-Verlag.

Young, E.A., and Cramer, E.W. (1971). Some Results Relevant to Choice of Sum and Sum-of-Product Algorithms. *Technolometrics*, 13, 657-665.

Young, F.W., Easterling, D.V., and Forsyth, B.N. (1984). The General Euclidean Model for Scaling Three-Mode Dissimilarities: Theory and Application. In *Research Methods for Multi-mode Data Analysis in the Behavioral Sciences*, edited by H.G. Law, G.W. Snyder, Jr., J. Hattie, and R.P. McDonald. New York: Praeger.

Young, F.W., and Lewyckyj, R. (1979). *ALSCAL-4 User's Guide.* Carrboro, NC: Data Analysis and Theory Associates.

Young, F.W., Takane, Y., and Lewyckyj, R.(1978). ALSCAL: A nonmetric multidimensional scaling program with several difference options. *Behavioral Research Methods and Instrumentation,* 10: 451-53.